A Garland of Satire, Wisdom, and History:

Latin Verse from Twelfth-Century France

(Carmina Houghtoniensia)

Edited by
Jan M. Ziolkowski and Bridget K. Balint
with
Justin Lake, Laura Light,
and Prydwyn Piper

Houghton Library of the Harvard College Library
Cambridge, Massachusetts
2007

Distributed by Harvard University Press

Houghton Library Studies

Series Editor: William P. Stoneman

Houghton Library Studies provides a forum for the scholarly analysis of the wide-ranging materials in the collections of Houghton Library, the primary repository for rare books and manuscripts at Harvard University.

Library of Congress Cataloging-in-Publication Data

A garland of satire, wisdom, and history : Latin verse from twelfth-century France (Carmina Houghtoniensia) / edited by Jan M. Ziolkowski and Bridget K. Balint, with Justin Lake, Laura Light, and Prydwyn Piper.

p. cm. — (Houghton Library studies)

Introduction and commentary in English; poems in Latin with facing English translation.

Includes bibliographical references and index.

ISBN 0-9765472-7-9 (pbk. : alk. paper)

1. Songs, Latin (Medieval and modern)—Texts. 2. Latin poetry, Medieval and modern—France—Texts. 3. Latin poetry, Medieval and modern—France—Translations into English. 4. Manuscripts, Latin (Medieval and modern)—Massachusetts—Cambridge. I. Ziolkowski, Jan M., 1956- II. Balint, Bridget K. III. Houghton Library. Manuscript. MS Lat 300. IV. Title: Carmina Houghtoniensia.

PA8164.G37 2007

871'.0408—dc22

2007036723

In memory of

RODNEY G. DENNIS
(1930–2006)

Curator of Manuscripts (1965–1991)
Houghton Library

Contents

Acknowledgments

THE EDITIONS AND TRANSLATIONS WITH COMMENTARIES that follow have been produced as a team effort over more than fifteen years. Encouraged by Rodney Dennis, who was for much of that time Curator of Manuscripts in Houghton Library, Jan M. Ziolkowski was first drawn to Houghton MS Lat 300 in the late 1980s. In 1990 he published in a journal article the poems in Group Two, along with a provisional description of the other contents. From the early 1990s through the present, Ziolkowski encouraged three Harvard University graduate students, now both present and former, to study the long poems in Group Five. This book represents a fusion of all this work, and its dedication conveys gratitude on the part of its editors to a bookman who would have been delighted to see a manuscript he loved made better known to a larger world. We regret that Rodney did not live to see the publication of this book.

Within Group Five, Poem 90 has been primarily the responsibility of Bridget K. Balint, Poem 91 of Justin Lake, and Poem 92 of Prydwyn Piper, but there has been considerable sharing among the three and equally active involvement at all stages from Ziolkowski. The general introduction incorporates the codicological work of Laura Light, but most of it embodies the efforts and insights of Balint, who also produced the introduction to Poems 90 to 95, with indispensable contributions from both Lake and Piper. To complete the work of editing the materials unique to Houghton MS Lat 300, Piper edited Group One, the rhythmic poem on the first folio, while Balint took in hand Group Six, the prose prophecy on the final folio. Balint also edited a small cento of moralizing aphorisms found on an earlier folio. Since Groups Three and Four comprise poems that have been edited already elsewhere and that consequently do not require full presentation here, the text for the whole of Houghton MS Lat 300 is now readily available in modern editions.

All of the contributors are beholden to William Stoneman of Houghton Library for having arranged for the manuscript to be digitized and made available through the electronic catalogue of Harvard College Library (HOLLIS), as well as to Peter Accardo and Duncan Todd for having overseen the final stages of the project from electronic files into print. For two rounds of copyediting and much more, our warmest thanks go to Thomas Kozachek. To the President and Fellows of Harvard College we are grateful for permission to incorporate into this study revisions and expansions of the *editio princeps* of the short poems in Group Two, which were published first in *Harvard Library Bulletin* in 1990, and to make available in facsimile here MS Lat 300 in its entirety. As a result the reader who consults the present volume can engage with the texts in both their modern and medieval guises.

In his preliminary research Ziolkowski was indebted to Rodney Dennis, Richard Tarrant, Peter Dronke, and George Rigg for helpful comments and suggestions. In the more recent round of investigations Ziolkowski became especially grateful to Peter Dronke and Jean-Yves Tilliette, who offered dossiers of reactions to the poems, especially in Group Two, that improved the edition and commentary, and to George Rigg, who also perused the whole book and offered the fruits of his extensive knowledge about Medieval Latin anthologies. Ziolkowski renders additional thanks to Thomas Bisson, for having commented upon the map and other features of the edition; Jean-Loup Lemaître, for having furnished him with a copy of an article on Monteil while it was still in press; M.T. J. Webber, for having answered (via David Ganz) queries about the hands that took part in producing the manuscript; Kathleen Coleman, Leofranc Holford-Strevens, and James Zetzel, for wrestling with Poem 9; Inez Lynn, for supplying pages of her unpublished Oxford University MA thesis on a related manuscript; and Justin Haynes, for sorting out a few embroiled questions relating to a Toronto dissertation.

Piper expresses appreciation to David Howlett as well as to his fellow assistant editors—Theodore Christchev, Carolinne White, and Trevor Evans—at the *Dictionary of Medieval Latin from British Sources*, all of whom looked over his transcript of Poem 1 and provided helpful suggestions.

All the collaborators benefited from the attentions of the two readers, Christopher J. McDonough and Paul Edward Dutton. Their copious and careful comments enabled a final polishing that much improved the book.

Abbreviations

CCCM	Corpus Christianorum, Continuatio Mediaevalis (Turnhout, 1966–)
CCSL	Corpus Christianorum, Series Latina (Turnhout, 1954–)
CSEL	Corpus Scriptorum Ecclesiasticorum Latinorum (Vienna, Leipzig, Prague, 1866–)
G	Gdańsk, Bibliotheka Gdańska PAN, MS Mar. F. 286 (fifteenth century)
H	Houghton, MS Lat 300 (1160–1190)
Luchaire	Achille Luchaire, *Louis VI le Gros: Annales de sa vie et de son règne (1081–1137)* (Paris, 1890; repr., Brussels, 1964)
MGH	Monumenta Germaniae Historica (1826–)
Monteil	Amans-Alexis Monteil, *Traité de matériaux manuscrits de divers genres d'histoire*, 2 vols. (Paris, 1835)
OLD	*Oxford Latin Dictionary*, ed. P.W.G. Glare (Oxford, 1982)
PL	*Patrologiae cursus completus, Series Latina*, ed. J.-P. Migne. 221 vols. (Paris, 1841–1864)
R	Reims, Bibliothèque municipale, MS 1275 (thirteenth century)
Rg	Oxford, Bodleian Library, MS Rawlinson G.109 (ca. 1200)
T	London, British Library, MS Cotton Titus A.xx (late fourteenth century)
Waquet	Abbot Suger of Saint Denis, *Vie de Louis VI le Gros*, ed. and trans. Henri Waquet, Les classiques de l'histoire de France au moyen âge 11 (Paris, 1929)
Walther	Hans Walther, *Initia carminum ac versuum medii aevi posterioris Latinorum: Alphabetisches Verzeichnis der Versanfänge mittellateinischer Dichtungen*, Carmina medii aevi posterioris Latina 1, 2nd ed. (Göttingen, 1969)

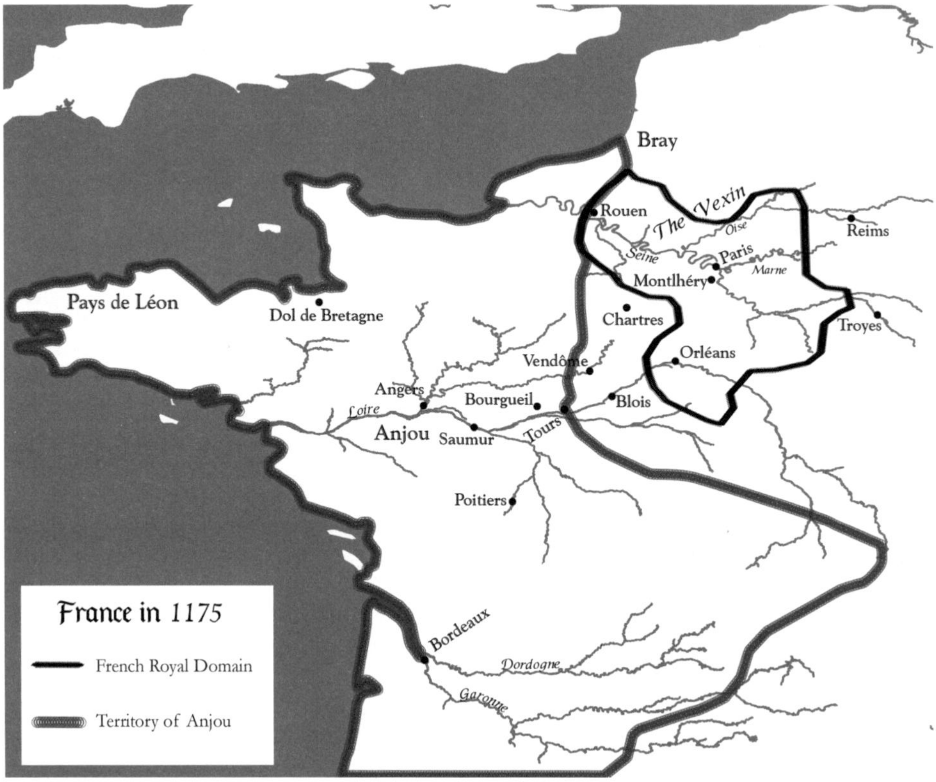
France in 1175
French Royal Domain
Territory of Anjou
Bray
Rouen
The Vexin
Oise
Reims
Seine
Paris
Marne
Montlhéry
Pays de Léon
Dol de Bretagne
Chartres
Troyes
Orléans
Vendôme
Angers
Bourgueil
Blois
Loire
Anjou
Saumur
Tours
Poitiers
Bordeaux
Dordogne
Garonne

INTRODUCTION

THE PARCHMENT LEAVES OF HOUGHTON MS LAT 300 make up a booklet that in its present state comprises only five bifolia and a singleton, for a total of eleven folios that may have once formed (and indeed probably did constitute) part of a larger manuscript. It transmits an anthology of twelfth-century Latin compositions, with ninety-four poems in quantitative verse (all different types of dactylic verse), flanked by a rhythmic poem at the beginning and a prose work at the end.

These ninety-six items have been subsumed into six groups. The poems in Groups Three (Poems 18 through 87) and Four (Poems 88 and 89) have long been available in print, as edited from other manuscripts, while an *editio princeps* with at least provisional texts and English translations of the poems in Group Two was published in 1990 in *Harvard Library Bulletin*.[1] This study not only revises the first edition of Group Two, but also completes the process of disseminating the contents of MS Lat 300 by offering editions, translations, and commentaries for all six poems in Group Five (all in elegiac distichs and all apparently unique to this manuscript) as well as for the rhythmic poem that by itself has been labeled Group One and the prose text that has been tagged as Group Six.

For whom will the items in this assembly be enticing? Historians of France will encounter in the occasional poems of Groups Two and Five collections of praise and blame poems that shed light on individuals from the first half of the twelfth century, a few of them quite prominent, others barely familiar or altogether unknown. Literary historians who explore this verse will also find grist for their mills, especially since the poet or poets who composed these items shared acquaintances and preoccupations, both literary and otherwise, with the so-called Loire Valley poets, such as Hildebert of Lavardin (1056–1133), Baudri of Bourgueil (1046–1130), Marbod of Rennes (1035–1123), and Fulk of Beauvais (born in the first half of the eleventh century).[2] Palaeographers may be intrigued by the distinctive characteristics of the script employed by the scribes, as well as by the slightly enigmatic character of the manuscript as a whole. Last but not least, the path followed by the booklet as it wended its way across centuries and continents to reach Houghton Library holds mysteries that warrant further study. [JZ]

1. Jan Ziolkowski, "A Bouquet of Wisdom and Invective: Houghton MS. Lat 300," *Harvard Library Bulletin*, n.s. 1, no. 3 (1990): 20–48.

2. Baudri's name is sometimes spelled Baudry. Alternative spellings of Fulk's name include Fulcoius, Fulco, and Fulcoie. For two attempts from the past decade or so to set the love lyrics of such poets in a broader context, see Gerald A. Bond, *The Loving Subject: Desire, Eloquence, and Power in Romanesque France* (Philadelphia, 1995), 42–98; and Thomas C. Moser Jr., *A Cosmos of Desire: The Medieval Latin Erotic Lyric in English Manuscripts* (Ann Arbor, 2004), 17–65.

Codicological Description

Parchment (several different types, of moderate to poor quality), fols. ii (paper; fol. i, marbled) + i (unnumbered parchment, blank, but ruled) + 11 (parchment leaves, foliated in pencil, bottom, inner corner, 1–11 [cited]; now interleaved with modern paper leaves that are continuously foliated together with the original parchment leaves, top, outer corner in pencil, 1–21) + i (blank, ruled parchment, foliated top, outer corner, as fol. 22), + ii (paper; fol. ii^{v}, marbled). Outer dimensions vary; assembled from unevenly shaped leaves, often notably irregular along the bottom and outer margins, 208–167 × 147–130 mm.

Layout varies. Poetic texts, fols. 1–10v, ruled space (158–140 × 123–103 mm.). Two columns, 31–25 lines. Ruled in hard point (fols. 1–2v, 5rv, 9v, 10rv) with full-length double vertical bounding lines inside, outside, and between the columns, used for the first letter of each line of verse, horizontal rules full across; or in brown crayon (fols. 3rv, 4v, 6v, 7rv, 8) or lead (fols. 4, 6, 8v, 9, 11v), generally with double full-length vertical bounding lines inside, outside, and between the columns; horizontal rules are not full-length. Ruling indiscernible, fol. 11, and very faint, fols. 7 and 9rv. Prickings for vertical bounding lines, top and bottom margins, on most folios ruled in crayon or lead. Fol. 11 (prose text), written space (145 × 113–110) mm., 32 long lines; fol. 11v (prose text), ruled space (145 × 92) mm., 24 long lines.

1^{12} (−3, following fol. 2; possibly canceled since there is no obvious loss of text; original parchment leaves now interleaved with modern paper leaves): see Figure 1.

Written above the top line by at least three scribes. The first scribe copied fols. 1–2v and fols. 4v–10v in a very small, upright twelfth-century minuscule. Fol. 3r–v^{A} was copied in a mature twelfth-century minuscule, approaching gothic; letter forms are fuller and ascenders and descenders notably smaller, giving the script a two-line appearance. Fol. 3v^{A}–4 was copied in a script that is larger and less controlled than the script identified with the first scribe; it has been suggested that this may be the work of a third scribe.[3] However, the similarity of the letter forms suggests that this is also the work of the first scribe. In parallel fashion, the prose text on fol. 11r is copied using very similar letter forms to fols. 3v–4 and is thus likely also by this first scribe. Fol. 11v seems to have been copied by another scribe, whose hand is not found elsewhere in the manuscript.

Each poem, fols. 1v–4, begins with 1-line red initials; red rubrics, fols. 1v–2. Blank lines for rubrics and spaces for initials in the remainder of the manuscript. Marginal ink drawings by the first scribe, fol. 2v (fox or dog), fol. 8r (animal heads), fol. 8v (fox head with long tail), and fol. 9v ("caper," "leo," and "aries").

3. See Ziolkowski, "A Bouquet of Wisdom and Invective," 23, and notes by Richard Rouse included in Houghton Library, files on MS Lat 300.

Bound, s. XIX, in mottled green leather, now rubbed; gold tooled borders, front and back covers; front cover: "Poésies latines avec lettres initiales et finales distinctes. Manuscrit du XIe siècle appartenant à Monsieur Monteil." Rebacked; spine preserved in library files with red leather label titled "Accrostiches" [*sic*], and added green paper label at bottom: "3[?]25." Marbled paper endleaves. [LL]

Figure 1
Collation: Houghton Library, MS lat 300

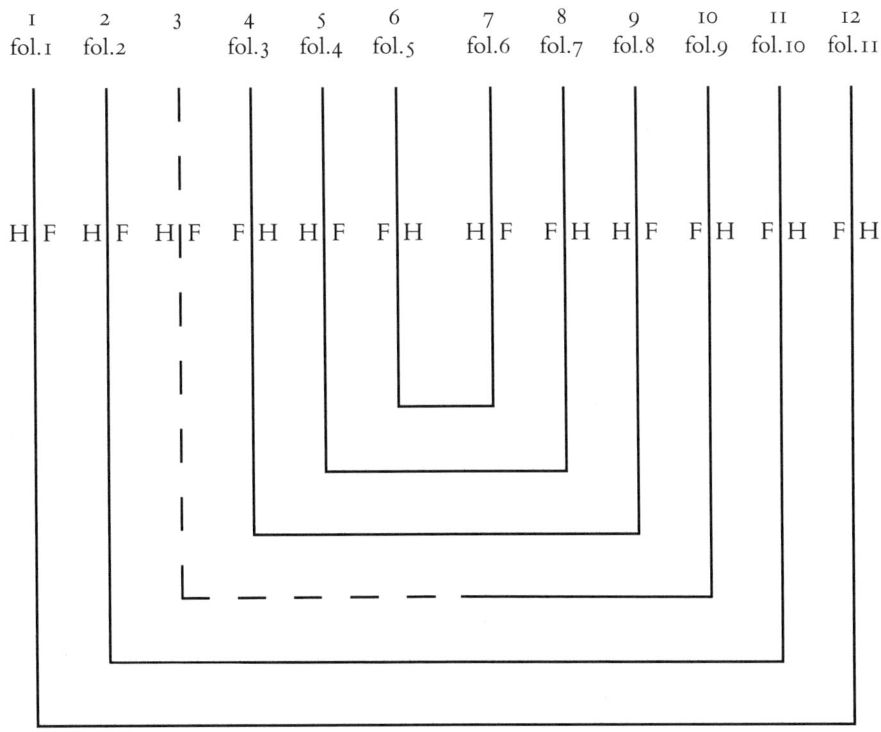

H = hairside; F = fleshside

Note that the missing leaf posited between fol. 2 and fol. 3 would have been positioned fleshside/hairside, preserving Gregory's rule. The quire is unusual in that Gregory's rule is broken between the first two and last two leaves.

Date

Written in France in the second half, probably in the final third, of the twelfth century. Brief added notes, s. XII–XIII, in a number of hands include fol. 1v (bottom margin; possibly by the second scribe), fol. 4 (far outer margin, mostly trimmed, s. XIII^{ex}), fol. 7v (top margin, "Ave maria gratia," s. XIII), fol. 8 (added cento of moral aphorisms in prose in bottom margin [see Appendix], s. XIII^{2}, possibly English; top line, fol. 3, probably also in this hand), and fol. 11 (bottom margin, s. XII/XIII).

Provenance

Dealers' notes: in ink, s. XIX, front paper flyleaf, fol. ii: "Satirae Epigrammata et alia. XIème siècle"; and in pencil on added paper leaf (p. 18): "Feuillets séparés d'un Ms du XIe siècle avec dessins à la plume." Purchased by Houghton Library from Nicolaus Rauch, Switzerland; received February 23, 1965.

The manuscript belonged to a collector and amateur historian named Amans-Alexis Monteil (1769–1850), who obtained it from a private collection in Paris and who interleaved the manuscript with paper leaves. Monteil attempted, not very successfully, to produce transcriptions (most of them partial) and published a description of the manuscript as well as an edition of one poem.[4] It was not included in the 1833, 1850, or 1851 sale catalogues of his library.[5]

As the foregoing information indicates, MS Lat 300 has been at Harvard for little more than forty years. Before its acquisition by Houghton Library from the Swiss bookdealer, the only certainty is that it belonged in the 1830s to the library of Monteil, who offered it for sale in Paris in 1836. It appears to have remained in private hands through the middle of the twentieth century, when it was reportedly in a Parisian collection.[6]

Monteil was a pioneer in the study of French national history, in which he was exceptional (though not unique) in aspiring to trace the history of the French people as a whole rather than exclusively of kings and ecclesiastics.[7] His signal

4. Monteil, 2:177–179. Although Monteil replaced the title page of this book with a new one to claim that the first edition had been exhausted and that a second one had been produced in 1836, the first and allegedly second editions are otherwise identical.

5. Amans-Alexis Monteil, *Catalogue des manuscrits et d'une partie des livres imprimés composant la bibliothèque de feu M. Amans Alexis Monteil* (Paris, 1850). For the bibliographic details of the 1833 and 1851 sale catalogues, see Jean-Loup Lemaitre, "Amans-Alexis Monteil (1769–1850) et les manuscrits," *Bibliothèque de l'École des Chartes* (forthcoming).

6. In the only published notice of the manuscript, André Vernet described it as being in the hands of "un amateur parisien." "Séance du 16 Avril," *Bulletin de la société nationale des antiquaires de France* (1952–53): 52–53.

7. Chris Warne, "Amateurs and Collectors: Amans-Alexis Monteil and the Emergence of a Professional Archive Culture in Nineteenth-Century France," *Australian Journal of French Studies* 33 (1996): 45–72.

achievement was the ten-volume *Histoire des Français des divers états aux cinq derniers siècles* (Paris, 1827–1844), in which he endeavored to characterize the different classes of French society from the High Middle Ages down to his own day. To facilitate his historical researches, he collected manuscripts in great numbers. Often he rebound manuscripts, which he interleaved with sheets of paper, as was done with Houghton MS Lat 300. Although this interleaving causes those who work with manuscripts today to shudder, one of Monteil's aims in having leaves of paper placed between the folios was to protect the parchment from damage. Another was to furnish a convenient place for the transcriptions and translations that he often attempted.[8]

The resale of manuscripts from his working collection generated revenues for Monteil to underwrite his own expenses, his further researches, and his further acquisitions. In fact, his description of Houghton MS Lat 300 was published in the sale catalogue of his manuscripts he had printed in 1836. Although many of these manuscripts passed into the library of the celebrated bibliomane, Sir Thomas Phillipps (1792–1872), this was not one of them.

As Monteil assembled his holdings, the libraries and archives of France persisted in the upheaval into which they had fallen in the aftermath of the Revolution. Paper and parchment were sometimes sold in bulk for commercial purposes, while in other cases unscrupulous officials gutted collections on the sly in order to line their own pockets with the proceeds from the sales. Millions of volumes were lost or destroyed, while additional millions changed ownership. Against this backdrop, it is not surprising that the provenance of MS Lat 300 is murky. Since Monteil did not keep systematic records of his suppliers, we cannot divine where he obtained MS Lat 300, whether it was already a separate booklet (although this would seem unlikely), or whether it was detached by him or by his supplier from a larger manuscript. The tantalizing annotation, penciled in French on one of the added paper leaves (fol. 18r), that refers to "separated leaves of an eleventh-century manuscript" (or "leaves separated from an eleventh-century manuscript"?) is the only modern discussion of the matter.

Perhaps the booklet belonged to the Bibliothèque municipale of Tours, a library that suffered infamously after the Revolution.[9] We know of many instances of manuscripts stolen from there around 1830 that came somehow into the possession of Monteil.[10] In one case Monteil dismembered a manuscript and rebound it in three volumes.[11] Although Monteil was hardly alone in profiting from the disorder

8. Warne, "Amateurs and Collectors," 55.

9. For preliminary information on the losses, see Léopold Delisle, "Notice sur les manuscrits disparus de la bibliothèque de Tours pendant la première moitié du XIXe siècle," in *Notices et extraits des manuscrits de la Bibliothèque nationale et autres bibliothèques* 31, no. 1 (1884): 157–356.

10. Warne, "Amateurs and Collectors," 50.

11. Lemaitre, "Amans-Alexis Monteil (1769–1850) et les manuscrits," forthcoming.

into which the library of Tours had fallen, he stands out for his activity in retailing codices pilfered from the Bibliothèque municipale to the Bibliothèque nationale de France in Paris.

The final folio side of MS Lat 300 contains, below the prose text written there, an erasure that could represent an attempt to abrade an *ex libris*. Would the writing obliterated have pointed to the celebrated abbey of Saint-Martin of Tours? This location would dovetail ideally with the places mentioned repeatedly in the anthology. [LL and JZ]

Script

Of the three scribes who wrote this manuscript, the first contributed the most. He produced a small, labored, and somewhat inconsistent example of a twelfth-century transitional script that has been labeled "protogothic documentary" or, more generally, "praegothica."[12] His inconsistency is evident, for instance, in his final *s*, which takes on a wide variety of shapes and sizes, sometimes superscript, sometimes not—even within the same line. Characteristics of the documentary script include the persistent use of the uncial *d* (round, shaft angled left), the 7-shaped Tironian *et* sign,[13] the lengthening of ascenders in the top line of text and of descenders in the bottom one, and superscript final *s*, which is simply the top half of the long two-stroke *s* often seen in documents of this period.[14] The first scribe has the habit of extending letters at the bottom of columns four or even five lines toward the lower edge of the folio. According to M. T. J. Webber, traits that allow more specific dating of this particular protogothic script to the last third of the twelfth century include the long undulating tail of *g* (fol. 1v^{B}, line 14), the trailing round *s* (fol. 2v^{B}, line 14), the very long limb of *h*, and the narrow initials: "The first two features can be found in documents of the 1160s, but are very rare; they become more common from the 1170s onwards."[15]

12. "Protogothic documentary" hands are illustrated and discussed by Michelle P. Brown, *A Guide to Western Historical Scripts from Antiquity to 1600* (Toronto, 1990), 78–79. On "praegothica," see Albert Derolez, *The Palaeography of Gothic Manuscript Books: From the Twelfth to the Early Sixteenth Century*, Cambridge Studies in Palaeography and Codicology 9 (Cambridge, 2003), 56–71. Derolez established earlier in the book (pp. 4–6), that changes in the generally conservative bookhands are usually borrowed from the more flexible and practical documentary script.

13. Tironian notes were a kind of shorthand named after Cicero's scribe, Marcus Tullius Tiro (reportedly died 4 BCE).

14. Examples in Françoise Gasparri, *L'écriture des actes de Louis VI, Louis VII et Philippe Auguste*, Centre de recherches d'histoire et de philologie de la IVe section de l'École Pratique des Hautes Études 5: Hautes Études Médiévales et Modernes 20 (Geneva, 1973), esp. pl. 8.

15. E-mail communication, November 9, 2005. In handwritten notes concerning the manuscript, Richard Rouse posited that the three hands were "contemporary with each other, working around 1160–80 or 1170–90." In conversation, Malcolm Parkes inclined to roughly the same dating. Vernet dated it at the beginning of the thirteenth century: see "Séance du 16 Avril," 52.

Abbreviation is common throughout the manuscript, but it is not uniform. For example, the first scribe occasionally writes the ending *-bus* as *b* with modern semicolon (Poem 5, fol. 1v^{B}, line 7, and Poem 90, fol. 9r^{A}, line 19), but elsewhere in the same poems (for example, fol. 2r^{A}, line 10, and fol. 9r^{A}, line 20) he resorts to the more common *b* with an apostrophe-shaped superscript. The ligature known as the *de*-monogram, which figures so prominently in this manuscript, is not as unusual as once proposed,[16] but its frequency here nonetheless remains notable. In other manuscripts it generally appears at line ends where a scribe would otherwise run out of room, and it is employed almost exclusively for the preposition *de*. Our scribe, however, incorporates the monogram within words as well (for example, *vide*re, *fide*s). (He also includes the Tironian *et* within words—for example, *docet*—and in combination with the tilde for the ending *–ent*.) The scribe of a Paris manuscript dated 1167 also found the *de*-monogram versatile, using it six times in five lines on one folio, in such forms as *videbat* and *corde*, a similarity that lends further support to the proposed dating of 1160–1190.[17] [BKB]

Orthography

The first scribe occasionally reveals something about the local conventions of pronunciation by the way he spells his words. These spellings include the very common substitution of *c* for *t* before *i* (for example, *iusticie*, 90.34, *tucius*, 90.42), which would presuppose a [ts] or even [s] pronunciation of *t* in this position. The scribe presents evidence as well for homophonic *c*, *s*, and *sc* (for example, *sciet*, 90.43, *ceptra*, 91.14).[18]

One of the more arresting and less common orthographic variations marks the scribe as Francophone: the substitution of *a* for *e* before a nasal consonant (and on a few occasions, *e* for *a*), reflecting an equivalence or near-equivalence in

16. On the *de*-monogram in this manuscript, see Ziolkowski, "A Bouquet of Wisdom and Invective," 23. The *de*-monogram appears in the Oxford manuscript of the *Song of Roland*, and has figured in attempts to date that manuscript. Ian Short, "The Oxford Manuscript of the *Chanson de Roland*: A Palaeographic Note," *Romania* 94 (1973): 221–231, argued that the monogram placed the manuscript in the 1170s or later. In contrast, Charles Samaran, "Sur la date approximative du *Roland* d'Oxford," *Romania* 94 (1973): 523–527, and Malcolm B. Parkes, "The Date of the Oxford Manuscript of *La Chanson de Roland* (Oxford, Bodleian Library, MS. Digby 23)," *Medioevo Romanzo* 10 (1985): 161–175, contend that the *de*-monogram is not a reliable indicator of date, and adduce other evidence to date Digby 23 earlier in the twelfth century.

17. S. Harrison Thomson, *Latin Bookhands of the Later Middle Ages, 1100–1500* (Cambridge, 1969), pl. 4 (Paris, Bibliothèque nationale, MS lat. 2702, fol. 102, dated 1167) provides this example of a protogothic documentary hand used to copy an anthology, in this case a collection of prose works.

18. The interchange of *c* and *t* is attested before the end of the fourth century; assibilation of *c* also perhaps had begun to occur by that early date. See József Herman, *Vulgar Latin*, trans. Roger Wright (University Park, 2000), 43–45.

then-current (and present-day) French pronunciation. Examples of *a* for *e* include *Burdegalanses* (12.2); *attandit* and *sentancia* (90.23); and *sapiancia* (92.13), *uiuandi* (95.1), and *splandentes* (Tiburtina, fol. 11r [line 13]). One instance of the less usual *e* for *a* is *testens* (92.9). These spellings were not always deemed acceptable by others involved in the manuscript production, however: several are expunged and corrected in the manuscript. For example, *sapiancia* is corrected above the line to *sapiencia* in the Sibylline text (Tiburtina, fol. 11r [line 10]).

Obviously such spellings could have resulted from sheer ignorance, but that is not the only feasible explanation. The variation in the vowels could be due to the scribe's being more accustomed to penning charters than *belles lettres*. In charters the spelling of place names would have sometimes reflected their pronunciation in the spoken language, and it is easy to see how the acceptability of such onomastic forms could have led scribes to employ similar orthography in regular Latin words.[19] [BKB]

Drawings

Drawings accompany four of the poems.[20] Since all of the drawings appear on folios where hand 1 wrote the text, hand 1 could have been the draftsman. In this case the drawings would take us into what remains largely a terra incognita in scholarship, especially at this early date:

> One as-yet-little-studied form of marginal imagery is the product of the scribe rather than the illuminator. As the work of scribes such imagery consists largely of pen-drawn text articulations, responses, explications, and commentaries, which range in form from manicules to figural vignettes.[21]

Whoever devised these unsophisticated drawings, it would be a mistake to regard them as impromptu sketches. In the twelfth century, and especially in a humble manuscript like Houghton MS Lat 300, drawings take the place of illuminations for

19. Peter Stotz, *Handbuch zur lateinischen Sprache des Mittelalters*, vol. 3: "Lautlehre" (Munich, 1996), 31–32, addresses this substitution, and provides as an example Bernard of Cluny's rhyme of *commendo* and *supplicando*. Other examples are available in Helmut Drevin, *Die französischen Sprachelemente in den lateinischen Urkunden des 11. und 12. Jahrhunderts* (Halle an der Saale, 1912), who finds in the Cartulary of the Abbey of Notre Dame de Ronceray *agripannus*, circa 1115 (p. 11), for *arpennus*, and *esamplas*, circa 1105 (p. 13), for *exempla*.

20. In the words of Monteil, 2:178, "Je veux du bien à ce poète du XIe siècle, qui dessinait mal, de ne pas s'être cru un grand dessinateur, d'avoir mis par dessus la représentation de quelques animaux qu'il a figurés sur les marges leurs noms, *leo, caper.*"

21. Lucy Freeman Sandler, "The Study of Marginal Imagery: Past, Present, and Future," *Studies in Iconography* 18 (1997): 44n6.

reasons of economy.[22] Such drawings are likelier to hew to model-books than to a draftsman's imagination or to observation of nature.[23]

These drawings may have served several possible functions, none of which excludes any of the others. Ornament could have been one aim. Although the parchment of Houghton MS Lat 300 is of poor quality, the compiler took pains to collect and arrange the texts. Those involved in the production of the manuscript may have wished to add a bit of visual variety to relieve the drabness of the parchment. At the same time, the images look to be more than simply ornamental.

On 2v a barking dog or open-mawed wolf is drawn between Poems 13 and 17, perhaps to exemplify the poor hospitality of the Diomedes described in Poem 13. In the left margin of 8r^{A} two open-mouthed grotesques face the text: one is placed to signal a transition in the *De gemellis* (line 53); the other to indicate a change of speakers in the same poem (line 65). In the left margin of 8v, beside the first column of Poem 90 ("Omnibus in rebus quas, mi Philippe, uidemus" lines 11–19), is a serpentine drollery with two loops in its tail. At the foot of 9v is a picture of a rampant lion (labeled *leo*) with its right paw and claws pressing into the right flank of a goat (*caper*) before it and its left paw and claws on the verge of doing so to a ram (*aries*) beneath it—perhaps a comment on political events related or implied in Poem 91 ("Francia dulcis, aue, regio bona, bella, salubris").

The drawings could have served any and all of these purposes—to furnish ornament pleasing to the eye, to signal textual divisions, and to comment on matters of content—but they could have also functioned as mnemonic devices, helping readers to remember the texts more readily. Such use as aides-mémoire does not necessarily presume that the texts of MS Lat 300 either originated in a classroom or ended up being employed there. [JZ]

Inferences about MS Production

Whether or not the scribes consciously implemented abbreviation to save space, there are certainly symptoms that this manuscript was assembled with efficiency in mind. The irregular shapes and sizes of the leaves and the poor quality of the parchment may presuppose that the producers of the manuscript welcomed whatever materials came to hand. Fol. 11r, most strikingly, may have been pressed into service already as a scrap before it reached our scribe: the decorative lengthened descenders seem carefully to avoid words already written at the foot of the page, which look to be pen-tests for a liturgical text. The scribes also began columns *in campo aperto*, above the top line of the writing frame, but this practice cannot be construed as an effort

22. See M.W. Evans, *Medieval Drawings* (London, 1969), 10–15.

23. The most recent and definitive study of model-book drawings is Robert W. Scheller, *Exemplum: Model-Book Drawings and the Practice of Artistic Transmission in the Middle Ages (ca. 900–ca. 1470)*, trans. Michael Hoyle (Amsterdam, 1995).

to utilize writing space efficiently: scribes routinely began above the top line in the twelfth century and indeed until about 1230.

The compilers appear to have assembled the quire in stages, perhaps as additional leaves became available. This hypothesis would help to explain why the layout varies, since the folios may have been obtained at different times from different sources. Even poor parchment of irregular shape was acceptable to the compilers and was used with efficiency by the scribes. At the same time, the efficiency was hardly obsessive. It would be an exaggeration to argue that the manuscript was ruthlessly economical of space since the verse is written as verse, with adequate if not generous spacing between columns.

The picture that emerges is paradoxical. Although Monteil termed Houghton MS Lat 300 a "manuscrit autographe," there are too many mistakes throughout the manuscript for any part of it to have been a poet's holograph.[24] The texts in the manuscript are not authorial fair copies. They were selected by an individual, possibly one of the scribes, who employed or at least involved others in the production of the manuscript. The quire was not written exclusively by one person in a hand that would have been readable by him alone, but by the same token the script shows signs of being less formal and more reliant on abbreviations than many bookhands would have been. All in all, the evidence points toward the possibility that the manuscript was produced at the instigation of an individual (and perhaps for him or even with his participation) by a small coterie of scribes who relied for their parchment on institutional leftovers, which might otherwise have been coopted for the classroom, use in binding, or other purposes.

Although the letter forms and the manner and extent of abbreviation reflect the habits of the chancery more than the scriptorium, the scribe made concessions to the conventions of book writers, most notably by writing the first letter of every line of verse in the outside left margin, separated from the body of the text, and, in several poems, attaching the concluding rhymed syllables of a couplet to both lines of verse with long pen strokes. The generous distance between the columns emphasizes the beginnings and endings of the lines—a visually pleasing effect that shows consideration for the particular experience of someone reading verse. [BKB]

MS Lat 300 as a Booklet or *Libellus*

Although MS Lat 300 may have been conceived and maintained as a separate little volume, the odds are stronger that it was bound with other gatherings into a bigger manuscript, from which it was later separated. But this supposition cannot be either proved or denied on the basis of the frustratingly equivocal note penciled in a

24. Monteil, 2:177.

nineteeth-century hand on the recto of the interleaved page facing 9v, numbered 18: "Feuillets séparés d'un Ms du XIe siècle avec dessins à la plume."[25]

George Rigg, expert on poetic anthologies, especially in the Anglo-Latin context, notes that many of them were compiled in one- or two-quire booklets that were later bound together.[26] Such booklets—in vernacular languages as well as in Latin—have attracted growing attention over the past quarter century from a strictly codicological point of view, from the perspective of the motives and principles that governed the selection and presentation of their poetic contents, and from the vantage point of the fiendishly intertangled relations among the surviving manuscripts.[27] Much work remains to be done before we will have attained a comprehensive understanding of the progressions that led from their assembly as individual units to their inclusion in larger codices.

MS Lat 300 may well be part of such a *libellus*, although whether it was ever actually bound with similar booklets is not known. Another engaging question is, How much, if at all, did conceptions that motivated production of this and other *libelli* of Latin poetry in the twelfth century influence the thinking of authors and collectors who assembled songs in the vernacular languages, especially but not solely those of Occitan troubadours and Old French trouvères known variously today as *Liederbücher*, *chansonniers*, and *canzonieri*?[28]

Whatever may be discovered about the relationship of MS Lat 300 to any extant manuscripts or parts of manuscripts, the booklet that has survived may well have started out as a collection of epigrams by Hildebert. Codicological evidence

25. The note could mean either that the folios were detached from a larger manuscript or that the folios of the manuscript were detached from one another during the process of interleaving.

26. A[rthur] G[eorge] Rigg, *A History of Anglo-Latin Literature 1066–1422* (Cambridge, 1992), 148. For a précis of his findings, see his "Anthologies and Florilegia," in *Medieval Latin: An Introduction and Bibliographical Guide*, ed. F. A.C. Mantello and A. G. Rigg (Washington, D.C., 1996), 709–712. Rigg's work extends the groundwork that was laid in the 1930s and 1940s by André Wilmart and André Boutemy.

27. See J. Peter Gumbert, "Codicological Units: Towards a Terminology for the Stratigraphy of the Non-Homogeneous Codex," *Segno e testo* 2 (2004): 17–42; Ralph Hanna, "Booklets in Medieval Manuscripts: Further Considerations," *Studies in Bibliography* 39 (1986): 100–111; P. R. Robinson, "Self-Contained Units in Composite Manuscripts of the Anglo-Saxon Period," *Anglo-Saxon England* 7 (1978): 231–238; and P. R. Robinson, "The 'Booklet': A Self-Contained Unit in Composite Manuscripts," *Codicologica* 3 (1980): 46–69.

28. For a review of the various terms and for concise bibliography, see Massimo Sannelli, "Raccolta, canzoniere, *Liederbuch*. *Ratio* e *ordo* delle raccolte poetiche mediolatine," in *Poesía latina medieval (siglos V–XV): Actas del IV Congreso del "Internationales Mittellateinerkomitee" (Santiago de Compostela, 12–15 de septiembre de 2002)*, ed. Manuel C. Díaz y Díaz and José M. Díaz de Bustamante (Florence, 2005), 303–307. The best attempt to present the Latin anthologies and *libelli* against the backdrop of the vernacular ones is Pascale Bourgain, "Les chansonniers lyriques latins," in *Lyrique romane médiévale: La tradition des chansonniers; Actes du Colloque de Liège, 1989*, ed. Madeleine Tyssens (Liège, 1991), 61–84.

points toward a separate initial production for fols. 3–8, which contain the epigrams, from fols. 1–2 and 9–11. For instance, crayon ruling appears only on fols. 3–8, even though not on every folio side there. Likewise, the arrangements of hairside and fleshside on fols. 3–8 and 9 follow "Gregory's rule," while those on fols. 1–2 and 10–11 do not.[29] The presence on fol. 2v of Poem 17, which serves as a preface to the biblical epigrams that begin on fol. 3r, does not necessarily disprove the idea of production in two stages, since it could have been an addition by a clever compiler with the aim of incorporating the earlier collection more comfortably into the new whole. It is also possible (see Figure 1) that the manuscript originally contained a leaf between the present fol. 2 and fol. 3, which, if oriented with its flesh side first and hair side second, would have meant that the only leaf in violation of Gregory's rule would have been the bifolium comprising fol. 1 and fol. 11. [BKB and JZ]

MS Lat 300 as an Anthology

In the twelfth century, anthologies were the most common form in which short poems in Latin such as lyrics, epigrams, and occasional verse circulated in written form among the reading public.[30] One vast Latin anthology from the early thirteenth century is famous throughout the West. German composer Carl Orff's oratorio of 1937 made the *Carmina Burana* a household word—if it had not attained this status as soon as the first edition appeared in 1847.[31] Yet Orff's twenty-five songs are just a small sampling of the anthology's more than two hundred twenty-five quantitative and rhythmic poems, which are organized in four groups: moral-satirical poems (1–55), love lyrics (56–186), and, less distinctly, first drinking and gaming poems and then religious dramas (187–228).[32]

Beyond the possible quality and the certain diversity of the poetry they contain,

29. Gregory's rule is named after the nineteenth-century German scholar, Caspar René Gregory (1846–1917). Gregory was the first to observe that medieval manuscripts present a regular alternation, in which every opening has facing each other a verso and a recto that are both either hairside or fleshside. For discussion, see Jacques Lemaire, *Introduction à la codicologie* (Louvain-la-Neuve, 1989), 46–47.

30. André Wilmart, "Le Florilège de Saint-Gatien: Contribution à l'étude des poèmes d'Hildebert et de Marbode," *Revue bénédictine* 48 (1936): 3: "La grande masse, si l'on peut dire, de petits poèmes, religieux et profanes, qui furent composés en latin depuis la fin du XIe siècle jusqu'en plein XIVe, nous a été conservée dans le cadre des florilèges. . . ." For a bibliography of published descriptions of anthologies, see A. G. Rigg, "Medieval Latin Poetic Anthologies (I)," *Mediaeval Studies* 39 (1977): 282–284. Rigg's work has continued in four subsequent articles with the same title, numbered II through V, the last authored with David Townsend, published in *Mediaeval Studies* 40 (1978): 387–407; 41 (1979): 468–505; 43 (1981): 472–497; and 49 (1987): 352–390.

31. J. A. Schmeller, ed. *Carmina Burana* (Stuttgart, 1847).

32. The standard edition of the Latin text is *Carmina Burana*, ed. Alfons Hilka, Otto Schumann, and Bernhard Bischoff, Band 1, vols. 1–3 (Heidelberg, 1930–1970), with the uncompleted commentary in Band 2, vol. 1 (Heidelberg, 1961).

anthologies are important for many reasons. No two medieval Latin anthologies are exactly the same. Rather, they vary according to the tastes and values of individuals or communities. Thus they are literary museums or, to take a metaphor from within the world of books, they are scrapbooks or commonplace books that reveal what was available and considered worth preserving and displaying. Accordingly, the anthologies sometimes constitute useful guides to medieval reading tastes and of cultural influences.[33] In many cases they provide tacit bestseller lists for their periods, since their contents indicate which poets and poems were in vogue in a given time and place. In short, anthologies have been recognized to hold considerable value for understanding the literary milieus of the Middle Ages.[34]

Since in the manuscript culture of the Middle Ages every anthology is unique, each one may provide insight into the relationships among other anthologies. Even a quick survey of the poems in Houghton MS Lat 300 suggests that the collection could eventually help in determining the filiation of some other, later anthologies. For instance, it is noteworthy that Houghton MS Lat 300 shares with Rg six items, Poems 2, 3, 7, 11, 12, and 88. Rg is itself closely connected with T: the two have in common sixteen items.[35] In turn, Houghton MS Lat 300 shares two items with T, Poems 5 and 88, the *De gemellis*; but the first piece is not found in Rg.

To look in a different direction, Houghton MS Lat 300 shares with Saint-Omer, Bibliothèque municipale, MS 115 (s. XII^2) both Poems 18 through 87, which are the biblical epigrams (including the "Natus homo, uitulus moriendo, leoque resurgens"), and Poem 89, *De paupere ingrato*.[36] Another codex that shows many proximities to Houghton MS Lat 300, more in themes and poetic language than in specific individual poems, is Zurich, Zentralbibliothek, MS C 58.[37]

The complex relationships between the Houghton manuscript and various other manuscripts confirm how freely Latin anthologies circulated and medieval anthologists rearranged, added, and subtracted poems in assembling new anthologies

33. Paul Lehmann, "Eine Sammlung mittellateinischer Gedichte aus dem Ende des 12. Jahrhunderts," *Historische Vierteljahrsschrift* 30 (1935): 22.

34. For a sampling of the approaches that have been taken to medieval anthologies in recent years, see Roberto Antonelli, ed., "L'antologia poetica," special issue, *Critica del testo* 2/1 (1999).

35. See Rigg, "Medieval Latin Poetic Anthologies (IV)," 480.

36. For descriptions of this manuscript, see Charles Fierville, "Notices et extraits des manuscrits de la Bibliothèque de Saint-Omer, nos. 115 et 710," in *Notices et extraits des manuscrits de la Bibliothèque nationale et autres bibliothèques* vol. 31, part 1 (Paris, 1884), 49–145, and André Boutemy, "Notes additionelles à la notice de Ch. Fierville sur le manuscrit 115 de Saint-Omer," *Revue belge de philologie et d'histoire*, 22 (1943): 5–23.

37. For detailed and perceptive analysis, see Jean-Yves Tilliette, "Le sens et la composition du florilège de Zurich (Zentralbibliothek, ms. C 58): Hypothèses et propositions," in *Non recedet memoria eius: Beiträge zur lateinischen Philologie des Mittelalters im Gedenken an Jakob Werner (1861–1944); Akten der wissenschaftlichen Tagung vom 9./10. September 1994 am Mittellateinischen Seminar der Universität Zürich*, ed. Peter Stotz (Bern, 1995), 147–167.

on the basis of old ones. The tradition we should envisage is one in which compilers blended their choice of poems from a constantly changing reservoir of regionally, nationally, or even internationally popular poems with the best of their own poems or those of local poets.[38]

Some anthologies present the collected or selected works of a single poet. Others are concatenations of poems that were employed as models in composition classes, poems that were produced in such classes, and poems such as epitaphs and eulogies that were composed by local artists for local audiences or addressees.[39] Houghton MS Lat 300 combines features of both these sorts of anthology. It also sheds light on medieval thinking about genres. Complementing the theoretical statements that can be found in Latin grammarians and rhetoricians, it offers concrete evidence about the kinds of poems that at least one medieval reader—namely, the compiler—associated with one another.[40] To commemorate the library that houses Houghton MS Lat 300, the poems have been given the name *Carmina Houghtoniensia* in the title of the present book. [JZ]

38. A slightly later anthology, probably from the area of Leicester and dating from 1180-1230, that is loosely comparable with Houghton MS Lat 300 is found in Cambridge, University Library, MS Ff.i.17 (1): see John Stevens, ed., *The Later Cambridge Songs* (Oxford, 2005).

39. André Wilmart, "Le Florilège de Saint-Gatien . . . Première partie," p. 11, defines the Tours florilegium as "un livret quasi officiel, où l'enseignement qui avait été donné de la rhétorique, au cours d'une assez longue période, vingt, trente ans peut-être, dans l'école capitulaire, se trouve mis au net et codifié, sous forme d'exemples variés."

40. A. G. Rigg, "Medieval Latin Poetic Anthologies (I)," *Mediaeval Studies* 39 (1977): 281.

EDITION

Principles of the Edition

THIS EDITION AIMS TO PROVIDE the Latin text and English translations, together with commentaries on literary features and discussions of historical contexts, for all the unedited items in Houghton MS Lat 300. For texts edited elsewhere, incipits and bibliographical information are supplied.

Each poem has a general introduction that furnishes literary and historical analysis, as appropriate. Before presenting the Latin texts, the editors offer guidance on where readers may find previously edited items, as well as on their incipits, the numbers assigned to them in Walther and in the electronic database *In principio: Incipit index of Latin texts*, manuscripts not listed in the incipitarium, and their lengths and metrical forms. Numbers for *In principio* are not provided for the poems by Hildebert, for which we supply incipits as well as references to the standard edition and to the numbers in Walther.

Within the editions, italics indicate letters or words that have been supplied or modified by the editors. The obelus † is placed before and after uncertain readings. Square brackets [ ] enclose indications of the folio, recto or verso, and column. These indications are preceded by a backslash \ if the column begins at that point.

The translations that come after the Latin texts do not pretend to be literary, but instead to convey the literal sense of the Latin. The English prose translations are followed in turn by textual notes. Then each section concludes with line-by-line commentary. The commentary is meant to gloss individual words and constructions that may pose especial difficulties, as well as to identify sources and analogues for wording and thinking in the texts. In presenting information on formulaic expressions and phrases, the commentary makes no effort to list all occurrences before the twelfth century. When an expression or phrase is documented widely, the commentary instead lists its earliest known occurrence in Latin literature. Obviously, such a listing does not necessarily indicate that the earliest occurrence of the expression or phrase is to be regarded as the source for its use in the Houghton anthology. [JZ]

Group One: "Medicamen et solamen"

Codicological Information

On the recto of the first folio is Poem 1, "Medicamen et solamen est paupertas homini." Although written in the same hand that copied Poems 2 through 17, "Medicamen et solamen" was probably added later: although it appears to be complete, it has neither a title, nor a red initial, nor even the unfilled space for a red initial. The folio is ruled in the same way as the others, but whereas the other folios with poems have few empty lines, this one has nearly twenty unfilled lines in the second column. These facts suggest that "Medicamen et solamen" was written after the other poems, on a folio side that had been left blank originally because the compiler intended or expected it to be placed at the front of his manuscript, where it would receive heavy wear.

Accentuation and Rhyme

Whereas all the other poems in the Houghton anthology are quantitative, this one is rhythmic. It is written in forty-four fifteen-syllable lines. Technically these lines are trochaic septenarii, usually described as having the pattern 8p + 7pp, where p signifies paroxytone—a word that carries an accent on the penultimate syllable—and pp, proparoxytone—a word accented on the antepenultimate syllable.[39]

These lines are end-rhymed in fifteen strophes of three lines (except lines 34–35). These tercets have been called sometimes *versus catapultini*, since the appearance of the three lines drawn from the common ending bears more than a slight resemblance to a sling—a little catapult.[40] In addition, each line is rhymed internally: (4p + 4p) + 7pp or (4pp + 4pp) + 7pp. With / indicating a syllable with a primary accent, ~ an unaccented syllable, and \ a syllable with a secondary accent, the line may be represented as / ~ / ~ | | / ~ / ~ | | / ~ / ~ / ~ \. This combination of internal and end-rhyme became popular from the early twelfth century.

39. Dag Norberg, *An Introduction to the Study of Medieval Latin Versification*, trans. Grant C. Roti and Jacqueline Skubly, ed. Jan Ziolkowski (Washington, D.C., 2004), 107–116.

40. For a reproduction of similarly arranged structure rhymes, see Pascale Bourgain, "La poésie lyrique médiévale," in *Mise en page et mise en texte du livre manuscrit*, ed. Henri-Jean Martin and Jean Vezin (Paris, 1990), 167 fig. 105 (Paris, Bibliothèque nationale, MS lat. 16208, fol. 135v). Such verses appear repeatedly in the *Historia Theophili*, a poem of 559 hexameters on the legend of Theophilus that has been ascribed to Marbod: 1.43–46, 51–56; 2.47–58, 63–66, 78–79; 3.28–29, 34–36, 40–41, in PL 171.1593–1604.

Content

The poem, which satirizes the power of money, belongs to the genre that is known as venality satire.[41] The power of money is embodied in the coin, designated most often as *nummus* but also three times as *denarius* (which could be translated slavishly as *denier*, after an old French coin with a name that derived ultimately from the Latin). The potential of coins to breed corruption, especially within the system of ecclesiastic justice, attracted much witty comment from the late eleventh century on. Line 4, line 13, and others suggest that this whole poem may be spoken in the voice of Nummus, the coin personified. [JZ]

POEM 1 Incipit "Medicamen et solamen est paupertas homini." Not included in Walther. *In principio*, reference 223363. Forty-four lines of fifteen syllables.

[1r^{A}] Medicamen et sol*a*men est pa*u*pertas homini
Qui scincere uult *t*enere caritatem Domini,
Ne molestus ac infestus fia*t* eius nomini.

Si quis credat, ut me ledat, munda cogitatio
Quo minuat uel destruat nummum, maliloquio,
Nunc audiat quid ueniat mali pro denario.

Quid ualeat, quid habeat nummus efficatie,
Ecclesias, prouincias quas corrumpat sanie:
Si queritur, disnoscitur in hac libri serie.

Paruus nummus princeps summus in Romana curia:
Causas regit, culpas tegit potestate regia;
Et disponit et exponit prout nil consilia.

Papa Rome fecit pro me: uidet nummi speciem!
Omnes uolunt, omnes colunt ipsius effigiem;
Imperantes et regnantes timent nummi faciem.

41. For general information, see John A. Yunck, *The Lineage of Lady Meed: The Development of Mediaeval Venality Satire* (Notre Dame, 1963). Interesting parallels may be found in the poems cited by Helga Schüppert, *Kirchenkritik in der lateinischen Lyrik des 12. und 13. Jahrhunderts* (Munich, 1972), 75–90 and 151–153.

Optimates et primates nummi uoluntatibus
Obsecuntur, et nituntur maximis conatibus
Ut placerent et fauerent nummosis hominibus.

Quod est iustum fit iniustum si nummo placuerit;
Inimici sunt amici si nummus dictauerit;
Inhonesti sunt honesti si nummus decreuerit.

Inter reges, inter leges fit quod nummi cupiunt;
Denario cum gaudio canones obediunt;
Tam clerici quam laici prompte nummo seruiunt.

Ut cineres caracteres atque priuilegia
Estimantur et dampnantur absente pecunia;
Carte stabunt quibus dabunt nummorum obsequia.

Criminales cardinales fiunt pro denario;
Qui furantur ordinantur mediante precio;
Qui dampnantur liberantur p*ro*curante premio.

[1r^{B}] Expectatur et amatur inter causas precium:
Qui rogabit nec donabit fundet *uani*loquium;
Qui prebebit, hic placebit tenenti consilium.

Compelleris et traheris ad cause negocium.
Denarius fit preuius: molliet iudicium.

Hostis premit, tua demit, et iniusta pateris;
Tua capit, tua rapit, et ad causam traheris;
Nec prebebit, nec spondebit; frustra loqui *n*iteris.

Si ueneris nec dederis, iudex dicet, "Langueo.
Inducias ut capias opus est; uix sedeo.
Nunc habito. Cras redito, quia cap*u*t doleo."

Si redeas nec habeas quid possis tribuhere,
Stultus redis et incedis, quia cares munere;
Ad ultimum stultis*s*imum poteris te dicere.

Poverty is remedy and solace to a man
who truly wishes to retain the Lord's affection,
so that he doesn't become troubling or hostile to His name.

If anyone, in order to damage me, gives credence to the disparagement
by which pure thinking aims to diminish or destroy the coin,
let him now hear what evil comes in return for cash.

Of what the coin is capable, what potency it has,
the churches and provinces it corrupts with its venom:
if this is sought, it will be discerned in the contents of this book.

The little coin is the highest prince in the Roman curia:
with regal power it rules over lawsuits, conceals guilt;
it arranges and expounds counsels, as if they were nothing.

The pope of Rome has acted in my behalf: he sees the beauty of the coin!
All desire, all worship its image;
those who command and those who rule fear the face of the coin.

Magnates and primates are submissive to the coin's
desires, and they strive with their utmost efforts
to be pleasing and well disposed to coinful men.

What is just becomes unjust if it is pleasing to the coin;
enemies are friends if the coin so dictates;
the dishonest are honest if the coin decrees it so.

Among kings, among laws what the coins desire happens;
with joy canons obey cash;
clerks as well as lay folk readily serve the coin.

As so many ashes are warrants and privileges
appraised and condemned where money is absent;
charters will stand firm, for which [people] grant the services of coins.

Criminals become cardinals in return for cash;
when payment intervenes, those who steal are ordained;
when a reward sees to things, those condemned are set free.

Payment is expected and loved in lawsuits:
whoever pleads and doesn't give will squander empty speech;
whoever offers, he will please the one who holds counsel. 33

You will be summoned and dragged to the action of the suit.
Cash leads the way: it will soften the judgment. 35

Your enemy oppresses, he takes what's yours, and you suffer injustices.
He seizes what's yours, snatches what's yours, and you're dragged into a lawsuit;
he'll neither offer, nor pledge; in vain you'll strive to speak. 38

If you come and do not give, the judge will say, "I'm tired.
You have to take a recess; I can hardly stay in my seat.
For now, go off! Come back tomorrow, because I have a headache." 41

If you return and do not have something you can pay,
then you return and enter as a fool, because you lack a gift;
to the end you'll be able to call yourself most foolish. 44

Textual Notes

1] sol*a*men: solomen, *with second* o *expunged.* pa*u*pertas: papertas.

2] uult *t*enere: uultenere *written as single word.*

3] fia*t*: fia.

4] le*d*at: legat, *with* gat *underlined, and correction* dat *added above line.*

12] nil, *with extra minim preceding.*

17] conatibus: cognatibus.

22] cupiunt: cupitunt, *with first* t *expunged.*

25] *The first word of this line is extremely unclear.*

30] pr*o*curante: precurante (*initial* p *with a stroke above to signify* re).

32] *uani*loquium: *Between* fundet *and* loquium *three letters have been erased in an uncompleted correction. Sense and meter are both well-served by* uaniloquium *(compare* frustra loqui niteris *in line 38), although* maliloquium *(compare line 5) would be another possibility.*

38] prebebit: prem, *with* m *underlined and* bebit *written supralinearly.* *n*iteris: miteris.

40] uix sedeo: indicio *written on the line,* uix sedeo *added above it although without any indication of deletion.*

41] cap*u*t: capit.

44] stultis*s*imum: stultisimum.

Commentary

2. **scincere** = *sincere.*
4. **credat, ut me ledat**: The syntax of this line is embroiled. **me**: Here as in line 13, the personal pronoun refers to a personified "Coin," who serves as the narrator of the poem.
5. **nummum:** By "the coin" is perhaps meant more broadly "(the power or the influence of) the coin." **maliloquium:** Franz Blatt, *Novum glossarium mediae Latinitatis ab anno DCCC usque ad annum MCC* (Copenhagen, 1969–), "Ma," col. 75, lines 35–40, and David Howlett, *Dictionary of Medieval Latin from British Sources*, fasc. 6 "M" (London, 2001), 1694.
6. **denario:** The coin in question is strictly speaking a *denier.*
9. **disnoscitur** = *dinoscitur.* **in hac libri serie**: Literally, "in these contents of the book." On *series* meaning "contents (of a book, etc.)," compare Aldhelm, *Carmen de virginitate* 772–773, ed. Ehwald, 385 ("Non pigeat prorsus seriem spectare libelli, / in quo scribuntur virtutes illius amplae").
17. **Obsecuntur** (Obse9tur in MS) = *obsequuntur.*
25. **caracteres**: R. E. Latham, *Dictionary of Medieval Latin from British Sources*, fasc. 2 "C" (London, 1981), 323, *character* 2c.
30. **procurante**: The MS reading is clearly *precurante*, which could be construed as meaning "tending to beforehand" or "taking care of in advance." But rather than struggle with an awkward hapax legomenon, it is worth noting that the preceding line ends with *precio* and that the following word is *premio*, either of which could have easily led the scribe to dittography for the initial word element.

34–35. These verses are not written as part of a threesome. Presumably a verse has dropped out, which could have happened easily since 31–35 share the same rhyme. Alternatively, two verses may have been added here to a shorter, earlier version. [PP]

Group Two

POEMS 2 THROUGH 17 (fols. $1v^A$–$2v^B$) amount to an anthology within the anthology. The arrangement of these poems evinces a deliberate thematic progression that should probably be credited to the care of the anthologist in the selection (or composition?) and organization of his materials. Although nine of these pieces bear titles (Poems 2 through 6 and 8 through 11), in no case here or elsewhere in the manuscript is authorship indicated. The first three poems in this group, Poems 2 through 4, handle the interrelated topics of illness, medicine, and death. In this connection, Inez Lynn has noted that Rg contains two clusters of poems concerned both with the status of poets and their sources of inspiration and with antimedical satire.[42] These themes come to the fore in Rg 55/57–61 and 126–128. Interestingly, these runs of poems contain four that also appear in Houghton MS Lat 300: Rg 60 = Poem 2, Rg 126 = Poem 3, Rg 57 = Poem 7, and Rg 55 = Poem 88. But the relationship between the two manuscripts is not a simple one, in which either is directly indebted to the other or even in which the two clearly derive from a common ancestor.[43] Instead, the two derive from different but perhaps related exemplars.

The poems in Group Two provide a pleasing sample of the various techniques available to medieval writers of dactylic verse. Seven of the sixteen poems are in elegiac couplets, the others in hexameters, and all but three (Poems 6, 7, and 8) use rhyme as a principle of composition. Rhyme is incorporated in several different ways. Verses with end-rhyme, known as *caudati*, occur in a few different configurations. Three of the poems use a single end-rhyme throughout (2: -ore, 9: -orum, 15: -eri). Another two are grouped in quatrains of end-rhymed verses (12, 13), and there are three poems written in rhymed pairs (4, 11, and 14, with 4 and 11 more specifically designated as *elegi caudati*). A second species of medieval dactylic rhyme occurs within the line of verse. When, as in Poems 3, 16, and 17, the rhyme falls at the penthemimeral caesura and the line-end, the verses, whether hexameter or elegiac, are categorized as leonine (*leonini*). Poem 5 has the most complex rhyme structure (*versus bicipites* or *sinodati*) with each line containing two rhyming pairs, one in the

42. See Inez T. P. A. Lynn, "A Critical Edition of Latin Poems from Oxford, Bodleian Library MS. Rawlinson G.109" (M.Litt. thesis, University of Oxford, 2001). Lynn, librarian of the London Library, has in progress an article to make available the unpublished poems from Rg that were omitted from Rigg, "Medieval Latin Poetic Anthologies (IV)," *Mediaeval Studies* 43 (1981): 472–497.

43. Lynn, "Critical Edition," 32, points out that in lines 10–11 the Houghton manuscript and R share a reading against Rg, whereas in lines 4 and 6 R and Rg are opposed to the Houghton manuscript. She reaches the conclusion that I have restated in the sentence that follows above.

first penthemimer, the second in the final hepthemimer; each line-division ends with a rhyme. This form, along with the leonines, marks out the main caesura in each verse as the most important point of articulation. Such a well-defined sense of the division of the line was not characteristic of dactylic poetry before the Middle Ages.

Adherence to the classical norms of dactylic composition varies. Elision is infrequent, found only twice in Group Two, in the unrhymed elegies (7.2, 8.2). Hiatus does not occur. The poets represented here were generally careful about quantities: even lengthening of short syllables at a caesura is rare, though it does occur (torto*ris*, 15.4; cup*is*, 17.1). Strong fifth-foot caesuras, resulting in a word-group of four syllables at the line end, were avoided by classical poets, and here too, for the most part, they are absent. The classicizing authors of poems 7 and 8 allowed four-syllable Greek names at the line-end, however (Eliconem, 7.1; Epicurus, 8.3). This convention also gives way when faced with the exigencies of leonine and bicipital rhyme: fifth-foot caesuras occur with some frequency in the leonines (e.g., 3.3 and 5; 16.3), and quite often in Poem 5, where the rhyme scheme makes the greatest demands on the poet's Latinity (lines 3, 6, 11, 23, 26, 29, 30, 36, 37, 38). Poem 5 is also the only poem in Group Two whose verses sometimes end with monosyllables. In general then, the poems of Group Two hold carefully to basic prosodic conventions, although the construction of rhyme within a verse may take precedence over these.

POEM 2. Incipit "Flebilis hora redit: reditum fle flebilis hore." Twenty lines of the end-rhymed hexameters known as *caudati*.[44] Walther 6601. *In principio*, references 141917 and 2048683. Edited from R, fol. 189, in Wilhelm Wattenbach, "Beschreibung einer Handschrift der Stadtbibliothek zu Reims," *Neues Archiv der Gesellschaft für ältere deutsche Geschichtskunde* 18 (1893): 514. In addition, the poem is extant in Rg: see A. G. Rigg, "Medieval Latin Poetic Anthologies (IV)," *Mediaeval Studies* 43 (1981): 487, no. 60.

In R this poem is immediately preceded by one that is closely related in both form and content: twenty end-rhymed hexameters on the topic of a persistent fever.[45]

44. See Wilhelm Meyer, "Radewins Gedichte über Theophilus und die Arten der gereimten Hexameter," in *Gesammelte Abhandlungen zur mittellateinischen Rythmik*, vol. 1 (Berlin, 1905; repr., Hildesheim, 1970), 82–83; and Paul Klopsch, *Einführung in die mittellateinische Verslehre* (Darmstadt, 1972), 78.

45. Incipit "Ut medici perhibent, mea febris in ossibus heret" (Walther 19830): see Wilhelm Wattenbach, "Beschreibung einer Handschrift der Stadtbibliothek zu Reims," 513–514. For a twenty-six line poem (incipit "Musa iocosa veni, mihi carmina suggere vati") the final twenty lines of which are all end-rhymed on *-ore*, see Peter Dronke, *Medieval Latin and the Rise of European Love-Lyric*, 2 vols., 2nd ed. (Oxford, 1968), 2:451.

In Rg an unrelated poem intervenes between the two.[46] Presumably "Flebilis hora redit," which begins by mentioning that a fever is returning (*redit*), was a sequel to the other poem, which the compiler of the Houghton manuscript did not include.

IV[A] De accessu febris

Flebilis hora redit: reditum fle flebilis hore,
In cuius reditu febris incumbente calore
Afficitur curis animus corpusque labore.
Vis perit exterior, quia ui caret interiore;
Singula membra iacent, proprio uiduata uigore.
Lux caligat, *hebent aures* nec gaudet *od*ore
Naris, et esca gulam non mitigat ulla sapore,
Priuanturque manus tactu rerumque tenore.
Forma decens roseo spectabilis ante decore
Quam deformauit macies, fugiente rubore,
Posset spectantes subito turbare timore,
Et me terribili perterret bubo canore,
Et super humano strix uisa dolere dolore,
At quociens quouis soluuntur membra sopore,
Me terrent lemures aspersaque monstra cruore,
Et furie que corda mouent humana furore
Tesifone*q*ue minax et peior utraque sorore
Verbera seua parat Stigio perfusa liquore,
Et Stigium carmen laruali persona*t ore*,
Hirta comas uultuque ferox et opaca colore.

About the Onset of Fever

The mournful hour returns: lament the return of the mournful hour,
at the return of which, as the heat of a fever attacks,
the soul is afflicted by cares and the body by distress.
Outward strength perishes, because it lacks inward strength.
All the limbs lie idle, bereft of their characteristic vigor.
Vision grows blurred, hearing turns dull, the nose takes no pleasure
in scent, no food assuages the throat with taste,
and the hands lose their capacity for touching and holding objects.
One's graceful appearance, formerly outstanding for rosy beauty,
could alarm onlookers with sudden fright,
once gauntness has disfigured it and dispelled its ruddiness.

46. See Rigg, "Medieval Latin Poetic Anthologies (IV)," 487, nos. 58–60.

The horned owl frightens me with frightful song
and, in addition, the owl seems to grieve with human grief;
but however often my limbs are released in any sleep,
ghosts and blood-spattered monsters frighten me,
and furies which stir human hearts with madness;
and Tisiphone, threatening and worse than either of her sisters,
readies savage blows, drenched in the water of the river Styx;
and, shaggy-haired, fierce-faced, and dark-colored,
she sounds out a hellish song with ghoulish mouth.

Textual Notes

Title and initial letter rubricated.

1] fle: fleo *R*, *Rg*.
2] incumbente: inconbente *Rg*.
4] exterior: interior *R*, *Rg*. ui: *omitted Rg*. interiore: exteriore *R*.
6] aures hebent: hebent aures *R*, *Rg*. hore: odore *R*, *Rg*.
9] roseo: reseo *Rg*.
10–11] fugiente rubore / . . . turbare timore: turbare timore / . . . fugiente rubore *Rg*.
13] strix: stirx *Rg*.
14] At: Et *R*. sopore: dolore *corrected above line to* sopore.
15] aspersaque: asperaque *Rg*.
17] Tesifone que: Thesiphoneque *R*, Tesiphoneque *Rg*.
18] parat: parit *Rg*. stigio: stygio *Rg*.
19] stigium: stygium *Rg*. laruali: laruari *Rg*. persona: personat ore *R*, *Rg*.
20] et opaca *added above line in same hand*.

Commentary

1. **flebilis hore**: Compare the line ending "flebilis hora," conventional since Prudentius, *Hamartigenia* 943, ed. Cunningham, 148.
2. **In cuius reditu**: Compare the line opening "pro cuius reditu" in Ovid, *Remedia amoris* 548, ed. Kenney, 226.
5. **Singula membra**: This pairing is trite in Latin verse, both classical and medieval. **membra iacent**: An opening in Ovid, *Metamorphoses* 11.50, ed. Tarrant, 315, stock thereafter. **uiduata uigore**: The same ending appears later in Nigel of Canterbury, *Miracula* 2177, ed. Ziolkowski, 84.

6–8. These lines detail the effects of the fever upon the five senses.

9. **Forma decens**: An opening already in Ovid, *Amores* 3.1.9, ed. Kenney, 67.
11. **turbare timore**: The same ending is attested from Lucretius, *De rerum natura* 1.106, ed. Bailey (unpaginated).
12. **terribili . . . canore**: Compare "terribilem . . . canoro" in the same metrical positions in Vergil, *Aeneid* 9.503, ed. Mynors, 322. **bubo**: On the owl as harbinger of death, see Baudri, *Carmina* 23.5, ed. Tilliette, 1:44 ("bubo

canens"); and Marbod, *Carmina* 1.39.1, in PL 171.1672D ("Bubo ferum nomen, dirum mortalibus omen").

13. **humano . . . dolore**: This adjective and noun appear in these metrical positions already in Propertius, *Carmina* 1.16.25 and 2.1.57, ed. Barber, 22 and 32, and in Ovid, *Metamorphoses* 1.246, ed. Tarrant, 10. **dolere dolore**: Compare the pentameter ending "dolere dolor" in Ovid, *Heroides* 20.4, ed. Kenney, 66.
14. **membra sopore**: A line ending repeatedly (with variations in the case of the final word) after Lucretius, *De rerum natura* 4.453, ed. Bailey.
17. **Tesifoneque**: For metrical reasons the name appears most often in this metrical position in dactylic poetry, and there is no allusion here to any specific earlier appearance. **utraque sorore**: Allecto and Megaera.
18. **Verbera seua**: This phrase, attested first as a hexameter ending in Vergil, *Georgics* 3.252, ed. Mynors, 72, appears first as a line opening in Ovid, *Ibis* 157, ed. Owen (unpaginated). **perfusa liquore**: Attested as a hexameter ending already in pseudo-Vergil, *Culex* 14, ed. Clausen, 10.
19. **personat ore**: This line ending is attested first in Silius Italicus, *Punica* 2.43, ed. Delz, 29.
20. **Hirta comas**: Compare Lucan, *De bello ciuili* 8.680, ed. Shackleton Bailey, 218 ("Regibus hirta coma"). **uultuque ferox**: It may be chance that the similar phrase "uultu ferox" appears as a line ending in Seneca the Younger, *Troades* 1152, ed. Zwierlein, 94.

POEM 3. Incipit "*N*e uetitis cenis inhiet gula, comprime frenis!" Ten lines of internally rhymed elegiac distichs. Not in Walther. *In principio,* reference 2075502. Edited from Rg by Rigg, "Medieval Latin Poetic Anthologies (IV)," 493, no. 126.

The compiler happens (or is determined?) to create a medical section of sorts within his anthology, for he follows Poem 2 ("Flebilis hora redit") with a composition that describes a major cause of illness and its consequences. The third poem tells of two perennial battles, with the waistline and with doctors.

[1v^{A}] De custodia diete et falsis medicis

*N*e uetitis cenis inhiet gula, comprime frenis!
    Comprime, ni malis non caruisse malis.
Si mihi cauissem, si frena gule posuissem,
    In me quartanas non reuocasset anas.
Quot tot Cloto notat uexatque febris, gula potat;
    Ergo si sapias, frena gule facias.
[1v^{B}] Viscera torquentur, quia felle *lut*oque replentur:
    ad medici nutum fel bibo, ceno lutum.

Hec mihi causa necis sit amare potio fecis,
    sed pereat per eam quod facit ut peream!

About Adhering to a Diet and about False Doctors

The gullet opens wide for forbidden foods. Clamp it shut!
    Clamp it shut, unless you prefer to suffer illnesses.
If I had watched out for myself, if I had clamped my gullet shut,
    a duck would not have caused my quartan fever to return.
The gullet absorbs just as many as Clotho marks and as fever ravages.
    Therefore, if you have your wits, clamp your gullet shut.
My intestines are tortured, because they are filled with bile and mud.
    I drink bile, I eat mud at the doctor's behest.
This potion of bitter dregs may be the cause of my death,
    but may it perish, because it causes me to perish through it!

Textual Notes

Title and first letter in rubrics.

1] De: Ne *Rg*.

3] cauissem: cauisem *H*.

5] notat: necat *Rg*, secat *conjectures Rigg*. potat (*emended to fit rhyme scheme*): portat *H*, necat *Rg* (*against the meter*). *Probably the scribe incorrectly wrote* notat *and then produced* portat *in order to supply a rhyme, of sorts.*

7–10] *Transposition rubric after 6 leads to rubric below column two, where the four lines are written (in a different hand?)*

7] ciboque: lutoque *Rg*.

9] Hec (*with first letter corrected and third one difficult to interpret)*: Hoc *Rg*. *An additional* sit *written above potio.*

10] pereat *Rg*: perit *H* (*against the meter*).

Commentary

2. **caruisse malis**: Compare the pentameter ending in Ovid, *Ex Ponto* 1.3.46, ed. Owen ("caruisse malum").
3. **frena gule posuissem**: Compare this phrase as well as the similar "frena gule facias" in 6 with Hildebert, *Carmina miscellanea* 27.12, in PL 171.1391D ("Frena gulae posuit, non gula frena viro"). Lynn, "Critical Edition," 153n90, makes the case for interpreting *gula* in this poem as carrying connotations of greed, on the grounds that greed was viewed in ancient and medieval medical theory as being conducive to fever.
5. "just as many *people* as Clotho marks *for death*."
7. **Viscera torquentur**: This line opening is attested first in Venantius Fortunatus, *Carmina* 9.2.57, ed. Leo, 207; ed. Reydellet, 2:17.

9. **Hec**: The reading **Hoc** in Rg could be translated as having the neuter *fel* in line 8 as its antecedent and as being in apposition to *potio*: "This [poison], a drink of bitter dregs." But construing the words in this fashion seems tortured. Although the reading *Hec* is uncertain in both its first and its last letters, it produces better sense. **causa necis**: A phrase commonplace from Ovid, *Heroides* 10.144 (pentameter line ending), ed. Knox, 72, on.
10. **quod**: Determining what should be understood as the subject of this line and what as the antecedent of *eam* is tricky. The strongest likelihood is that both *pereat* and *facit* have as their subject *gula*, while *eam* refers to *potio*. Since both manuscripts read *quod*, this word would have to be emended to *qui* to allow for the possibility that the line means "may he perish through it who causes me to perish." Without emendation it could also be translated as "but may he perish through it because he causes me to perish," in which case the "he" would refer to the *medicus* mentioned two lines earlier (in 8).

POEM 4. Incipit "Mors furit et mortis emancipat omne furori." Four lines: two hexameter couplets with end-rhyme. Not in Walther. Not in *In principio*. Published from this manuscript by Monteil, 2:178.

[\1v[B]] De morte

Mors furit et mortis emancipat omne furori.
    Nil morti demens, mors facit omne mori.
Mors indiscrete maiora minoribus equat;
    Omnia mors equa condicione necat.

About Death

Death rages and frees everything from the rage of death.
    Depriving death of nothing, death causes everything to die.
Death renders the great equal to the humble, without distinction;
    death slays all on the same terms.

Textual Notes

Title and first letter in rubrics. Published from this manuscript by Monteil, 2:178: "Mors furit et morti somnicipat omne furo / Nil morti dirimus, mors facit omne mo / Mors indistincte majora cratieribus equat / Omnia mors equa conditione necat."

Commentary

1. **Mors furit**: A similar idea, though expressed differently, appears in Baudri, *Carmina* 46.1, ed. Tilliette, 1:55 ("Mors uelut effrenis ruptis bacchatur habenis").
2. **Nil mort***: A common line opening.

3–4. These two lines could function well as a versified gloss on Horace, *Odes* 1.4.13–14, ed. Shackleton Bailey, 7: "pallida Mors aequo pulsat pede pauperum tabernas / regumque turris." Horace's *sententia* was much cited in the Middle Ages: see Hans Walther, *Proverbia sententiaeque Latinitatis medii aevi: Lateinische Sprichwörter und Sentenzen des Mittelalters in alphabetischer Anordnung*, vol. 3 (Göttingen, 1965), 695, no. 20578.

4. **Omnia mors**: Routinely found as an opening from Seneca the Younger, *De qualitate temporis* 7, in *Anthologia Latina*, no. 224, ed. Shackleton Bailey, 164.

POEM 5. Incipit "Ve, quid agam? Plagam sub mesto pectore gesto." Thirty-nine hexameter lines, internally rhymed with the pattern aabb. In medieval handbooks on metrics such verses were designated *bicipites* and *sinodati*.[47] In the medieval definition cited by Meyer, the consonances are purportedly at either end of the verse, in the first and second and in the fifth and sixth feet, respectively; but Meyer points out variations in this pattern. Here the consonances in the first half of the line most commonly rhyme the first foot with the end of the second and beginning of the third, in the second half of the line the fourth foot with the sixth. But the placement of the consonances varies considerably, not only falling sometimes at the beginning and sometimes at the end (or even in the middle) of a foot, but also even moving to another foot altogether. Thus the consonance that usually joins together the fourth foot with the sixth may begin instead with a rhyme that runs from the end of the third to the beginning of the fourth or from the end of the fourth to the beginning of the fifth foot or, exceptionally, that falls in the third (see 25) or fifth (see 9) foot. What might appear to be the most daring departure from the usual scheme comes on a single occasion when the four rhymes are concentrated in the third, fourth, fifth, and sixth feet, but this unique arrangement is likely to have arisen from a textual corruption (see 21). Not in Walther.[48] *In principio*, references 412392, 412437 (Paris, Bibliothèque nationale, MS lat. 3343, fol. 93v [fifteenth century]), and 412438. Also extant in T: see Rigg, "Medieval Latin Poetic Anthologies (I)," *Mediaeval Studies* 39 (1977): 307, no. 58.

47. Meyer, "Radewins Gedichte über Theophilus," 92–93.

48. Before the manuscript came into the possession of the Houghton Library, this poem was listed by Dronke, *Medieval Latin and the Rise of European Love-Lyric*, 2:575 (on the basis of Vernet's brief description).

The fifth poem is linked with its predecessors through its closing description of illness and death, but it is mainly on the theme of desperate love (as its title indicates).

[1v[B]] Conquestio amantis

Ve, quid agam? Plagam sub mesto pectore gesto;
Saucius interius, doleo nimis ossibus imis;
Torqueor et teneor, laqueo captus Cithereo;
Sollicitus penitus, loris constringor Amoris.
Quem sequor, ille decor me lesit et intus adhesit.
Hic meus est laqueus, hinc cure non habiture.
Constituam statuam Veneri morboque mederi.
Qui dolet, intro uolet; cadet hinc data uic*t*ima grata
Igne nec indigne pona*m* deuotus ego tus,
Hancque colam solam, si purget dura quod urget.
Hactenus ergo, Venus, fer opem, queso, michi leso.
Quero michi misero, michi mesto, micior esto.
Quod peto, completo. Gere morem, pelle dolorem;
Vulnera letifera, dea, comprime, redde michi me.
Nam tenere, misere sum captus, sum michi raptus.
Me tenet ut penet Ioue digna superba Corigna.
Querit sponte, *g*erit michi bella superba puella.
Cum fleo, cum doleo miser eque nocte dieque,
*Ac*rior asperior id curat ut acrius urat.
Enecor, excecor, quia quod precor inflat ere cor.
Tu cor ad hoc, dea, uelle pelle rebelle puelle.
Expuit et renuit michi mente pari sociari.
Ridet quando uidet commotum me fore totum.
Estus et questus lacrimantis ridet amantis.
[2r[A]] Mens igitur quatitur, foris extant signa doloris,
Nec latet, immo patet certis signis meus ignis.
Nam caro dum raro quod uul*t* habet, arida tabet.
Risus abest, uisus lacrimis tabescit opimis.
Sed dolor, ira, color, gemitus tociens repetitus.
Quid sibi na*mque* cibi? Cibus eius quod michi peius.
Est rudis in ludis, effrenis parque leenis.
Tu, dea nectarea, distilla nectar ut illa
Effrenis lenis, infesta sit inde modesta.
Muneribus, precibus cum tempto domumque frequento,

Quid paro? Litus aro, cui tandem semina mandem?
Cum secor atque precor, aures claudit, nichil audit.
Plus ideo doleo, crescit furor et magis uror.
Fessus et oppressus tandem morbum fero grandem.
Mors prope: nudus ope, uicinam cerno ruinam.

A Lover's Lament

Alas, what am I to do? I bear a wound within my sad heart;
smitten within, I grieve exceedingly to the very marrow of my bones;
I am tortured and held fast, captured by the snare of Venus;
troubled through and through, I am bound by the bonds of Love.
The beauty that I follow has wounded me and has clung to my heart.
It is my snare, from it come cares that will not pass away.
I will erect a statue to Venus and will arrange to be healed of sickness.
Let the person who suffers pain hurry inside: a pleasing sacrificial animal given by him
will fall and, not undeservedly, I will place incense devoutly in the fire.
I will worship her alone, if she dispels the trouble she harshly threatens.
Therefore bring aid, Venus, I ask, to me here because I am wounded.
I ask, be gentler to me, sad and wretched as I am.
Carry out what I ask. Indulge me, banish my sorrow;
bind my fatal wounds, goddess, return me to myself,
for I have been lovingly captured, wretchedly wrenched from myself.
Haughty Corinna, fit for Jupiter, holds me to punish me.
Of her own free will the proud girl seeks and wages war against me.
When I weep and grieve, wretched equally by night and day,
she grows keener and harsher; and she takes care that passion burns me more keenly.
I am tortured and blinded, because my entreaties puff up the heart of my mistress.
Impel you, goddess, the rebellious heart of the girl to this wish.
She spurns and refuses to be joined with like mind to me.
She laughs when she sees that I am entirely distraught;
she laughs at the frenzy and lamentation of a weeping lover.
Therefore my mind is shattered: the signs of grief can be seen outwardly,
and my passion is not hidden, but is displayed with sure indications;
for when the flesh seldom has what it wishes, it withers and wastes away.
Laughter is gone, power of sight wastes away from plentiful tears.

But grief, passion, the flush of emotion, and moans are many times repeated.
What is her food? Her food is what is worst for me.
She is graceless and unruly in play, no different from lionnesses.
You, goddess sweet as nectar, sprinkle nectar so that that
unruly and violent girl may then be gentle and mild.
When I court her with gifts and entreaties and visit her home constantly,
what do I achieve? I plow a shore, to which in the end I should consign seeds?
When I follow her about and beg, she shuts her ears and hears nothing.
Therefore I grieve more, the frenzy grows, and I am inflamed more.
Tired and overpowered, at length I suffer a great illness.
Death is close: stripped of resources, I see my demise nearby.

Textual Notes

Title (in red): not in T.

1] Ve *initial in red.* iesto (i *expunged,* g *above line*): gesto *T.*

2] ossibus: osibus *H.*

2–3] *Or punctuate* "Saucius interius doleo nimis; ossibus imis / Torqueor et teneor . . ."

5] ille decor: iste decor *T.*

6] hinc cure non habiture: hec insita corde sagitta *T.*

7–8] *Or punctuate* "Constituam statuam Veneri; morboque mederi / Qui dolet . . ."

8] intro: intra *T.* uictima: uitime *H,* uictima *T.*

9] Igne: Digne *T.* pona*m*: pona *H,* ponam *T.* tus: thus *T.*

10] dura: diua *T.*

12] michi s misero (s *expunged*): michi misero *T.*

13] gere morem: gero morem *T.*

14] Vulnera: Wlnera *T.*

17] *g*erit: ierit *H,* gerit *T.*

18] cum doleo *or* condoleo: cum doleo *T.* docteque (d *expunged,* n *above line*) dieque: nocte dieque *T.*

19] *A*crior: Ascrior *H,* Acrior *T.*

21] dea, uelle: uelle dea *T.*

24] Estus et questus: us *written in red on line,* et questus *written in red in margin.*

25] foris extant signa doloris: *ink thick.*

26] patet *written above line. In T the letters before* signis *are smudged and* ignis *is oddly abbreviated* ig^{i}s.

27] Nam: Iam *T.* dum: de *T.* uul: uult *T.* arida: arrida *T.*

29] tociens: tocies *T.*

30] na*m*que: nape *H,* namque *T.* quod michi: *word written in between and inked out.* cibus: cibet *T.*

34] cum tempto *or* contempto: cum tempto *T.*

35] semina: femina *H*, femine *T*.
36] Cum secor *or* consecor: Cum sequor *T*
38] tandem morbum: morbum tandem *T*.
39] *Final letter of* Mors *smudged T*.

Commentary

1. **Ve, quid agam**: The comparable opening "Heu, quid agam" is commonplace in hexameter poetry.
2. **ossibus imis**: A line ending in *Ilias Latina* 25.
3. **Torqueor**: To open a line with this word is characteristically Ovidian. **laqueo captus Cithereo**: The net or toils of Venus are a commonplace image. Compare pseudo-Ovid, *De Piramo* 2.17, ed. Lehmann, 47 ("Cipridis in laqueo captiuus uterque iacebat").
4. **loris constringor amoris**: For a very close parallel (or source of inspiration?), see Marbod, *Carmina* 1.17.1 (incipit "Strictus eram loris vesani nuper amoris"), in PL 171.1655D. The poem is also found in Zurich, Zentralbibliothek, MS C 58, fol. 40v, ed. Jakob Werner, *Beiträge zur Kunde der lateinischen Literatur des Mittelalters aus Handschriften gesammelt*, 2nd ed. (Aarau, 1905; repr., Hildesheim, 1979), 88, no. 199.
5. The phrasing shows similarities to the "elegiac comedy" known as *Pamphilus de amore* 455, ed. Rubio and González Rolán, 138 ("Spes mea me lesit! Per spem Venus ossibus hesit!").
6. Although the combination of *cure* and *habiture* is by no means unique, it may be significant that Marbod was fond of it: see *Versus de sancto Laurentio* 31, in PL 171.1608B, and *Carmina* 1.4.19, in PL 171.1718B.
7. It is probably merely fortuitous that a poem attributed to Hildebert has a pentameter ending "constituit statuas": see *Carmen in libros Regum* 4.530, in PL 171.1261C. **morboque mederi**: The line ending "morboque medere" is attested already in Cyprian of Gaul, *Heptateuchos*, "Numeri" 313, ed. Peiper, 127. Although *medeor* was only a deponent verb in Classical Latin, in Late Latin and Medieval Latin it is also attested as a regular transitive verb: see Howlett, *Dictionary of Medieval Latin from British Sources*, fasc. 6 "M," 1741. If understood as a deponent here and not in a passive sense, it could be translated alternatively here as "[for her] to heal the sickness."
8. **uictima grata**: This phrase is Ovidian in origin (*Fasti* 1.440, ed. Alton, Wormell, and Courtney, 15), but was also used at least twice each by Baudri (*Carmina* 142.22 and 210.4, ed. Tilliette 2:51 and 143) and Hildebert (*De mysterio missae* 194, in PL 171.1182C, and (possibly pseudo-Hildebert) *Inventio sanctae crucis* 262, in PL 171.1319D).
11. **Hactenus ergo**: This opening is attested at the latest from Milo of Saint-Amand (Elnonenis: died 871/872), *Vita Amandi* 2.190, ed. Traube, 583.

15. **tenere:** Emending *tenere* (tenderly) to *temere* (recklessly) could be tempting, but preserving the manuscript reading allows for a hyperbaton that alludes to the bittersweet effects of love.
16. **Corigna**: This is Corinna, subject of many of Ovid's love poems (*Amores* 1.5, 1.11, 2.6, 2.8, 2.11–13, 2.17, 2.19, 3.1, 3.7, and 3.12, ed. Kenney, 11–12, 26–27, 43–45, 46–47, 51–56, 61–62, 64–66, 66–69, 82–85, 94–96).
19. **acrius urat**: Compare the line ending in Ovid, *Amores* 2.19.3, ed. Kenney, 64 ("acrius urit").
20. **inflat**: puff up (with pride).
21. The line has evidently suffered in transmission, as the violation of the rhyme scheme and as the false quantity in *uelle* betoken. The reversal of two words to "uelle, dea" in T fixes the latter shortcoming (since the prolongation of the second vowel in *uelle* is permissible in its new metrical position at the penthemimer), but does not resolve completely the former (because the first half line still lacks a rhyme).

    One approach, in keeping with T, would be to endeavor to redistribute the unique congestion of four rhymes in a row at the end of the hexameter, so that two words would be shifted to positions earlier in the line and consistent with what the rhyme pattern allowed. The resultant line would be extraordinary, like its immediate predecessor, in being monorhymed. And what rearrangement of the words would serve? "Pelle rebelle cor ad hoc, tu dea, uelle puelle" comes close, but the second rhyme in the first half of the line is placed irregularly.

    Another tack would be to ignore the arrangement of words in T as a failed attempt to correct the problems and to emend instead so as to create a rhyme that builds upon the sounds in "Tu cor." For example, consider "Tu cor (ad hoc ducor), dea, pelle rebelle puelle." Two drawbacks to this emendation are that it provides no noun to specify *hoc* and that it leaves the three rhymes as the end of the line.

    In any case, it makes best sense to construe "ad hoc" as two separate words together with "uelle" (the infinitive used as a neuter noun). To understand them as one word "adhoc" (= *adhuc*) that modifies "rebelle" would render interpretation of "uelle" highly problematic.
25. **signa doloris**: This phrase is Ovidian in origin: see *Heroides* 19.107 (hexameter line ending), ed. Kenney, 63, and *Tristia* 4.3.28, ed. Owen (at the beginning of the second half of a pentameter).
26. The phrase **certis signis** is linked with *ignis* uniquely in the *Historia Theophili* ascribed to Marbod, 393 "Hic certis signis erit omne probans opus ignis," in PL 171.1601A.
28. **Risus abest**: The line opening is Ovidian: see *Metamorphoses* 2.778, ed. Tarrant, 60. **uisus . . . tabescit**: This conceit is attested already in Catullus, *Carmina* 68.55–56, ed. Mynors, 83 ("maesta neque assiduo tabescere lumina fletu / cessarent"). Here it is difficult to gauge whether the poet means to

refer to the physical appearance of the eyes, marred by frequent weeping, or to the vision that they would enable, if not clouded by tears. **lacrimis . . . opimis**: The pairing appears often in dactylic poetry, perhaps most relevantly in Baudri (*Carmina* 36.3, ed. Tilliette, 1:50), Hildebert (*Vita beate Marie Egiptiace* 316, ed. Larsen, 252), and Embrico of Mainz, *Vita Mahumeti* 543, ed. Cambier, 69.

29. **color**: It would be tempting to interpret *color* as referring to the pallor, the lack of color, that was conventionally associated in ancient and medieval medicine and literature with the lovesick, but the Latin noun was employed routinely to describe the presence rather than the absence of coloring.

35: This proverb seems to reflect knowledge of Ovid, *Heroides* 5.115, ed. Knox, 53 ("quid facis, Oenone? quid harenae semina mandas?"). For different versions, see August Otto, *Die Sprichwörter und sprichwörtlichen Redensarten der Römer* (Leipzig, 1890; repr. Hildesheim, 1988), 159, no. 789, and Reinhard Häussler, ed. *Nachträge zu A. Otto Sprichwörter und sprichwörtlichen Redensarten der Römer* (Hildesheim, 1968), 57 and 169–170.

36. **nichil audit**: A line closing attested already in Catullus, *Carmina* 17.21, ed. Mynors, 15.

39. **Mors prope**: Although not as a line opening, the phrase is found in Seneca the Younger, *Troades* 575, ed. Zwierlein, 73, and in Hildebert (or pseudo-Hildebert), *Carmen in libros Regum* 4.12, in PL 171.1252C.

POEM 6. Incipit "Infelix duplici Landricus peste laborat." Seven elegiac distichs. Not in Walther. Not in *In principio*.

The topic of love leads to a sixth poem, which focuses upon lust and gluttony. The poet of this poem emphasizes a moral point, but he does so with touches of both crudity and elegance. The former quality is evident in his description of the interaction between the gullet (*gula / venter*) and phallus (*priapus / mentula*). The latter shows in his casual but deft allusions to classical poets such as Ovid and Horace. The most important of these allusions (in line 5) draws a parallel between a man named Landri and an Ovidian glutton, Erysichthon, who was stricken with insatiable hunger as punishment for violating a sacred grove. The poet's easy familiarity with Latin poetry may extend even to the works of contemporaries, since lines 7–8 seem to imitate the opening of Bernard Silvestris's *Cosmographia*.

The Landri in the sixth poem could have been a real person, since some of the poems in Group Two are directed against actual people. Alternatively, he could have been a literary figure of some sort, and once again this section of the anthology would offer parallels. If Landri is a fictitious character, he could have been a stock scoundrel, as he appeared in Latin poetry,[49] or a burlesque of the hero in a lost Old

49. For a possible example of such a poem, see Wilmart, "Le Florilège de Saint-Gatien," *Revue*

French *chanson de geste* that is known from four or five witnesses to have existed in the twelfth century and that has been hypothesized to have been about Count Landri of Nevers, about Landri le Timonier, or about either or neither.[50] In any event, Landri seems to have been old hat to twelfth-century audiences of poetry, for in a passage about the repertoires of minstrels Peter the Chanter (about 1120–1197) commented:

> Qui videntes cantilenam de Landrico non placere auditoribus, statim incipiunt de Narciso cantare, quod si nec placuerit, cantant de alio.[51]
>
> *[These minstrels,] when they see that their song [or chanson de geste] about Landri fails to please their listeners, at once begin to sing about Narcissus; and if that doesn't work, they sing about another character.*

[2r^{A}] De Landrico edace et luxurioso

Infelix duplici Landricus peste laborat;
    Alterius uires altera pestis alit.
Clades prima gule cladesque secunda Priapi.
    Mentula nec nouit nec gula frena pati.
Quod prebet tellus, nutrit mare, sustinet aer,
    Id recipit uenter, mentula spergit idem.
Res elementorum sedem confundit in unam,
    Cogit in anticum sic elementa cahos.
Ventris eum dampnosa lues, damp*nosa* libido
    Priuat amicitia presulis atque domo.
Vendidit ergo domos, prebendas uendidit idem,
    Et iam principibus displicet ille uiris.
Quod stomacus commisit edax commisit et inguen,
    Fabula Landricus factus in urbe luit.

---

bénédictine 48 (1936), 20, no. 8: "Landricus medicus faciens quod factor iniquus. / De muliere uirum fit merito neutrum. / Amodo clareret sua quid medicina ualeret: / Vertere si neutrum posset in alterutrum."

50. For the first, the locus classicus is Ferdinand Lot, "La chanson de Landri," *Romania* 32 (1903): 1–17. The most recent study is Claude Hohl, "Le comte Landri de Nevers dans l'histoire et dans la geste de *Girart de Roussillon*," in *La Chanson de Geste et le Mythe carolingien. Mélanges René Louis publiés par ses collègues, ses amis et ses élèves à l'occasion de son 75e anniversaire*, 2 vols., ed. Emmanuèle Baumgartner (Saint-Père-sous-Vézelay, 1982), 2:779–806. For the second, see Maurice Delbouille, "La chanson de Landri," in *Revue belge de philologie et d'histoire* 5, nos. 2–3 (1926): 339–350. On the reasons for not declaring in favor of the one or the other, see Joseph Bédier, *Les légendes épiques*, vol. 4 (Paris, 1921), 386–387.

51. *Verbum abbreuiatum* (composed 1187–1197), Chap. 27, in PL 205:101AB: compare 1.22, lines 68–72, ed. Boutry, 195. The passage was repeated, with Wacherius for Narcissus, by Gerald of Wales (Giraldus Cambrensis), *Gemma ecclesiastica*, ed. Brewer, 2:290.

About Gluttonous and Lecherous Landri

Unfortunate Landri labors under a two-fold affliction:
one affliction builds the strength of the other.
The first pestilence is of the gullet, the second of the phallus.
Neither the penis nor the gullet can endure restraints.
What the land offers, sea nourishes, and air sustains,
the stomach receives and penis shoots it out.
He conflates the substances of the four elements into one location,
he compels them into primordial chaos.
Ruinous corruption of the stomach and ruinous lust
deprive him of the bishop's friendship and home.
Therefore he sold his homes and sold his prebends;
and now he is displeasing to the leading men.
For that which the ever-hungry stomach and loins caused,
Landri, having become the talk of the town, atones.

Textual Notes

Title and first letter in rubrics.

8] anticum: ti *written again above line.*

9] damp*nosa* libido: damp libido *H.*

14] *Ink thick* Landricus *and* urbe *rewritten above line.*

Commentary

2. **Alterius uires altera pestis alit**: This line plays upon Ovid, *Remedia amoris* 444, ed. Kenney, 222 ("Alterius uires subtrahit alter amor").
5. **Quod prebet tellus, nutrit mare, sustinet aer**: The closest parallel to the thought is Ovid, *Metamorphoses* 8.830–831, ed. Tarrant, 248: "quod pontus, quod terra, quod educat aer / poscit et appositis queritur ieiunia mensis" ("he demands what the sea, land, and air bring forth, / and he complains of hunger even when the tables are laden"). For similar constructions, see Lucretius, *De rerum natura* 1.278, ed. Bailey, and Ovid, *Ex Ponto* 1.10.9, ed. Owen. For the line ending, compare Marius Claudius Victorius, *Alethia* 2.442, ed. Hovingh, 162 ("Qua sua tellus alit, quae non sua sustinet aer").
6. **Id recipit uenter, mentula spergit idem**: This association between an overindulged appetite for food and a sexual hyperactivity is often drawn in patristic (especially Jerome) and medieval sources. See for example Bernard Silvestris, *Commentary on the First Six Books of the "Aeneid" of Vergil*, Book 4, ed. Jones and Jones, 24, lines 7–21; trans. Schreiber and Maresca, 25–26.
7. **confundit in unum**: Compare Ovid, *Metamorphoses* 4.472, ed. Tarrant, 111 ("Imperium, promissa, preces confundit in unum").

8. The wording of this line reflects Ovid, particularly the opening of *Metamorphoses* 2.299, ed. Tarrant, 42 ("in Chaos antiquum confundimur"), but also the opening of *Fasti* 1.103, ed. Alton, Wormell, and Courtney, 4 ("me Chaos antiqui").
9. **dampnosa libido**: The ending was known through Horace, *Epistles* 2.1.107, ed. Shackleton Bailey, 296.
14. **Fabula . . . factus**: The idiom *fabula fio* can be traced to Horace, *Epistles* 1.13.9, ed. Shackleton Bailey, 274 (line ending: "fabula fias"), and Persius, *Satires* 5.152 (see the *OLD* 665, *fabula* 1d).

POEM 7. Incipit "Exposuere suum mihi Pierides Eliconem." Four elegiac distichs. Not in Walther. Not in *In principio.* Edited from Rg by Rigg, "Medieval Latin Poetic Anthologies (IV)," 487, no. 57.

The seventh poem contains one further substantiation of the hypothesis that the anthology originated near Tours. With their mention of a philosopher named Thierry these couplets bring us again to the neighborhood of this town, since this fellow is likely to be Thierry of Chartres. Thierry taught philosophy in Chartres (one of his students styled him "totius Europae philosophorum praecipuus"), and from 1142 to 1150 or thereabouts he was chancellor of the cathedral chapter there.[52] One of his predecessors in the second capacity was a man known as Bernard of Chartres (died around 1126), who was long presumed (without any convincing evidence) to have been Thierry's brother.[53] Whereas identifying Thierry is easy, the poet Gualo (Galo) is elusive. The most widely preserved Medieval Latin poem that is attributed to a Galo is an *Inuectio in monachos* (Invective against Monks), but nothing certain is known of this supposed author except that he was a Breton (as was Thierry).[54]

52. See Peter Dronke, "Thierry of Chartres," in Peter Dronke, ed., *A History of Twelfth-Century Western Philosophy* (Cambridge, 1988), 358–385, 455; Édouard Jeauneau, "Thierry de Chartres," in Georges Grente, ed., *Dictionnaire des lettres françaises*, vol. 1, *Le Moyen Age*, ed. Robert Bossuat, Louis Pichard, and Guy Raynaud de Lage (Paris, 1964), 710; Édouard Jeauneau, "Thierry v. Chartres," in *Lexikon für Theologie und Kirche*, ed. Josef Höfer and Karl Rahner, vol. 10 (Freiburg i. B., 1965), 114; Vera Rodrigues, "Thierry de Chartres: Profil philosophique d'un maître Chartrain," in *Roma, Magistra Mundi: Itineraria Culturae Medievalis; Mélanges offerts à Père L. E. Boyle à l'occasion de son 75e anniversaire*, 3 vols., ed. Jacqueline Hamesse (Louvain-la-Neuve, 1998), 3:317–328; André Vernet, "Épitaphe de Thierry de Chartres," in *Recueil de travaux offert à M. Clovis Brunel, membre de l'Institut, Directeur honoraire de l'École des Chartes, par ses amis, collègues et élèves* (Paris, 1955), 2:660–670; and Berthe Widmer, "Thierry von Chartres, ein Gelehrtenschicksal des 12. Jahrhunderts," *Historische Zeitschrift* 200 (1965): 552–571.

53. On the extreme unlikeliness that Thierry of Chartres was Bernard of Chartres's brother, see Paul Edward Dutton, *The "Glosae super Platonem" of Bernard of Chartres* (Toronto, 1991), 40–42.

54. Walther 17011, incipit "Sacrilegis monachis, emptoribus ecclesiarum," ed. Thomas Wright, *The Anglo-Latin Satirical Poets and Epigrammatists of the Twelfth Century*, vol. 2 (London, 1872), 201–207. On manuscripts, see André Boutemy, "Notice sur le recueil poétique du manuscrit Cotton

This "Gualo the Breton" ("Gualo Brito") could be identical with Galo, a bishop of Léon (and monk of Landévennec?) in Brittany whose existence is attested during a twenty-year period between 1108 and 1128.[55] This bishop has been credited with a poem of hexameters in tercets *De mundi contemptu*.[56] In a poem found in at least three anthologies an otherwise unspecified Galo laments the absence of his friend Girard.[57] To complicate matters, another Galo (who seems to have had an uncle with the same name) is mentioned in an epitaph entitled "Gualo ad episcopum successorem patrui sui."[58] And a philosopher and dialectician in Paris who appears to be one more Galo is discussed in two other poems.[59] Once more evidence has been collected, it should be possible to sort out the biographies and writings of the various Gualos.

The author of the anthology poem to Girard is probably the Gualo to whom Baudri of Bourgueil (1046–1130) addressed two of his poems.[60] Once again, there is reason to believe that Gualo was a Breton: from 1107 Baudri was bishop of Dol in Brittany, where one of the Galos attended a council in 1128.[61] But is Baudri's Gualo one and the same as Bishop Galo? And is Bishop Galo the author of the *Inuectio in monachos*? And is any of these identical with the Gualo to whom Rodulfus Tortarius (about 1063–1114), monk of Fleury, addressed one of his letters?[62]

Vitellius A xii, du British Museum," *Latomus* 1 (1937): 284, no. 32, fol. 127r. Manitius refers to this Galo as Gualo of Caen: see Maximilian Manitius, *Geschichte der lateinischen Literatur des Mittelalters*, vol. 3 (Munich, 1931): 644, 870n3, and 943. For another opinion on the authorship, see Ronald E. Pepin, *Literature of Satire in the Twelfth Century: A Neglected Mediaeval Genre*, Studies in Mediaeval Literature 2 (Lewiston, N.Y., 1988), 6 and 26n16.

55. See *Gallia christiana*, ed. Barthélemy Hauréau, vol. 14 (Paris, 1856), col. 975.

56. Incipit "Heu stolidi qui tam cupidi dubiis inhiatis." Ed. from fol. 135r2 of London, British Library, MS Cotton Vitellius A.xii by Boutemy, "Notice sur le recueil poétique du manuscrit Cotton Vitellius A xii," 289, no. 66, fol. 135r, and 310–311. For discussion, see Wilmart, "Le Florilège de Saint-Gatien," 15–16.

57. On the manuscripts of this twenty-six-line poem (Walther 13561), see Rigg, "Medieval Latin Poetic Anthologies (IV)," 485–486, no. 41. Rigg notes: "Galo regrets Girard's absence and advises him not to work too hard. Galo and Girardus may be the friends of Baudri of Bourgueil to whom he addressed his poems. . . ."

58. See André Boutemy, "Le recueil poétique du manuscrit latin 5129 de la Bibliothèque nationale de Paris," *Scriptorium* 2 (1948): 49, item 22, fol. 103r; and, on Paris, Bibliothèque nationale, MS lat. 5129, Wilmart, "Le Florilège de Saint-Gatien," 165, item 44.

59. See Barthélemy Hauréau, *Les mélanges poétiques d'Hildebert de Lavardin* (Paris, 1882), 30–33; and Werner, *Beiträge*, 40, no. 101, and 58, no. 138.

60. *Carmina* 193 and 252, in Tilliette, 2:113–116 and 158–159. Manitius identifies Baudri's Galo with Gualo of Caen: see Manitius, *Geschichte*, 3:888 and 943.

61. See *Gallia christiana*, ed. Hauréau, 14: col. 975.

62. Rodulfus Tortarius is also known as Raoul Tortarius, Raoul Le Tourtier, and similarly. For his letter to Gualo, see *Epistula* 7, "Ad Gualonem," ed. Ogle and Schullian, 298–316. Manitius identifies this Galo with Bishop Galo of Paris and dates the verse epistle to 1108, when Galo and

Another intriguing question is the identity of the anonymous poet who studied under both Thierry and Gualo.[63] Although younger than Baudri, he could have been a member of Baudri's circle of friends and correspondents. A definite trace of Baudri's coterie in Houghton MS Lat 300 is Poem 93, three elegiac distichs that eulogize a certain Frodo: Baudri left three eulogies in distichs for a scholar named Frodo who left Anjou to seek his fortune in England.[64] Both Baudri and the poet of the Houghton poem use the commonplace of referring to Frodo as an "Aristotle."[65]

[\2r^{B}] Exposuere suum mihi Pierides Eliconem
Atque aditus aperit Philosophia suos.
Non ars una tamen, non unus contulit actor
Ut uates fierem philosofusque simul.
Carmina Gualo mihi, Terricus philosophiam
Inspirat. Nostrum pectus utrumque sapit.
Lingua diserta sonat Terrici philosophiam;
G*ua*lonis redolent carmina nostra stilum.

The Muses exposed their Helicon to me
and Philosophy opened her approaches to me.
But, just the same, one single art, one single author did not contribute
to my becoming at once poet and philosopher:
Gualo inspires me with poetry, Thierry with philosophy.
My heart smacks of both men.
(My) eloquent tongue sounds out the philosophy of Thierry;
my verses have the air of Gualo's style.

Textual Notes

1] *First letter in red.* Exposuere suum mihi: Exposuere michi *Rg*.
5] Carmina Gualo mihi: Carmina conuallo mihi *H*, Carmina Galo michi *Rg*. philosofiam: *corrected in same hand to* philosophiam *by addition of* phi *above last syllable.*
8] G*ua*lonis: Gaulonis *H*, Galonis *Rg*.

---

other prelates brought the body of Philip I to be buried in Fleury: Manitius, *Geschichte*, 3:874.

63. Rigg, "Medieval Latin Poetic Anthologies (IV)," 487, comments, "The identity of a philosopher-poet indebted to Galo and Thierry of Chartres (died 1155) is tantalizing."

64. *Carmina* 28–30, ed. Tilliette, 1:46–48.

65. *Carmina* 29, line 2, ed. Tilliette, 1:47.

Commentary

1. **Pierides Eliconem**: The Muses and the landscape associated with inspiration in classical mythology were well known in the Middle Ages: see Jan M. Ziolkowski, "Classical Influences on Medieval Latin Views of Poetic Inspiration," in *Latin Poetry and the Classical Tradition: Essays in Medieval and Renaissance Literature*, ed. Peter Godman and Oswyn Murray (Oxford, 1990), 15–38.
2. **aditus aperit**: Compare *Carmina Burana* 102.7.2, ed. Hilka and Schumann, 160 ("Fraus aditus aperit, hostis ab hoste perit").
3. **ars**: In conjunction with *Philosophia*, the noun must refer to a liberal art. The seven liberal arts were understood allegorically to be the daughters of Lady Philosophy. **actor**: On the nuances of this word in medieval usage, see M.-D. Chenu, "*Auctor, actor, autor*," *Bulletin du Cange: Archivum Latinitatis medii aevi* 3 (1927): 81–86.
6. **utrumque sapit**: Also, presumably by coincidence, a line ending in Hugh of Mâcon, *Gesta militum* 3.374, ed. Könsgen, 1:157.
7. **Lingua diserta**: The first medieval attestations of this phrase are in Baudri, *Carmina* 173.4, ed. Tilliette 2:104, and Marbod, *Carmina* 2.22.4, in PL 171.1721C.
8. **carmina nostra**: The phrase is jejune in this metrical position (to open the second half of a pentameter), from Ovid, *Ars amatoria* 3.792, ed. Kenney, 199.

POEM 8. Incipit "Materiam rerum proponit Eraclitus ignem." Two elegiac distichs. Not in Walther. Not in *In principio.*

Mentioning the philosopher Thierry induces the anthologist to include the eighth poem, a brief exposition of the doctrines of prominent ancient philosophers.

[2r^B] Ponit opiniones philosophorum

Materiam rerum proponit Eraclitus ignem,
    Aera Anaximenes primo fuisse putat,
Id Tales ascribit aquis, athomis Epicurus,
    Pitagoras numeris Esiodusque solo.

He puts forward the opinions of the philosophers

Heraclitus proposes that the substance of things is fire,
    Anaximenes thinks that air was first,
Thales attributes it to water, Epicurus to atoms,
    Pythagoras to numbers, Hesiod to earth.

Textual Notes

Title and first letter in rubrics.

2] Anaximanes: *last* a *expunged and* e *added above line.* fuisse: fuise H.

4] Pitagogas: *corrected through addition of* or *above line.* numeris: *could be read alternatively as* minimis.

Commentary

1–4. Two parallels to the first three lines of this listing can be found in Tertullian, *Adversus Marcionem libri quinque*, 1.13, ed. Kroymann, 307 ("deos pronuntiauerunt, ut Thales aquam, ut Heraclitus ignem, ut Anaximenes aerem, ut Anaximander uniuersa caelestia, ut Strato caelum et terram, ut Zeno aerem et aetherem, ut Plato sidera") and Augustine, *De civitate Dei* 8.5, ed. Dombart and Kalb, 1:328, lines 9–14 (" . . . alii quoque philosophi, qui corporalia naturae principia corpori deditis mentibus opinati sunt, cedant his tantis et tanti Dei cognitoribus uiris, ut Thales in umore, Anaximenes in aere, Stoici in igne, Epicurus in atomis, hoc est minutissimis corpusculis, quae nec diuidi nec sentiri queunt . . .").

4. Because of the succession of minims and the ambiguity of the abbreviation signs, it is hard to be certain that the second word in the line was written as "numeris" (num'is) rather than as "minimis" (mini'is). Whatever the scribe wrote here, the poem must originally have had "numeris." In the Middle Ages Pythagoras was credited with having established all four of the so-called mathematical arts in the quadrivium, arithmetic, geometry, astronomy, and, above all, music. An ancient legend ascribed to him the discovery of a numerical relationship among basic musical intervals. See Barbara Münxelhaus, *Pythagoras musicus: Zur Rezeption der pythagoreischen Musiktheorie als quadrivialer Wissenschaft im lateinischen Mittelalter* (Bonn, 1976). It is Epicurus whom we might expect to find associated with "smallest (particles)."

POEM 9. Incipit "Basse pilos odis neque cernis quanta pilorum." Four lines of end-rhymed hexameters. Not in Walther. Not in *In principio.* From praise of wisdom the anthologist passes to invective. The full sense of these four lines may have been impossible to decode outside a small coterie, even before a scribe who had trouble reading, writing, or both, copied the text.

The ninth poem bears the no-nonsense title "An Invective against Bassus" (*Inuectio ad Bassum*). The name would seem to reflect classical poetry, since a drinker with the cognomen Bassus occurs in the verse of both Horace and Martial, and poets of the same name also appear in the works of Propertius and Ovid.[66] Bassus

66. For drinkers named Bassus, see Horace, *Odes* 1.36.14, ed. Shackleton Bailey, 39, and Martial, *Epigrams* 1.37, ed. Lindsay (unpaginated). For poets, see Ovid, *Tristia* 4.10.47, ed. Owen (unpaginated);

also carries social connotations. Not only does the Late Latin adjective *bassus, -a, -um* (low, lowly) have a social application, in reference to juridical inferiority, but in addition *bassus* is an alternative spelling of *uassus* (vassal): compare *Mittellateinisches Wörterbuch*, 1 (Munich, 1963), 1390, lines 57–63, and 1391, 4.

The key to the poem may well be the Bassus (Caesius Bassus, to be exact) to whom Persius casts his sixth satire as a letter. The opening of Persius's satire presents this Bassus, a friend of the satirist's who reportedly perished in the eruption of Vesuvius (79 CE) and who is reputed in Quintilian's *Institutio oratoria* to be a lyric poet, as a master of stringed instruments and as a good artisan.[67]

In Poem 9 Bassus may well be a pseudonym. Interestingly, the name is often used by Martial to mock people and it can be impossible to determine whether in these cases the name is real or fictitious.[68] The twelfth-century poet here makes matters equally uncertain as to whether Bassus is the actual name of a real person, a pseudonym for a real person, or a name borrowed from earlier literature as part of a poetic game that has no connection with reality.

The poem has a riddling quality and might involve a play on words. Could the word *pilos* nod toward the horsehair of a bow for a stringed instrument or to horsehair strings of a harp? A major impediment to either interpretation is that any component of a stringed instrument that could be described as a vessel would not be the bow or any other part that could be produced with horsehair. No more easily determinable is the precise shortcoming of the person designated as Bassus in Poem 9. Maybe he created strings made of horsehair rather than of catgut, but he could not however realize the value of his creation.

All the uncertainties notwithstanding, the fact remains that Poem 9 has a notable density of terms relating to music, with *canorum*, *strepitus*, *modus*, and *sonorum* (as well as perhaps the uncertain *uox*). Furthermore, the adjective *bassus* and the noun *bassum* both acquired in Medieval Latin senses that anticipate their usage in modern music: see *Mittellateinisches Wörterbuch*, 1: 1390, lines 52–56 and 63–65, and *Lexicon musicum Latinum medii aevi = Wörterbuch der lateinischen Musikterminologie des Mittelalters bis zum Ausgang des 15. Jahrhunderts = Dictionary of Medieval Latin Music Terminology to the End of the 15th Century*, ed. Michael Bernhard (Munich, 1992–), fasc. 3, cols. 211, lines 44–212, line 63.

Propertius, *Carmina* 1.4.1 and 1.4.12, ed. Barber, 6; and Persius, *Satires* 6.1, ed. Clausen, 25.

67. Quintilian, *Institutio oratoria* 10.1.96, Russell, 4:304–305. For information on Bassus that could have been known through the commentary tradition, see *Commentum Cornuti in Persium*, ed. Clausen and Zetzel, 141. For close commentary on the opening lines, see Hugo Beikircher, *Kommentar zur VI. Satire des A. Persius Flaccus* (Vienna, 1969), 17–29, and Aules Persius Flaccus, *Satiren*, ed. and trans. with commentary by Walter Kissel (Heidelberg, 1990), 763–788.

68. *Thesaurus Linguae Latinae* (Leipzig, 1900–), 2:1779, lines 72–76. For a concise account of real versus fictitious names in Martial, see Lindsay Watson and Patricia Watson, ed., *Martial: Select Epigrams* (Cambridge, 2003), 12–15.

The neuter substantive *bassum* is documented in the thirteenth century as a designation for a saddle-pad or neck-pad (for a horse): see R. E. Latham, *Dictionary of Medieval Latin from British Sources*, fasc. 1 "A-B" (London, 1975), 186. Not only is this word attested too late to hold much hope of being relevant, but in addition its relation to horses does not prove that it had anything to do with horsehair.

[2r[B]] Inuectio ad Bassum

Basse, pilos odis neque cernis quanta pilorum
Munere *g*aza tibi. Pater olim pauper, equorum
Rarificans caudas, ua*s* texuit inde canorum,
Cui nomen tribuit strepitusque modusque sonorum.

Invective against Bassus

Bassus, you hate hair and you do not see how great
a treasure you have, by the munificence of hair. [Your?] father, once poor,
thinning the tails of horses, constructed by this means a melodious vessel,
to which the loud noise and tune granted a resounding name.

Textual Notes

Title and first letter in rubrics.

2] Munere gaza tibi: Gaza (*with large initial*) tibi, *with* munere (*reading uncertain*) *written above.*

3] ua*s*: *uax H.* inde: . īn (*preceded by full stop*) *H.*

4] nomen (*reading uncertain*).

Commentary

Title **Inuectio ad Bassum**: Even the title has its puzzles. How exactly does the poem qualify as an invective? On a more mundane level, *inuectio* is usually paired with *in* or *contra*: see *Thesaurus Linguae Latinae* 7/2: 124, lines 37, 40, 42, 44, 49, 60, 62 (*in*) and 45–46 (*contra*). Although forms of *inuectio* are occasionally juxtaposed to the preposition *ad*, the constructions are not to express "invective against" but rather "invective to the purpose of" or another unrelated meaning.

1. **pilos odis**: Why does Bassus hate hair? Does this assertion allude to an assertion or episode in an earlier, perhaps classical, poem, or does it represent a private joke for which the context has been lost? **odis:** The verb *odi, odisse* acquired present, fourth-conjugation forms already in late antiquity, which became entirely routine in the Middle Ages: see Peter Stotz, *Handbuch zur lateinischen Sprache des Mittelalters*, vol. 4 (Munich, 1998), 219, VIII § 126.1.

2. **Munere gaza**: Two arguments speak in favor of inserting *munere* as the initial word in the line. One is that *munere* is written directly above *Gaza tibi*. Another is that this opening is attested at least once, in Arnulf of Orléans, *Miles gloriosus* 48, ed. Pareto, 62. Yet it remains difficult to construe *munere* syntactically in the first clause. **Gaza tibi, pater olim munere pauper equorum**: Although *munere* (if the reading is correct) is written above *gaza*, a case could be made for this alternative placement, the only other that is metrically possible. First, it seems likelier that a word other than the initial one would be omitted. Second, the phrase *munere pauper* is attested in Propertius, *Carmina* 2.16.9 (line ending), ed. Barber, 53, and Ovid, *Ex Ponto* 4.9.122 (as opening of the second half in a pentameter), ed. Owen. But if *munere* is placed in this position, there is no caesura. **pater olim pauper, equorum**: The combination of the father's poverty and the horses' tails suggests that the father worked as a groom. This humbleness of the father's profession would add a social dimension to the lowness to which Bassus's name alludes.

2–3. **equorum / Rarificans caudas**: The plucking of hairs from the tail of a horse is mentioned by Horace, *Epistles* 2.1.45–46, ed. Shackleton Bailey, 293, to exemplify the kind of logical conundrum known technically as a sorites. The question posed implicitly by the Roman poet seems to be: how many hairs constitute a tail? If the hairs of a tail are removed one by one, the moment comes when the tail is no longer a tail—but what determines that moment? Does the dividing line between what is and what is not a tail depend upon a single hair, or is such an approach mere hairsplitting?

To different effect, Plutarch relates in *The Parallel Lives* an anecdote about how, so as to demonstrate the superiority of perseverance over abrupt action, Sertorius had a weak man who by plucking hairs one by one stripped bare the full tail of a healthy horse more easily than did a strong man who tried to tug out all the hairs at once from the thin tail of a weak, old horse: see *Sertorius* 16.5-11, ed. Konrad, 16–17. The same anecdote is also related in Valerius Maximus, *Factorum et dictorum memorabilium libri novem*, 7.3.6, ed. Kempf, 337, and in Sextus Iulius Frontinus, *Strategemata*, 1.10.1, ed. Ireland, 23.

3. **ua*s***: The manuscript reading *uax*, if correct, is nonsensical. Emendation to *uix* would help little, since it would necessitate either construing *canorum* as a substantive or making another emendation elsewhere to produce a different object for the verb. The palaeographically minimalist change to *uox* would accord with the other musical terminology (and with Persius, *Satire* 6), but makes little sense. I emend to *uas*, on the grounds that final -x for -s is attested in some manuscripts. For example, see Hugh Primas, *The Oxford Poems*, 9.2 ("ligustrix" for "ligustris"), ed. McDonough, 41. On the interchangeability of *s*(*s*) and *x*, see Stotz, *Handbuch zur lateinischen Sprache des Mittelalters*, vol. 3 (Munich, 1996): 316–317, VII § 279.5, and 320–322, VII § 281.9–282.2. Furthermore, the scribe may have slipped under the influence of the following *texuit*.

A problem could remain, in that a "vessel" is not the part of a stringed instrument that horsehair would produce—and *inde* seems to connect this clause to the preceding mention of horse tails. In the plural, *uasa* is attested, albeit slimly, in reference to musical instruments. For instance, Osbern of Canterbury (died about 1094) writes in the *Vita et miracula S. Dunstani*, Chap. 8, ed. Stubbs, 79: "Sicut ergo David nostri simphonista vasa cantici habuit, quia usum illorum non nisi in divinis laudibus expendit." Bartholomew the Englishman (Bartholomaeus Anglicus, died 1250) makes reference to "vasorum omnium musicorum": see *De proprietatibus rerum* 19.132, published under the title *De genuinis rerum coelestium, terrestrium et inferarum Proprietatibus libri XVIII* (Frankfurt am Main, 1601; repr. Frankfurt am Main, 1964), 1254. But although both of these passages confirm a possible connection with music, neither refers explicitly to horsehair as used in either the manufacture of the instruments or the devices used to extract sounds from them. Could *uas* mean more generally "implement" (*OLD* 2014, *uas*[2] 2a: usually plural, but note Cicero, *Letters to Quintus* 1.1.13, ed. Shackleton Bailey, 7)? In this case it could designate the string of a musical instrument.

Last but not least, could the conjectural *uas* be a sort of pot? The scholiast on Persius, *Satires* 5.148 has a relevant comment on *sessilis obba*: "obba genus uasis ex sparto factum." This conjures up the idea of a vessel made from reeds or marsh grass. A vessel plaited of horsehair or made of leather stuffed with horsehair, like a saddle, is no less plausible. In any case, leather buckets and pots were surely common, and if such a bucket or pot served as a chamberpot, the sounds emitted by its user when relieving himself could explain the references to noise in the final line of this poem. Supporting the supposition that the container signified here is a "night bucket" is Martial, *Epigrams* 1.37, ed. and trans. Shackleton Bailey, 1:66–67, a single elegiac couplet that faults Bassus (or Bassa, in other manuscripts) for defecating into a gold chamberpot more valuable than the glass out of which he drinks: "Ventris onus misero, nec te pudet, excipis auro, / Bassa, bibis vitro: carius ergo cacas" (You receive your belly's load, Bassa, in gold—unlucky gold!—and are not ashamed of it; you drink out of glass. So it costs you more to shit). The clever twist of the poet here would be to present the chamberpot as being made of an exceedingly humble material, rather than of a precious metal. **texuit**: The verb *texit* "covered" might be more appealing for some interpretations, but it is not possible metrically. If the reading is correct, the poet makes a transition from the second-person forms *odis* and *cernis* to the third person here, perhaps because he is speaking no longer of his addressee, Bassus, but rather of this man's father. **inde canor***: This line ending appears in Optatianus Porfyrius (third or fourth century), *Carmina* 10.2, ed. Polara, 118 ("inde canoros").

4. **strepitus**: Persius, *Satires* 6.4 refers to *strepitus* in a positive sense, which may have inspired the use of the word here. **sonorum**: Proximity would argue that it should be construed as a genitive plural with both *strepitus* and

modus: "to which the loud noise and manner of sounds granted a name." Yet since the line as a whole seems to imply that Bassus deserved to receive a name connoting the deep sound still associated with the word "bass" in musical usage, *sonorum* is here construed as an adjective agreeing with *nomen*. **strepitusque modusque**: The hendiadys could be put into English as "noisy music."

POEM 10. Incipit "Vis tua fracta perit fracto de cornibus uno." Four elegiac distichs. Not in Walther. Not in *In principio*.

The main device of this poem is to mock an unspecified person for being like the mythological Achelous, a river-god who lost a horn when struggling in the form of a bull with Hercules. The poet's familiarity with the ancient myth is apparent in line 4, where he alludes slyly to the cornucopia, which was reported to have been created from Achelous's lost horn. The poet's awareness of Ovid in particular stands out in the second line.

The inspiration to identify a vicious person with Achelous probably came to the poet as a result of reading a commentary on Ovid. No similar identification appears in early commentaries on Ovid, such as those of Arnulf of Orléans (late twelfth century), John of Garland (thirteenth century), or anonymous ones, such as the "Vulgate" commentary;[69] in early mythographic works, such as those of the three Vatican mythographers;[70] or in such literary works as the poetry of Theodulf or the *Ecloga Theoduli* (or in Bernard of Utrecht's commentary on the last-mentioned). The only tenuous leads to any particular preoccupation with Achelous before the High Middle Ages are that the anonymous St. Gall commentator on Boethius's *Consolation of Philosophy* mentions Achelous, out of confusion with Acheron, and that one of the ivory panels, "very likely made up in the Carolingian ivory workshop," on the

69. For Arnulf, see Fausto Ghisalberti, "Arnolfo d'Orléans, un cultore di Ovidio nel secolo XII," *Memorie del R. Istituto Lombardo di Scienze e Lettere, Classe di Lettere, scienze morali e storiche* 24, fasc. 4 (1932): 157–234; for John of Garland, see *Integumenta Ovidii: Poemetto inedito del secolo XIII*, ed. Fausto Ghisalberti (Messina and Milan, 1933). For checking on the "Vulgate" commentary, I am much beholden to Frank Coulson, who generously sent me his transcription of the text from Vatican, Biblioteca Apostolica Vaticana, MS Vat. lat. 1598, fol. 90v. In addition, he confirmed that nothing is said of Achelous's moral character in the commentary on the *Metamorphoses* in Munich, Bayerische Staatsbibliothek, clm 4610, or in the three commentaries in Munich, Bayerische Staatsbibliothek, clm 14482.

70. The antiquated standard edition of the three Vatican mythographers was Georgius Henricus Bode, ed., *Scriptores rerum mythicarum Latini tres Romae nuper reperti*, 2 vols. (Celle, 1834), 1:1–73 (First Vatican Mythographer), 1:74–151 (Second), and 1:152–256 (Third, referred to as Alberic of London). The first two have been reedited in *Mythographi vaticani I et II*, ed. Péter Kulcsár (Turnhout, 1987), 3–33 (First) and 33–62 (Second). For information on the dates of the three Vatican mythographers, see Richard M. Krill, "The *Vatican Mythographers*: Their Place in Ancient Mythography," *Manuscripta* 23 (1979): 173–177.

so-called *cathedra sancti Petri* represents the combat between Hercules and Achelous, which the *cathedra* integrates with the list of the Twelve Labors.[71]

In contrast to the dearth of evidence from the earlier centuries, a close parallel is found in the fourteenth-century moralization of Ovid's *Metamorphoses* by Petrus Berchorius (Pierre Bersuire), who equates Achelous with the devil, Deianira with the human soul, and Hercules with the son of God. Bersuire writes that Hercules broke Achelous's "horn of power" ("cornu suę potentiæ"), and he cites Psalm 74.11: "I will break the horns of sinners" ("Cornua peccatorum confringam").[72] The existence of this parallel raises the possibility that the inspiration for this poet's treatment of Achelous may derive from the commentary tradition, although evidence for similar interpretations of the mythological figure from the eleventh or twelfth century are lacking.[73]

[2r^{B}] Ad quemdam superbum et inuidum

Vis tua fracta perit fracto de cornibus uno;
Frons, Acheloe, suo trunca decore caret.
Frangitur in fracto frangenda superbia cornu
Et te tota simul copia deseruit.
Erepto cornu uis est erepta nocendi.
Posse cares sed non uelle nocere cares.
Impia mens assueta malis celerumque magistra,
Immo parens scelerum, corripit omne scelus.

To a Certain Haughty and Invidious Man

Your might is broken and perishes when one of (your) horns is broken;
(your) mutilated forehead, Achelous, lacks its (usual) charm.

71. It has been debated whether the imagery on the ivory plaques gives expression to an anti-Herculean tendency or not. The foundational discussions are Kurt Weitzmann, "The Heracles Plaques of St. Peter's Cathedra," *The Art Bulletin* 55 (1973): 1–37 (at 11-12 and 15 for Achelous), and Kurt Weitzmann, "An Addendum to 'The Heracles Plaques of St. Peter's Cathedra,'" *The Art Bulletin* 56 (1974): 250. Arguing for an anti-Herculean tendency, see Lawrence Nees, *A Tainted Mantle: Hercules and the Classical Tradition at the Carolingian Court* (Philadelphia, 1991), 104–105n51. On the *cathedra sancti Petri*, see Nees, *Tainted Mantle*, 205–207 (with the quotation here on p. 205). Offering a different reading of the throne, see Paul Edward Dutton, *Charlemagne's Mustache and Other Cultural Clusters of a Dark Age* (New York, 2004), 124–125.

72. Petrus Berchorius (= Pierre Bersuire), *Ovidius moralizatus*, Book 9, Fable 1: see *Metamorphosis Ouidiana moraliter a magistro Thoma Walleys anglico de professione predicatorum sub sanctissimo patre Dominico: explanata* (Venundatur in aedibus Ascensianis & sub pelicano in vico sancti Iacobi Parisijs, 1509), fol. LXVIIr = Petrus Berchorius, *Reductorium morale. Liber XV, cap. ii–xv: "Ovidius moralizatus" naar de Parijse druk van 1509* (Utrecht, 1962), 135.

73. For comments on the oddity of the similar and related interpretation advanced in the somewhat earlier *Ovide moralisé*, see Franco Gaeta, "L'avventura di Ercole," *Rinascimento* 5 (1954): 243–245.

Pride that should be broken is broken when a horn is broken
and all might at once forsook you.
When one horn is taken away, the power to injure is taken away;
you lack the power to cause harm, but you do not lack the desire to do so.
An impious mind, accustomed to wickednesses and the mistress of crimes—
no, the parent of crimes—seizes hold of every crime.

Textual Notes

Title and first letter in rubrics.

2] aquilone *H*: *corrected above line to* Acheloe.
3] frangend *H*: da *added above line.*
4] *Erasure above* deseruit.

Commentary

1. **Vis tua**: A line opening attested from Ovid, *Fasti* 4.915, ed. Alton, Wormell, and Courtney, 112.
2. **Frons . . . trunca**: The phrase recalls Ovid, *Metamorphoses* 9.1–2 and 9.86, ed. Tarrant, 251 ("truncaeque . . . frontis") and 254 ("truncaque a fronte reuellit").
6. **uelle nocere**: The wording is found repeatedly in dactylic verse, with the most important and earliest instance being pseudo-Ausonius, *Septem sapientum sententiae septenis versibus explicatae* (incipit "Quaenam summi boni est? mens quae sibi conscia recti"), 7, ed. Schenkl, 247 ("quid stulti proprium? non posse et uelle nocere").
7. **celerumque**: *scelerumque*.

POEM 11. Incipit "Errant qui credunt gentem periisse Ciclopum." Six end-rhymed elegiac distichs. Not in Walther. *In principio*, reference 123788. Also extant in Rg: see Rigg, "Medieval Latin Poetic Anthologies (IV)," 487, no. 63. These twelve lines, lightly ornamented with classical borrowings, are in end-rhymed elegiac distichs. The rhymes are brought home by the presentation of the text in the manuscript, since the rhyming final syllable is written only once and is connected by lines to the verses that it completes.

Like the tenth poem, this one equates an unnamed person with an ancient mythological figure. Although the Polyphemus here could be any selfishly grasping person, the poem later reveals that he is indeed, as the title proclaims, "A Certain Lustful and Greedy Prelate."[74] His failure may be emphasized in Christian terms, if the last verse is meant somehow to echo the Bible.

74. The title is written in the right margin, beside the last verse of Poem 10.

At least as important as the mythological backdrop is the specific historical context for Poem 11, which is also linked closely with that for Poems 12 and 13. Poem 11 deals with a high-ranking clergyman, presumably a bishop. Both Poems 11 (line 11) and 13 (line 5) refer to a papal legate. Poem 12 (line 1) places prominently a mention of "Hilarians" (Hilarienses), canons of Saint-Hilaire-le-Grand of Poitiers, dedicated to Saint Hilary (about 315–367; feast day, January 13), the patron saint of Poitiers, and (line 2) touches upon someone who holds power over the people of Bordeaux.

Putting together the scraps of information, we may hypothesize that Poems 11 through 13 relate to a particular violent episode as the Gregorian reform spread through France. In 1073–1074 the canons of Saint-Hilaire were pitted in a severe conflict against the bishop of Poitiers, the simoniac Isembert. He would be the Polyphemus singled out in Poems 11 and 12. The papal legate who intervened against him was the energetic Amatus (died 1101), bishop of Oloron (1073–1089), archbishop of Bordeaux (1089–1101).[75] As legate of both Popes Gregory VII and Urban II, Amatus, who oversaw the renewal of the Church in Bordeaux in 1080, was particularly vigilant against simony. His efforts were appreciated, at least by Baudri, who wrote a poem in praise of him. At the instigation of Amatus, Isembert was compelled to go to Rome to justify himself. Gozlin, the bishop of Bordeaux, was eventually charged with executing the measures that were to be taken against Isembert.[76]

De quodam prelato cupido et auar*o*

Errant qui credunt gentem peri*i*sse Ciclopum:
    E*n*, Poliphemus adest multiplicator opum,
[\2v^{A}] Excedens alios uultuque minisque Ciclopes,
    Tantalus alter, i*n*ops esurit inter opes.
Cum sit tam capitis quam mentis lumine cecus,
    Dedecus omne docet, dedocet omne decus.
Rupe caua latitans cupiendo, timendo laborat;
    Quosque tenere potest, ossa cutemque uorat.
Ecclesiam lacerat, deglutit publica fratrum,
    Nec saciare potest mentis hians baratrum.

75. For information on Amatus of Oloron, see Theodor Schieffer, *Die päpstlichen Legaten in Frankreich vom Vertrage von Meersen (870) bis zum Schisma von 1130* (Berlin, 1935), 88–152 (esp. 89–91 and 110–115), and Alfons Becker, *Studien zum Investiturproblem in Frankreich; Papsttum, Königtum und Episkopat im Zeitalter der gregorianischen Kirchenreform (1049–1119)* (Saarbrücken, 1955), 69, 73–74, 77, 80.

76. On the episode involving Isembert, Amatus, and Gozlin, see Augustin Fliche, *La réforme grégorienne*, vol. 2 (Louvain, 1925), 166n1.

Pontificum legat*e*, *decus*, pater optime patrum,
Ad solitum redeat, coge nefas, aratrum.

About a Certain Lustful and Greedy Prelate

Those people are mistaken who believe that the Cyclopes' clan died off:
look, a Polyphemus is here who makes his wealth manifold.
Outdoing the other Cyclopes in both his demeanor and threats,
he is a second Tantalus, hungering needily amid abundance.
Since he is blind spiritually as well as physically,
he teaches every dishonor and unteaches every honor.
Lurking in a cliffside hollow, he toils in desire and fear;
and those of whom he can lay hold, he devours their bones and flesh.
He tears apart the Church, he gobbles the brothers' communal property,
but he cannot satisfy the yawning chasm of his mind.
Pontifical legate, glory, best father of fathers,
force this wicked person to return to the usual plow.

Textual Notes

Title and first letter in rubrics. Last letter of title, which is written not on a line of its own but in the margin to the right of the final line of Poem 10, cropped away.

1] peri*i*sse: perisse *H*, periisse *Rg*.
2] E*n*: Et *H*, En *Rg*. Pholiphemus *H*: *first h expunged.*
4] ater *H*: al *written above line*. inops esurit: iops esurit (*suspension mark omitted*) *H*, inops exurit *Rg*.
6] docet, dedocet *H*: decet, dedecet *Rg*.
8] Quosque *H*: Quemque *Rg*.
10] hi*a*ns: hiens *H*, hians Rg.
11] Pontificum legat*e*: Pontificum legale (*no lacuna*) *H*, Pontificum legate decus *Rg*.

Commentary

4. **esurit inter opes**: compare Baudri, *Carmina* 5.29–30, ed. Tilliette 1:13 ("Quodsi diues eges, te tota sequatur egestas, / Ad mensam esurias, in Ligeri sitias").
5. **mentis lumine**: The earliest occurrence of the phrase in this particular metrical position is in Hildebert, *De mysterio missae* 718, in PL 171.1193C. **lumine cecus**: Though the line ending is cliché, the closest parallel to the thought here is in Hildebert, *Carmina miscellanea* 49, in PL 171.1401C ("Exterius velut interius fit lumine caecus"). To turn from wording to thought, was Isembert, the simoniac bishop of Poitiers, blind in one eye?
6. **Dedecus omne** and **omne decus**: Both wordings are commonplace.

7. **Rupe caua latitans**: The phrase seems to fuse Ovid's characterization in *Metamorphoses* 13.786, ed. Tarrant, of Polyphemus as "latitans ego rupe" (third, fourth, and fifth feet of a hexameter) with Vergil's description in *Aeneid* 3.641, ed. Mynors, 173, of the monster's cave as "cauo . . . in antro" (third-fourth and sixth feet of a hexameter).
8. **tenere potest**: The phrase originated as a pentameter line ending in Ovid, *Ars amatoria* 2.388, ed. Kenney, 156, and *Heroides* 1.106 (as a variant reading), ed. Knox, 44.
11. **pater optime**: The vocative comes in the same metrical position as the same phrase in Vergil, *Aeneid* 3.710, ed. Mynors, 175.
12. **aratrum**: Luke 9.62 "ait ad illum Iesus: 'Nemo mittens manum suam in aratrum et aspiciens retro aptus est regno Dei'" ("Jesus said to him: No man putting his hand to the plough, and looking back, is fit for the kingdom of God").[77]

POEM 12. Incipit "Exilaras mestos, hilaris pater, Hilarienses." Eight hexameters, end-rhymed in two groups of four lines. Not in Walther. Not in *In principio*. Also extant in Rg: see Rigg, "Medieval Latin Poetic Anthologies (IV)," 487, no. 63.

Following directly upon the Polyphemus poem are eight hexameters, end-rhymed in two groups of four lines, which are marked by a red initial as a new poem (the twelfth). In these lines, a poet calls upon an unidentified "father" to discipline a miscreant similar to the ones described in Poems 9 through 11.

Despite the change of meter between Poems 11 and 12 and the fact that the scribes of both the Houghton manuscript and Rg copy them as separate poems, the links between the two are so strong that a recent reader has argued for considering them a single poem.[78] The two poems are stylistically related: for example, the vocative "pater optime" appears in 12.4 in the same metrical position as in 11.11. More important, the poems are clearly concerned with the same malefactor, since 12.7 mentions the Polyphemus who is the topic of Poem 11.

If the title of Poem 12 is correct, then Polyphemus was probably a bishop of Poitiers who oppressed the *Hilarienses* (the monks or canons of Saint-Hilaire-le-Grand at Poitiers).[79] The episode in question was a conflict that pitted the canons of the cathedral against the canons of Saint-Hilaire. According to a traditional custom,

77. The Latin text of Bible quotations follows *Biblia sacra iuxta vulgatam versionem*, ed. Robert Weber, rev. Roger Gryson, 4th ed. (Stuttgart, 1994); the English comes from *The Holy Bible: Douay Rheims Version* (Baltimore, 1899).

78. Rigg, "Medieval Latin Poetic Anthologies (IV)," 487, no. 63.

79. *Graesse, Benedict, Plechl: Orbis Latinus; Lexikon lateinischer geographischer Namen: Lateinisch-deutsch, deutsch-lateinisch. Handausgabe*, ed. Helmut Plechl (Braunschweig, 1971), 178, identifies *Hilarii eccl.* as Antran (Vienne), France. On Saint-Hilaire-le-Grand, see Ulysse Chevalier, *Répertoire des sources historiques du Moyen Age: Topo-bibliographie* (Montbéliard, 1894–1903), col. 2709.

the canons of the cathedral would go on All Saints' Day to the church of Saint-Hilaire-le-Grand, where the bishop or, failing that, the dean or another dignitary would celebrate the Mass. In 1073 the canons of Saint-Hilaire ventured to impede the performance of this ritual. The business was taken ultimately to the pope, who settled in favor of the canons of the cathedral.[80]

Although Poems 11 and 12 were no doubt composed by the same author, the first poem is addressed to the pontifical legate, whereas the second invokes for aid "Father Hilary." The addressee—the one expected to restore peace and order to the people of Bordeaux, particularly to the monks of Poitiers—is probably not Amatus of Oloron, the legate mentioned at the end of Poem 11, but Archbishop Gozlin of Bordeaux.[81]

In any event, Poem 12 is the only one in Group Two to take us out of the region running from Anjou through Île de France (where most of the other poems in the manuscript seem to have been composed), since it refers to the people of Bordeaux (*Burdegalenses*, here spelled *Burdegalanses*) as well as to the religious of Saint-Hilaire-le-Grand.

[2v^{A}] Exilaras mestos, hilaris pater, Hilarienses,
Cuius uirga regit, docet accio Burdegalanses:
Iura foues reprimisque dolos, sed digna repenses
Qui delere uolunt *que tu*, pater optime, censes.
Luce tua remoue tenebras animosque serena;
Dumque redis nobis redeant solacia plena
Afficiatque semel Polifemum debita pena.
Tam caput elatum confringe minasque refrena.

You gladden, glad father, the sad followers of St. Hilary,
you whose rod rules the people of Bordeaux, whose conduct teaches them:
you cherish laws and restrain treachery, but may you make fitting returns
to those who wish to destroy what you recommend, best father.
Through your light remove darkness and brighten hearts;
and as you return, may complete solace return to us,
and may due punishment cause harm to Polyphemus once and for all.
Shatter the head that has risen so high and restrain the threats.

Textual Notes

1] *Initial rubricated.* exilaras: exilares *with* e *expunged and* a *above line in same hand H*, exhilaras *Rg*.

80. Fliche, *La réforme grégorienne*, 2:116.

81. Contrast Rigg, "Medieval Latin Poetic Anthologies (IV)," 487, no. 63.

2] docet *H*: beat *Rg*. Burdegalenses *Rg*: Burdegalanses *H*.
3] foues *H*: fouet *Rg*. digna *written unclearly*: na *added above line*.
4] uolunt *que tu* pater: uolunt pater *no lacuna in H*, uolunt que tu pater *Rg*.
7] Afficiatque *H*: Efficiantque *Rg*. Polifemum *H*: Poliphemum *Rg*.
8] minasque *H*: minaque *Rg*.

Commentary

1. **Exilaras mestos**: The line opening echoes Baudri, *Carmina* 194.22, ed. Tilliette, 2:117 ("Exhilaras mestos et stolidos reprimis"). **hilaris**: The choice of the verb *Exilaras* as well as of the adjective *hilaris* sets the stage for the closing mention of the *Hilarienses*, the canons of Saint-Hilaire-le-Grand. There is no natural way in English to convey the dense wordplay (for which the technical term would be *annominatio*) of *Exilaras-hilaris-Hilarienses*: the closest would be the unnatural and inaccurate "You exhilarate, hilarious father, the sad Hilarians [=denizens of Saint-Hilaire]."
2. **Burdegalanses**: The same substantive is used to close a hexameter by Baudri, *Carmina* 202.11, ed. Tilliette, 2:136.
3. **digna repen***: This line ending was common from Statius, *Thebaid* 9.50 and 11.182, ed. Klotz and Klinnert, 318 and 411, on.
7. **debita pena**: Compare especially Ovid, *Fasti* 5.648, ed. Alton, Wormell, and Courtney, 134 ("et tandem Caco debita poena venit").

POEM 13. Incipit "Edibus in nostris ferus hospitibus Diomedes." Eight hexameters, end-rhymed in two groups of four lines. Not in Walther. Not in *In principio*.

The untitled thirteenth poem lingers over the topic of ecclesiastic corruption, charging that an unnamed prelate turns over church property to his Ganymede—that is, his male lover. The reference to the legate in the fifth line recalls the eleventh line of Poem 11. As mentioned in the discussion of Poem 11, in both cases it is reasonable to infer that the pontifical legate Amatus is meant.[82] Amatus, future successor of Gozlin to the see of Bordeaux, was the addressee of at least two poems by Baudri.[83]

Poem 13 is also closely related to Poem 11 in form, inspiration, and technique. Like Poem 11, Poem 13 commences with a mythological allusion—this time to Diomedes, a Thracian king who fed his mares on the flesh of his visitors. The episode of "the horses of Diomedes" was conventionally one of the Twelve Labors of Hercules, who fulfilled the task by killing the king and feeding his body to the horses. After eating Diomedes, the horses became tame and could be led by Hercules to Argos.

82. This suggestion was made by Vernet, "Séance du 16 Avril," 53.

83. *Carmina* 146–147, ed. Tilliette, 2:55–56.

Like Achelous in Poem 10, Diomedes appears in Book 9 of Ovid's *Metamorphoses*. As was the case with Achelous, the sort of interpretation advanced in this poem is not found in the early commentaries on Ovid by Arnulf of Orléans and John of Garland, or in the three Vatican mythographers; but it resembles Bersuire's moralization of the passage (*Metamorphoses* 9.194):

> . . . Diomedes significat mundi tyrannos qui equis id est stipendarijs dant comedere carnes hominum laceratorum id est substantias hominum miserorum. Itaque presepia talium equorum id est talium oppressorum cadaueribus id est bonis sunt plena.
>
> *. . . Diomedes signifies the tyrants of the world who give the flesh of men torn apart—that is, the possessions of miserable men—to their horses—that it, tributaries—to eat. And so the stables of such horses—that is, of such oppressors—are filled with bodies—that is, with goods.*[84]

The allusion in the twelfth-century poem has a particular appropriateness, since male homosexuals were sometimes associated with mares in medieval literature.[85]

One further similarity between the eleventh and thirteenth poems is that both introduce into their mythological allusions a figure from an unrelated myth: just as the rapacious Polyphemus of Poem 11 is "another Tantalus," the Diomedes of Poem 13 has a protégé who is a Ganymede.

[$2v^{A}$] Edibus in nostris ferus hospitibus Diomedes
Intulit insidias, fecit manus impia cedes;
Nunc moriens hostis nostras sibi uindicat edes
Ut suus in dote*s* proprias habeat Ganimedes.
Iusticie legate rigor, defensio ueri,
Arbitrio cuius pendet moderatio cleri:
Hoc tantum fac*in*us prohibe dignum prohiberi;
[$2v^{B}$] Hostis frange minas et nos assuesce tueri.

84. Petrus Berchorius, *Ovidius moralizatus* Book 9, Fable 9: see *Metamorphosis Ouidiana* (1509), fol. LXIXv. The translation is quoted, with modification, from William Donald Reynolds, "The *Ovidius moralizatus* of Petrus Berchorius: An Introduction and Translation" (Ph.D. diss., University of Illinois at Urbana–Champaign, 1971), 333.

85. Such an association seems to underlie the comment in Geoffrey Chaucer's General Prologue (line 691) to *The Canterbury Tales*, ed. Robinson, 23, that the Pardoner resembled "a geldyng or a mare." For information on the same association in early Scandinavian societies, see Preben Meulengracht Sørensen, *The Unmanly Man: Concepts of Sexual Defamation in Early Northern Society* (Odense, 1983).

In our household a savage Diomedes
laid snares for guests, an impious hand caused bloodshed;
and the enemy, now dying, claims our house for himself
so that his Ganymede may have it as his dowry.
Legate, rigor of the justice, defense of truth,
upon whose judgment depends the governance of the clergy:
forbid this great crime, which deserves to be forbidden;
break the threats of the enemy and keep the habit of protecting us.

Textual Notes

1] *Initial rubricated.*
4] *Squeezed between lines 3 and 5.* in dote (*without final* s) proprias *H.*
7] faci*n*us: facimus *H.*

Commentary

2. **manus impia**: This phrase appears in the same metrical position in Ovid, *Metamorphoses* 8.761, ed. Tarrant, 245, and *Heroides* 7.127, ed. Knox, 65.

3-4. **edes . . . Ganimedes**: The name of the mythological Ganymede as a shorthand for a young male paramour is particularly common in the poems of Baudri. The same rhyme is found (within a leonine hexameter) in Baudri, *Carmina* 77.95, ed. Tilliette, 1:73, and in pseudo-Hildebert, incipit "Tot scelerum morbis totus prope subjacet orbis," line 37 in Hauréau, *Les mélanges poétiques*, 69. But the most relevant parallel in rhyme and thought is Hugh Primas, *Oxford Poems* 23.159-161, ed. McDonough, 72 "Qui, quod sacre datur edi / Aut inpertit Palemedi / Aut largitur Ganimedi." **Iusticie legate rigor**: The wording may be compared with Hildebert (or pseudo-Hildebert), *Carmina miscellanea* 49 ("Versus de quodam paupere"), line 4, in PL 171.1400B ("Iustitiae rigor et fidei uigor omnibus aequus").

POEM 14. Incipit "Intus et exterius uirtute lauemur et unda." Two end-rhymed hexameters. Not in Walther. *In principio*, reference 198322 (Paris, Bibliothèque nationale, MS lat. 3343, fol. 93 [fifteenth century]).

The mythological poems began with the pure invective of Poem 10, but they shifted in Poems 11 through 13 to balancing complaints with pleas for the punishment of the malefactors. In the last few poems before the biblical epigrams the anthologist guides the reader away from the acrimony of the mythological poems toward penance and theology. This route begins in the fourteenth poem, a single rhymed couplet on the theme of purity. In the remaining poems in the second group, the anthologist continues to escort the reader on a penitential path, so that the shift to the biblical epigrams seems in no way abrupt.

The poem bears a striking resemblance to opening words of the similarly proportioned and end-rhymed antiphon (Psalm 50.9) sung by the choir in the ceremony of the Asperges, as the priest sprinkles holy water during the purification of the altar at the beginning of the Mass: "Asperges me, Domine, hyssopo, et mundabor. Lavabis me, et super nivem dealbabor" (You will sprinkle me, Lord, with hyssop, and I will be cleansed. You will wash me, and more than snow will I be whitened).

[2v^{B}] Intus et exterius uirtute lauemur et unda;
Exteriora liquor, uirtus facit intima munda.

Inwardly and outwardly let us be washed by virtue and water;
water makes the outside pure, virtue the inside.

Textual Notes

1] *Initial rubricated.*

Commentary

1. **Intus et exterius**: A stock line opening.

POEM 15. Incipit "Solue graues penas celerum, committe, Loteri" (ductus of first three letters in last word uncertain). Six hexameters, all with the same end-rhyme. Not in Walther. Not in *In principio*.

Much is unclear about Poem 15, but no one would dispute that it opens with a firm directive to the addressee to accept punishment for his wrongdoing and concludes with a blunt statement of his failings. Presumably it is to be fitted within the same general context of the Gregorian reform as are Poems 11 through 13. This context would help to explain the mention of the appearance at Rome that the addressee is obliged to make, the crime of simony with which he is taxed, and the condemnation of the clergy that falls upon him. But who is the addressee?

[2v^{B}] Solue graues penas celerum, conmitte †loteri†;
Solue graues, sed que digne poterunt adhiberi.
Excicium maius te censet Roma mereri
Quam quod tortoris excogitet ira seueri.
Te simonia notat, domus eruta morsque Rogeri:
Quodlibet istorum te dampnat in ordine cleri.

Pay the heavy penalties for crimes, undertake to †confess† them;
pay the penalties, heavy but which will be able to be applied rightly.

Rome resolves that you deserve a greater destruction
than that which the anger of a stern torturer can devise.
Simony is charged against you, the destroyed house and death of Roger:
any one of these condemns you in the rank of the clergy.

Textual Notes

1] *Initial rubricated.* loteri (*or* lioteri), *with two-letter erasure afterward (apparently of letters* ri, *unnecessary because of markings to indicate shared rhyme of lines 1-3) H.*

3] moueri *corrected above line to* mereri *H.*

4] simonia *written poorly H.* eruta. mors *written above line H.*

Commentary

1 (and 2). **Solue graues penas**: Compare Seneca the Younger, *Phoenissae* 645, ed. Zwierlein, 121 ("Ne metue. Poenas et quidem soluet graues"). **celerum** = *scelerum*. †**loteri**†: The reading of the final word in the line is problematic. The first shaft resembles that of some *b*s and *h*s rather than *l*s, although in the text of this poem it is most like the *l* in "Solue." It is followed by a short upward stroke that fails to produce a typical *b*, a typical *h*, or a typical *li*.

"Loteri" would make sense only as a variant spelling of Lotari (vocative of the name Lothar). This interpretation would lead to the late 1130's, since shortly before dying Emperor Lothar III (1075–December 4, 1137) in fact attacked and harassed King Roger II (1095–1154) of Sicily in 1136–1137. Such a variant spelling, although rare, is attested elsewhere, since "Lothero" is found in the final position of a hexameter, in a phrase that designates Lotharingia as having received its name from Lothar: see Gunther of Pairis, *Ligurinus* 7.207–208, ed. Assmann, 376 ("Francia seu magno nomen sortita Lothero / terra"). But since Lothar predeceased Roger, this interpretation of the word would have to assume (most tenuously) that the poet wrote these six hexameters during a brief interval when people thought mistakenly that Lothar had gotten the better of Roger and killed him. The name Boterius is attested, but this reading of the letters would be equally strained.

The solution assumed in the translation is to emend to *fateri*, which places at the end the word with the ending *-teri* that is most commonly found at the ends of hexameters. An alternative way of proceeding would be to emend *scelerum committe* to *scelera commissa*, but this approach would still leave the problem in the final word of the line. Furthermore, *scelera commissa* appears not to be attested in this *sedes*, whereas *scelere commisso*, *scelerum commissa*, and *sceleris commissa* are found in this metrical position.

3. **Excicium** = *exitium*.

5. **simonia**: Scan short-short-long-short? **Rogeri**: If the name were taken as a vocative (which morphology could allow), Roger would be the addressee of the poem. In this case our thoughts might turn to Roger of Hainaut (died

1093), bishop of Châlons-sur-Marne in Champagne (1066–1093), who was summoned to Rome by Pope Gregory VII at the same time as Isembert of Poitiers: see Fliche, *La Réforme grégorienne*, 2:238. But Roger could be the person whose death is being laid at the feet of the addressee, as an additional misdeed on his part. In this case it is not clear who the Roger would be. Both Baudri and Hildebert left poems in praise of a Roger, but in each instance scholars disagree over the identity of the man to whom the poems were addressed. See Baudri, *Carmina* 192, ed. Tilliette, 2:111–113 (text) and 273 (discussion, in favor of Roger "Borsa" and against King Roger II), and Hildebert, *Carmina minora* 41, "Ad ducem R<ogerum>," ed. A. Brian Scott, 2nd ed. (Munich: K. G. Saur, 2001), 33 (text) and XXIX–XXX (discussion, in favor of King Roger II).

6. **ordine cleri**: A stock ending in Medieval Latin hexameters.

POEM 16. Incipit "Per loca culta parum, per aquas, per lustra ferarum." Eight leonine hexameters. Walther 13944: compare Walther 12932 ("De itinere Romano"). *In principio*, reference 274894. Also preserved (between poems by Hildebert) in G, folio 174 ("De difficultate itineris Romani"). For an edition and further information, see Otto Günther, "Die Handschriften der Kirchenbibliothek von St. Marien in Danzig," in *Katalog der Danziger Stadtbibliothek verfertigt und herausgegeben im Auftrage der städtischen Behörden*, Katalog der Handschriften, vol. 5 (Gdańsk, 1921), 379.

The mention of Rome in Poem 15 connects it to Poem 16, which is fortunately easier to decipher and interpret. Although most of Poem 16 describes the travails of the route that a wayfarer must travel to reach Rome, it is no mere verse itinerary. The phrase *curia diues* calls attention to the venality of the papal court, which was criticized for encouraging pilgrimages simply to increase its wealth.[86] The two words cast doubt upon the entire enterprise of risking life and limb to see the *menia Remi*, if they are nothing but the walls of a greedy and corrupt city.

[2v^{B}] Per loca culta parum, per aquas, per lustra ferarum,
Per iuga perque niues trait orbem curia diues.
Difficilis callis ubi nix, ubi mons, ubi uallis
Inpedit, infestat, trahit artus, corda molestat.
Dum tremulos pontes, gelidos dum transeo montes
Nil habeo tuti, proprie diffido saluti;
Undique cerno minas nemorum montisque ruinas.
Cladibus his emi quod uidi menia Remi.

86. On satire against Rome, see Josef Benzinger, *Invectiva in Romam: Romkritik im Mittelalter vom 9. bis zum 12. Jahrhundert* (Lübeck and Hamburg, 1968), and Yunck, *Lineage of Lady Meed*, 82–117, esp. 109.

The wealthy papal court drags the world through scarcely cultivated places—
through waters, lairs of wild beasts, mountain ridges, and snow.
A difficult path troubles the heart, where snow hinders,
a mountain assaults, and a valley drags down the limbs.
As I cross tottering bridges and frozen mountains,
I hold nothing safe and I fear for my own safety.
Everywhere I perceive the threats of groves and the ruins of a mountain.
Through these disastrous experiences I paid for seeing the walls of Remus.

Textual Notes

1] *Initial rubricated.* culta pa *H*: culta parum *added above line in same hand.*
2] trait *H*: trahit *G*.
4] trahit artus *H*: terit artus *G*.
7] Undique cerno *H*: Unde cerno *G*.

Commentary

1. **lustra ferarum**: A line ending commonplace from Vergil, *Georgics* 2.471, ed. Mynors, 61.

3–4. The translation is intended to preserve what appears to be a deliberate matching of three subjects (snow, mountain, valley) and three verbs (hinders, assaults, drags down). Alternatively, we could supply *est* with "Difficilis callis" to construe as: "Difficult [is] the path where snow, mountain, [and] valley hinders, assaults, and drags down the body, [and] troubles the heart." Finally, it is worth considering the reading "terit artus" in *G*, which would encourage the translation "wears out the body." Palaeographically it is easy to see how *trahit* could have entered the text in place of an original *terit*, especially under the influence of *trait* in line 2.

7. **montisque ruinas**: Compare Seneca the Younger, *Thyestes* 77, ed. Zwierlein, 297 ("Montis ruinam": line opening).

8. **Cladibus his**: A stock opening. **menia Remi**: This line ending plays upon that of Vergil, *Aeneid* 1.7, ed. Mynors, 103 ("moenia Romae"). The *variatio* achieved by the transformation of *Romae* into *Remi* could express a polemic intention, by implying that the walls have been contaminated by the blood of the fratricide who founded the city.

POEM 17. Incipit "Mira uidere cupis? Ascende cacumina rupis." Six lines: two elegiac distichs, followed by two hexameters. In each distich a leonine hexameter is followed by a pentameter with a different internal rhyme (. . b . . b . . b). The two hexameters at the end are leonine. Walther 11074 cites Munich, Bayerische Staatsbibliothek, Clm 17212 (s. XII/XIII), fol. 22 (also 6 verses). See "Codices latinos

(Clm) 15121–21313 complectens," in *Catalogus codicum manu scriptorum Bibliothecae regiae monacensis*, vol. 4, part 3, ed. Karl Halm, Friedrich Heinz, Wilhelm Meyer, and Georg Thomas (Munich, 1878), 88, item 709. Not in *In principio*.

Poem 16 contains three mentions of mountains. These afford the anthologist a link with Poem 17, which is set upon a mountain. Apart from their settings, the two poems have little common ground. Whereas Poem 16 is concerned with the routes that the poet follows to the papal court in Rome, 17 reformulates one verse in the Canticle of Moses:

> Constituit eum super excelsam terram ut comederet fructus agrorum, ut sugeret mel de petra oleumque de saxo durissimo (Dt 32.13: compare Ps 81.17).
>
> *He set him upon high land: that he might eat the fruits of the fields, that he might suck honey out of the rock, and oil out of the hardest stone.*

At first sight a poem based on this verse in Deuteronomy seems an odd choice for inclusion in the anthology, but this impression may be dispelled by two considerations. One is that the poem may be understood as celebrating a visit to the Holy Land, just as its predecessor dealt with pilgrimage to Rome. The other is that the poem may serve as preface to the text of the biblical epigrams, which begins on the next folio. In this light, Poem 17 becomes a hermeneutic exhortation to the reader to be prepared to interpret the Old Testament meaningfully. Possibly the poet had in mind the typological understanding of Deuteronomy 32.13 that Rabanus Maurus urged:

> Sed nusquam tale aliquid juxta historiam legitur, si tota Testamenti series Veteris recenseatur. Nusquam de petra mel, nusquam oleum populus ille suxit. Sed quia juxta Pauli vocem, petra erat Christus, mel de petra suxerunt, qui ejusdem Redemptoris nostri facta et miracula viderunt.[87]
>
> *But nothing of the sort can be read anywhere on the literal level, even if the whole progression of the Old Testament is considered. Nowhere did that people suck honey from a stone, nowhere oil. But because according to Paul's statement the rock was Christ, they who saw the deeds and miracles of this selfsame redeemer of ours sucked honey from a stone.*

87. *Enarrationes super Deuteronomium* 4.2, in PL 108.975CD.

Rabanus Maurus's interpretation is especially relevant to the biblical epigrams, which are arranged in an irregular alternation between Old Testament and New Testament topics. But Rabanus is hardly the only plausible source of inspiration for the poet, since the metaphor of drawing honey from rocks is commonplace in medieval discussions of biblical exegesis.[88] In fact, the second verse reveals a possible debt to Paulinus of Aquileia.[89]

[2v^{B}] Mira uidere cupis? Ascende cacumina rupis;
    Non alibi quam ibi dat petra mella tibi.
Quid sit et unde stupes quod manat nectare rupes:
    Non dedit illud apis quod capis immo lapis.
Ex apium cellis non est data copia mellis,
Fundit mella silex plus quam caua quercus et ilex.

You wish to see marvels? Climb the peaks of the mountain.
    Nowhere but there does a rock produce honey for you.
You are stunned why and for what reason it should be, that a crag flows with nectar.
    Not a bee, but a stone produced the honey that you take.
The abundance of honey was not produced by cells of bees.
Flint, rather than a hollow oak or holm-oak, pours forth honey.

Textual Notes

1] *Initial rubricated.* cacumina mo, *with* rupis *added above line. Probably the scribe began automatically to write* montis, *since the phrase* cacumina montis *was a hexameter line ending common after Lucretius,* De rerum natura *6.464, ed. Bailey, and Vergil,* Aeneid *3.274, ed. Mynors, 161.*

Commentary

1. **cacumina rupis**: The poet is here indebted to Venantius Fortunatus, *Carmina* 3.12.25, ed. Leo, 65; ed. Reydellet, 1:108 ("cacumine rupis").

88. See Klaus Lange, "Geistliche Speise: Untersuchungen zur Metaphorik der Bibelhermeneutik," *Zeitschrift für deutsches Altertum und deutsche Literatur* 95 (1966): 81–122, and Hans-Jörg Spitz, *Die Metaphorik des geistigen Schriftsinns: Ein Beitrag zur allegorischen Bibelauslegung des ersten christlichen Jahrtausends*, Münstersche Mittelalter-Schriften 12 (Munich, 1972).

89. *Carmina* 4.37–38, ed. Norberg, 109: (37) "Haec est illa petra, Moses de qua sanctus cecinit: / 'Suxerunt de petra mella, de saxo durissimo / Oleum,' quod docet sanctum per enigma spiritum, / Quem post gloriam triumphi flauit in discipulos. / (38) Potest accipi doctrina per mellis dulcedinem, / Quam rorauit totus dulcis et desiderabilis / Iesus, esset cum infirma passioni dedita / Eius caro, que surgendo facta est fortissima."

3. The line could be punctuated alternatively "Quid sit et unde? Stupes quod manat nectare rupes?" and translated "What could it be and where does it come from? Are you astounded that a crag flows with nectar?" The arguments against this alternative include the fact that it breaks the line into two sense units which do not coincide with the internal rhymes. **nectare rupes**: The line ending is identical with that of Statius, *Siluae* 2.2.99, ed. Courtney, 43. If the identity is a sign of indebtedness rather than a mere coincidence, then it could be relevant to a determination of the extent to which the *Siluae* were known in the Middle Ages. For the most current information on the transmission of Statius's texts during this period, see Birger Munk Olsen, "La réception de Stace au moyen âge (du IXe au XIIe siècle)," in *Nova de veteribus. Mittel- und neulateinische Studien für Paul Gerhard Schmidt*, ed. Andreas Bihrer and Elisabeth Stein (Munich, 2004), 230–246.
6. **quercus et ilex**: The line ending is attested in Horace, *Epistles* 1.16.9, ed. Shackleton Bailey, 278, and Baudri, *Carmina* 134.343, ed. Tilliette, 2:12. [JZ]

Group Three

POEMS 18 THROUGH 87 (fols. $3r^{A}$–$7r^{B}$) are epigrams. Poem 18, only two lines, is an anonymous versification of Gregory the Great, *Moralia in Job* 31.47: "Natus homo, uitulus moriendo leoque resurgens, / In pennis aquile Christus ad astra uolat" (Walther 11625).[90] It stands in a close relation to all the rest—Poems 19 through 87—of the sixty-nine biblical epigrams by Hildebert.[91] The epigrams in the Houghton manuscript follow the same order as those in the new edition, with the following exceptions: nos. 4–5 and 22–23 are reversed, and nos. 50.I and 61.I are included, but not 50.II and 61.II. This arrangement does not follow the biblical sequence of the passages to which the poems refer, and was probably the author's own.[92] Comparing the text of the poems in Houghton MS Lat 300 with the text in other early manuscripts could offer an additional means of localizing the anthologist (or the manuscripts upon which he drew). Several variants in the Houghton text also appear, for instance, in Saint-Omer, Bibliothèque municipale 115, a late twelfth-century manuscript from the Cistercian abbey of Clairmarais (Scott's C), and London, British Library, MS Royal 8.B.iv, from Bury St. Edmunds in the thirteenth century (Scott's D).[93] While their commonalities are suggestive, they are not definitive, since they are so few. Aside from the question of localization, the text of MS Lat 300, which presents all sixty-nine Epigrams, arranged quite nearly in the order supposed to be original, should also be taken into account by readers

90. The poem was published in André Boutemy, "Notes additionnelles à la notice de Ch. Fierville sur le manuscrit 115 de Saint Omer," *Revue belge de philologie et d'histoire* 22 (1943): 25.

91. See A. B. Scott, Deirdre F. Baker, and A. G. Rigg, "The *Biblical Epigrams* of Hildebert of Le Mans: A Critical Edition," *Mediaeval Studies* 47 (1985): 272–316 (which does not make use of Houghton MS Lat 300). Scott describes the other manuscripts of the Epigrams in "The Biblical Allegories of Hildebert of Le Mans," *Sacris Erudiri* 16 (1965): 404–424.

92. Wilmart, "Le Florilège de Saint-Gatien . . . seconde partie," 150. Four other extant manuscripts and three fragments share this arrangement. In another twelve manuscripts of the Epigrams, scribes attempted to rearrange them sequentially; their results vary: see Scott, "Biblical Allegories," 409.

93. In Epigram 17, line 2, the words *gentis dux* are reversed to *dux gentis*, as in C, D, and Houghton MS Lat 300. In Epigram 59, line 4, MS Lat 300, D, and K (London, British Library, MS Cotton Cleopatra C.i) presents *ardet*, for Scott-Baker-Rigg's *aret*. In Epigram 65, line 3, C, D, MS Lat 300, and A (London, British Library, MS Cotton Julius D.iii) have *tonsura*, for Scott-Baker-Rigg's *rasura*. C and D, along with X (Paris, Bibliothèque nationale, MS lat. 14958), invert the order of Epigrams 22 and 23, as does MS Lat 300; D also reverses 3 and 4, while MS Lat 300 exchanges Epigrams 4 and 5. MS Lat 300 and C also share some other compositions: Poem 18 ("Natus homo, uitulus") appears in C separately from Hildebert's Epigrams, and the *declamatio* and *controversia* that compose Group Four (Poems 88 and 89) are present in C as well.

of the Scott-Baker-Rigg edition, e.g., in Epigram 51, line 1, where MS Lat 300 has *beato*, for the otherwise universal *latino*.

The presence of the epigrams in MS Lat 300 may point toward a provenance for the manuscript in Tours, where Hildebert was archbishop from 1125 until his death in 1134—and where the invaluable Saint-Gatien anthology (Tours, Bibliothèque municipale, MS 890, destroyed in 1940), with its ample samplings of Hildebert's and Marbod's poems, originated. This anthology had also contained all but two of the epigrams, in their original order.[94]

Below are listed the Epigrams as they occur in MS Lat 300, with the Scott-Baker-Rigg number in parentheses, and incipit. Where the first line in MS Lat 300 differs from the printed edition, the variant incipit is noted. Red initials decorate the incipits on 3r–4r; blank spaces are left for them thereafter.

fol. 3r

19. (1) "Vicit Adam ueterem gula, gloria uana, cupido." Walther 20296.
20. (2) "Quattuor esse reum faciunt: suggestio primum." Walther 15296.
21. (3) "Ter Dominus Petrum rogat an se diligat, an non." Walther 19207.
H: Ter Dominus Petrum Dominus rogat an se diligat; an non *added above the line*
22. (5) "Cur uoluit de desponsata uirgine nasci." Walther 3957.
23. (4) "Quare ter Samuelem uox diuina uocauit." Walther 15259.
24. (6) "Dauid per cytharam potuit lenire furorem." Walther 4087.
25. (7) "Vinea culta Dei plebs est. Infantia mane." Walther 20356.
26. (8) "Sanson significat Christum, subuersio templi." Walther 17195.
27. (9) "Sunt hydrie mentes doctrine fonte replete." Walther 18334.
28. (10) "Plenus ager florum plenum uirtutibus orbem." Walther 1173.
ager H: hodor

fol. 3v

29. (11) "Per Iacob patrem, per Ioseph concipe Christum." Walther 13941.
30. (12) "Egiptus mundus, Pharao Sathan, Israelite." Walther 576.
mundus Pharao H: Pharao mundus
31. (13) "Peccatum sanies. Sanies hec defluit extra." Walther 13907.
32. (14) "Exit de Iherico Christus, dat lumen utrique." Not in Walther.
Compare Walther 6085 "Exit de Iericho Christus cecisque duobus," which Scott prints as the standard version (giving "dat lumen utrique" as part of a variant), and 6072a "Exit de Iericho" (three-word incipit only).
33. (15) "Est certum quod quinque modis gula damnat edacem." Walther 5627.
34. (16) "Mentis in excessu datus est liber Ezechieli." Walther 10960.

94. See Wilmart, "Le Florilège de Saint-Gatien . . . Première partie," 5.

35. (17) "Est Abrahae dictum: Terramque tuosque relinque." Walther 5560. After the opening line of Epigram 17, lines 10–11 of Epigram 11 were recopied here and canceled. On fol. 4r, line 12 of Epigram 11 and the first five lines of Epigram 12 were recopied and canceled; then Epigram 17 continues.
36. (18) "Asa Caleph nobis animam designat, asellus." Walther 1563.
H: Axa Caleph animam nobis
37. (19) "Qui res mundanas pro religione relinquit." Walther 15635.
38. (20) "Mons fumat, Deus hic loquitur, stat turba deorsum." Walther 11186.
39. (21) "Panis significat scripturam. Frangere panem." Walther 13626.
40. (23) "Respecxit Dominus ad Abel, respexit ad eius." Walther 16659 ("Respexit Deus ad Abel, respexit ad eius: Scott prints "Dominus").
41. (22) "Iudicium per aquam transiuit, eritque per ignem." Walther 9922.
42. (24) "Coram pennatis tenduntur retia frustra." Walther 3306.
43. (25) "Stulta decensque simul mulier quasi circulus auri." Walther 18642.

fol. 4v

44. (26) "Celum factum firmamentum mistica res est." Walther 2988.
45. (27) "Quando facit mihi iustitiam pro munere iudex." Walther 15216.
46. (28) "Vestem contextam lana linoque recusa." Walther 20268.
47. (29) "Anticus serpens mihi serpit pectore si quid." Walther 1330.
48. (30) "Exiit ignotas mulieres Dina uidere." Walther 6076.
Dina H: digna
49. (31) "In mensa Domini phiale ciatique parantur." Walther 8999.
50. (32) "In base sunt cherubim sunt et bos et leo sculti." Walther 8828a (three-word incipit).
51. (33) "Vult intrare, nequit fera gens Sodomita domum Lot." Walther 20874.
52. (34) "Loth fugit ardentem Sodomam, montesque requirit." Walther 10396.

fol. 5r

53. (35) "Aurea pontificis pendebant insita uesti." Walther 1804.
54. (36) "Accinctis gladio de porta precepit ire." Walther 236 ("Accinctus gladio de porta praecepit ire": Scott prefers "Accinctis").
55. (37) "Cum multas pecudes habuissent, pascua querunt." Walther 3679.
56. (38) "Exploratores Iherico tardasse diebus." Walther 6131.
diebus H: duobus
57. (39) "Terram Miffiboseth Dauid diuisit inique." Walther 19236.
58. (40) "Dum poscunt solui Baraban Christumque necari." Walther 3717 ("Cum poscunt": Scott prefers "Dum poscunt").
59. (41) "Cum sponsum Rebecca uideret, uecta camelo." Walther 3808.
60. (42) "Spelunca duplici Sarram sepelisse uir eius." Walther 18478.

fol. 5v

61. (43) "Per Nabuzardan destruxit rex Babilonis." Walther 13952.
62. (44) "Iob, Daniel, Noe sunt saluandi teste propheta." Walther 9862.
salvandi H: sauuandi
63. (45) "Traduntur seruis unum, duo, v talenta." Walther 19346a (three-word incipit).
64. (46) "Exprimitur per timpana mortificatio carnis." Walther 6134.
65. (47) "Accepit fruges ad semen seruus ad esum." Walther 228.
66. (48) "Mactatam uitulam comitantur cedrus, isopus." Walther 10553.

fol. 6r

67. (49) "In Sion ignis, in Ierusalemque caminus." Walther 9106.
68. (50) "Patrem significat Abraham, sua uictima Christum." Walther 13827.
69. (51) "Abner presbiteros signat; sermone latino." Walther 181.
latino H: beato
70. (52) "Archa Noe sursum fuit arcta, sed ampla deorsum." Walther 1423.
71. (53) "Israel est Moises et uirga superna potestas." Walther 9594a (three-word incipit).

fol. 6v

72. (54) "Angelus in cultu candorem, fulgur in ore." Walther 998.
73. (55) "Dum staret Moises in petra, pretereuntis." Walther 4962b (two-word incipit).
74. (56) "Nostre nature deitas unita refertur." Walther 12303.
75. (57) "Ut fertur salices sunt in medio Babilonis." Walther 19797.
76. (58) "Hostia turturis atque columba mistica res est." Walther 8488.
77. (59) "Petra capit semen, uia, sentes, optima terra." Walther 14025.
78. (60) "Absorbet fluuium Behemoth, speratque quod ori." Walther 198.

fol. 7r

79. (61) "Ad plus viii solent celebrari festa diebus." Walther 418.
80. (62) "Panes quinque duos pisces dat quinque uirorum." Walther 13608.
dat quinque H: dat quisque
81. (63) "Quomodo suscepit Salomon a matre coronam?" Walther 16341.
82. (64) "Doctrinam per aquam, per nubes sume prophetas." Walther 4686.
83. (65) "Ut capitis rasura docet, rex atque sacerdos." Walther 19775.
rasura H: tonsura
84. (66) "Mens mala, mors intus; malus actus, mors foris; usus." Walther 10911.
85. (67) "Est ratio quod pars altaris dextera misse." Walther 5831.
86. (68) "Scignant tres partes de Christi corpore; prima." Walther 18193.
87. (69) "Quid statio dextra signat, uel parte sinistra." Walther 15912 (with "signet"). [BKB and JZ]

Group Four

Poems 88 and 89 (folios 7v^{A}–8r^{B}) are modeled on ancient exercises in forensic rhetoric. Both of these declamations are sometimes ascribed to Bernard Silvestris.[95] Bernard's interest in such materials is confirmed by the fact that he took as source for his *Mathematicus* a pseudo-antique declamation: pseudo-Quintilian, *Declamatio maior* 4.[96] Although the attribution of these two forensic declamations to Bernard is insecure, they can certainly be considered the product of the "school of Bernard" or of the "school of Tours."[97] Thus they may well have originated in the same region as did Hildebert's epigrams.

Poem 88 is the *De gemellis* (although it is not entitled in Houghton MS Lat 300), based on pseudo-Quintilian, *Declamatio* 8.[98] Eighty-two hexameter lines. Incipit "*R*oma duos habuit, res est, non fabula vana."[99] Explicit "Definiuit eam sententia iudicialis." The text in MS Lat 300 is lacking lines that are found in other manuscripts, such as Rg.[100] Walther 16848. *In principio*, reference 1284121.

Poem 89 is *De paupere ingrato*, also known as *Pauper ingratus* (although it is not entitled in Houghton MS Lat 300), based on Seneca the Elder, *Controversia* 5.1.[101] Twenty-eight lines (14 elegiac couplets). Incipit "*M*esta parens misere paupertas anxietatis." Explicit "Res est iudicibus discucienda datur." Walther 10559.[102] *In principio*, references 226187–226191, 1283465, 2069603–2069607, 2072968–2072969. [JZ]

95. In favor of the attribution, Edmond Faral, "Le manuscrit 511 du 'Hunterian Museum' de Glasgow," *Studi medievali* n.s. 9 (1936): 18–119; against it, Mirella Brini Savorelli, "Il 'Dictamen' di Bernardo Silvestre," *Rivista critica di storia della filosofia* 20 (1965): 182n1.

96. *Declamationes XIX maiores Quintiliano falso ascriptae*, ed. Håkanson, 60–84.

97. Bernardus Silvestris, *Cosmographia*, ed. Dronke, 7.

98. The fullest study of the *Declamatio* is *I gemelli malati: Un caso di vivisezione (Declamazioni maggiori, 8)*, ed. Antonio Stramaglia (Cassino, 1999).

99. The best edition is Robert R. Edwards, "Poetic Invention and the Medieval *Causae*," *Mediaeval Studies* 55 (1993): 183–217, at 197–202. The poem is extant in many manuscripts, among which Rg (Oxford, Bodleian Library, MS Rawlinson G. 109): see Rigg, "Medieval Latin Poetic Anthologies (IV)," 487, no. 55, and T (London, British Library, MS Cotton Titus A.xx); see Rigg, "Medieval Latin Poetic Anthologies (I)," 306, no. 54.

100. For a table of the correspondences (in which MS Lat 300 is designated H and Rg is O), see Edwards, "Poetic Invention," 202.

101. For the source text, see Seneca the Elder, *Declamations*, ed. and trans. Winterbottom, 1:470–475.

102. The best edition is Edwards, "Poetic Invention," 211–213. At 213 Edwards prints the explicit more intelligibly as "Res hec iudicibus discutienda datur," but he notes the variant "est" in this manuscript and "ea" in another.

Group Five

Contents

THIS SECTION OF THE MANUSCRIPT (fols. $8v^A$–$10v^B$) encompasses six occasional poems, none of them listed in Walther, all in elegiac distichs, and all written to mark beginnings and endings. The poems celebrate a young count and a new king, and they mourn or mock some less widely known personages. As in the other sections of the manuscript, the poems are arranged in a thematic progression, so that each one has a relation of similitude or contrast with its predecessor and often relates by counterpoint of one sort or another to earlier and later poems within the section. In addition, the order of the poems follows a chronological progression.

Poems 90 and 91 open the section with glory and optimism, praising two young rulers, both of whom hold promise of surpassing their fathers. Poem 90 presents Geoffrey Martel le Jeune (about 1071–1106), scion of the house of Anjou (count of Anjou, 1103–1106), who is depicted as restoring to his territories the benefits of a golden age: *pax* (peace), *pietas* (devotion), *lex* (law), *ordo* (order), *fides* (faith), and *concordia* (harmony)—all are attributed to his rule and opposed to earlier disorder. Poem 91 continues in a panegyric mode, elaborating on the justice tempered with mercy that characterizes (or that the poet hopes will characterize) the young Louis, crowned king in 1108. Both Poems 90 and 91 complete their portraits with comparisons to noted historical and legendary figures from Greco-Roman antiquity: Aemilius Paulus, Scipio, Laelius, and the Caesars in the first poem, and Aeneas, Cato, Socrates, Nestor, Ajax, Ulysses, and Paris in the second. The more intricate, illustrious, and numerous comparisons in Poem 91 befit the higher rank of the king.

Poem 91 develops at length a theme that appeared only briefly in 90: the superiority of the new ruler over his base father. For example, the poet gives free rein to his ire in describing King Philip I of France (1052–1108) as the "badly twisted vine" from which the flower, King Louis VI (1081–1137), has sprung. The nexus between the incompetent fathers of Poems 90 and 91—Fulk "Rechin" (count of Anjou, 1043–1109) and Philip I, respectively—is Bertrada of Montfort (1059–1117), who was Fulk's fourth wife before abandoning him in 1102 for Philip. Bertrada also lay behind attempts made to prevent both Geoffrey Martel and Louis from taking power. Fulk had conspired to disinherit Geoffrey Martel, son of Ermengarde of Bourbon (born about 1045), in favor of a son by Bertrada, and Louis too had to surmount a challenge to his kingship by Bertrada and her partisans.

With Poem 92, an elegy for a certain Milo, the mood turns somber. The identity of this particular Milo has been debated and is discussed further below in the introduction to the poem, but the evidence for Milo II of Bray is reasonably convincing. The phrase "a victor even over himself" ("victor et ipse sui") might, for example, be seen as referring to Milo's somewhat inconstant support of Louis VI, with the poem's emphasis on his obedience to the king meant in turn to focus attention on the state of affairs at the time of his death. The statement (25–26) that Milo elected to die rather than forsake justice bespeaks a death in some kind of conflict; and the date of his death in October meshes with what we know of Milo II of Bray's history, namely, that he was strangled in October of 1116 or 1117 by his cousin Hugh of Crécy in a conflict over the possession of the castle of Montlhéry, which Louis VI had bestowed upon Milo in 1109.

A connection with the intrigues of Bertrada emerges, as well: Montlhéry had been ceded to the crown in 1104 by Guy II Trousseau (died 1109), Milo's older brother, on the condition that his daughter and heir, Elisabeth (died after 1141), marry the adolescent Philip of Melun, who was the son of Bertrada and Philip I, and the younger half-brother of the future Louis VI.[103] Eventually Montlhéry came into the younger Philip's hands, and he gave it to Hugh of Crécy. Given Philip's (and through him Bertrada's) own regal ambitions, Louis VI was unwilling to see this important castle in the possession of a partisan of his half-brother, and thus he confronted Hugh at Montlhéry in 1109: the outcome of Louis' victory was the installation of Milo II of Bray, at this moment a partisan of Louis, as seneschal of Montlhéry.[104] Hugh's subsequent murder of his cousin was widely deplored; Louis himself was present at Milo's interment at Longpont-sur-Orge, and his grief and subsequent revenge upon Hugh are well attested.[105]

In sum, Poem 92 is linked to 91 through Milo's association with Louis, and through the treachery of the king's enemies, including of course Bertrada and her son Philip. If Poem 90 was a lesson meant for the young Philip, perhaps Poem 92 spells out the consequences of neglecting such lessons. Milo's death at the hands of a traitorous enemy also resonates with the eventual fate of Geoffrey Martel, who was assassinated in 1106. Thus Poem 92 also interlocks with Poem 90.

Milo's epitaph sets the tone for the three brief poems that conclude this section. Poem 93, an epitaph for Frodo, plausibly refers to the scholar from Angers who was mourned by Baudri of Bourgueil in three epitaphs of his own.[106] Baudri

---

103. Once the marriage took place, King Philip and his heir Louis confirmed Philip "de Melun" as count of Mantes; hence his more familiar title, Philip of Mantes.

104. This much of the history of Montlhéry is found in Suger, *Vita Ludovici Grossi Regis* 8 and 18, ed. Waquet, 34–43 and 122–129, trans. Cusimano and Moorhead, 39–43 and 81–83.

105. For the record of the royal itinerary, see Jean Dufour, *Recueil des actes de Louis VI, roi de France (1108–1137)*, vol. 3 (Paris, 1993), 209.

106. *Carmina* 28–30, ed. Tilliette, 1:46–48. Milo's death and Louis' reaction are reported in the *Chronicon Mauriniacense (Chronicle of Morigny)*. See Léon Mirot, ed., *La Chronique de Morigny (1095–1152)*, 2nd ed. (Paris, 1912), 24; and Richard Cusimano, trans., *A Translation of the Chronicle of the Abbey of Morigny, France, c. 1100–1150* (Lewiston, N.Y., 2003), 47–51.

writes of Frodo's "mors inopina" (unexpected death), which likens the deceased to both Milo and Geoffrey, perhaps insinuating that death is equally unforeseeable and unavoidable, whether for a knight or a scholar.

Poem 94, the epitaph for one Julian, remains more mysterious. The name refers not to St. Julian, patron of monasteries in Le Mans and Tours, but rather to a real person. Yet despite forays into various cartularies and historical indices, no one by this name has surfaced who died at this time. Thus for the time being Julian remains unidentified.

Poem 95 is an epitaph for a man called Maurice that satirizes the deceased's engagement in bribery and perhaps also in simony. Two possible identifications tie this poem as well to the Angevin sphere of influence. In a letter written between 1107 and 1110, Geoffrey of Vendôme (about 1070–1132) complained to Ivo of Chartres (about 1040–about 1116) about the grasping practices of one Maurice, and about his controversial election, probably around 1106, as abbot of Saint-Laumer in Blois.[107] Apparently the abbot of Saint-Laumer, one Geoffrey, decided to retire to a hermitage, and named Maurice to replace him. Later the retiree decided that he preferred his former position, which resulted in several years of uncertainty about just who was in charge at Saint-Laumer.[108] A suspicion may have arisen that Maurice had suborned the former abbot, which would account for the unflattering portrait of Maurice here.

Another greedy Maurice in Vendôme is the baron named Maurice of Craon, whose unjust appropriations of revenues belonging to the abbey of La Trinité, Vendôme, were stopped by the cooperation of Geoffrey Martel and Renaud of Martigné, bishop of Angers (1102–1125).[109] Though it is unknown whether this Maurice committed bribery as well, it sounds as if doing so would have been in character for him. If the poem were indeed about him, we could identify the author of this poem, and possibly of the poem about Geoffrey Martel (Poem 90) as writers with a particularly *vendômois* outlook. Regardless of whether the Maurice named here is the sometime abbot, the greedy baron, or someone else entirely, the corruption criticized by the poet here contrasts nicely with the evenhanded justice meted out by Geoffrey Martel and Louis VI in Poems 90 and 91. [BKB]

Authorship and Style of Poems 90 through 92

The authorship of all these poems is undetermined. Also uncertain is whether all six of them, Poems 90 through 95, are the work of a single author. André Vernet (1910–1999) posited that one and the same writer should be credited with Poems 90

107. Letter 109, ed. and trans. Giordanengo, 210–211.

108. Some further details have been assembled in Noël Mars, *Histoire du royal monastère de Sainct-Lomer de Blois de l'ordre de Sainct-Benoist* (Blois, 1869), 139–141 and 283–284.

109. Olivier Guillot, *Le comte d'Anjou et son entourage au XIe siècle*, 2 vols. (Paris, 1972), 276.

through 92, though he did not reveal his reasons for this surmise.[110] Much in their style upholds the view that two or even more of these three poems are indeed by the same poet or at least by poets from within the same circle, as can be verified most easily by close comparison of individual poems in word choice and style, but even within the smaller cluster of Poems 90 through 92 it is not yet possible to assert firmly that one poet wrote all or even two of the poems.

Observations about stylistic tendencies and tone can point readers toward identification of an author, but by themselves such subjective determinations do not constitute proof. Criteria that are (or at least seem) more objective, such as statistical analysis of metrical and linguistic characteristics, often carry greater conviction in arguments about authorship, but here the sample—a grand total of 266 lines for Poems 90 through 92 together—proves to be unworkably small for many purposes. Still, a closer scrutiny of the word choice (and particularly of word choice influenced by phrasing in earlier literature) and style (especially rhetorical figures cultivated by the writer or writers) may suggest whether the three poems share an author, even if it does not permit a definitive answer.

Both consciously and reflexively, writers of Medieval Latin commonly drew upon their readings in earlier literature to furnish their own writings with elegant turns of phrase that sometimes facilitated the act of composition and often displayed the quality of their education. Patterns in the incorporation of borrowed words can help to distinguish one writer from another. While certain earlier authors belonged to the standard curriculum and so are quoted almost involuntarily by later writers, others were less widely read. As a consequence, a writer who habitually quotes less well-known texts stands out from the crowd. Additionally, if a poet turns out in his phraseology to echo texts nearly contemporary with him, that circumstance may enable an educated guess about when he composed his poem and maybe about his locality or literary circle as well.

In Poem 90, by far the most visible presence from earlier literature is Ovid, especially for phrases that fit in elegiac half lines. The poet of Poem 90 also frequently calls upon the Latin epic tradition, most often in the description of heroic traits and deeds. Vergil, Lucan, and Statius stand out, as would be expected. Poem 90 also announces its contemporary models, borrowing from some well-known classicizing poets of late eleventh and early twelfth centuries, particularly the so-called Loire Valley poets. On occasion, the verses of Poem 90 incorporate the same classical tidbits of which these earlier poets had availed themselves.

Poem 91 employs tags familiar from Ovid and Statius, and possibly from Vergil and Lucretius as well. One phrase ("ne quid nimis") is unmistakably Terentian in its origins, but it had become proverbial at the latest by the eleventh century: in his

110. André Vernet, "Séance du 16 avril," *Bulletin de la Société national des antiquaires de France* (1952–1953): 53.

Proverbia the poet Wipo states outright: "Prouerbium 'Ne quid nimis' laudatur in primis" (The proverb "Nothing to excess" is praised above all).[111] Clichés that derive directly or indirectly from Avienus and the *Ilias Latina* emerge. Like the author of Poem 90, the composer of 91 may evidence knowledge of works by the Loire Valley poets: his language may contain reminiscences of Baudri and Marbod, and the style of his panegyric, with an address to the ruler's country, follows that of Hildebert's panegyric on Henry I and Matilda of England.[112]

Poem 92 conforms with much the same pattern, with many phrases that are commonplace in Medieval Latin hexameter poetry but that may point particularly to Hildebert, Baudri of Bourgueil, and the canonical poems that were favored in their circles.

In some ways comparison is easiest between Poems 90 and 91 since both are praise poems for the politically powerful. All three poems, however, devote a goodly number of lines to delineating the virtues of their respective subjects. Poems 90 and 91 emphasize justice and courage as displayed by Geoffrey Martel and Louis VI, respectively. Each poet borrows phrases from poets such as Lucan to describe his subject's virtues, and each compares the ruler with a catalogue of classical figures to align the count and the king with heroes of ancient epic and history.

The chief difference between these two poems and Poem 92 is that in Poem 92 the virtues singled out for praise reflect an ecclesiastical point of view rather than a political one. The deceased Milo is lauded as a student of Holy Wisdom, a rich man who gave to the poor, and a moralist who remained on the straight and narrow, imposing a manner of martyrdom upon himself and playing host to Modesty personified. The praises heaped upon Milo come across as more appropriate for a bishop, an abbot, or an ecclesiastic of another kind, than for a lay nobleman. For instance, the epithet *uenerabilis* (3) would better qualify a prelate than a layman. Likewise, the assertion that "He overcame the world, a victor even over himself" (10) could describe a person who has made a monastic profession. The same surmise may hold true to a limited extent for the accentuation of Milo's purity (31–32) and modesty (33–40), which leads into the personification of Modesty as his inseparable companion. The remark about "the good things he taught" (42) may presume that Milo was a teacher or preacher; and the virtues singled out in the grand finale of panegyric (45–46)—*pietas* (righteousness), *spes* (hope), *pax* (peace), *gloria* (glory), and *fides* (faith)—again sound more ecclesiastical than political, though *gloria* may imply a prelate rather than just an everyday churchman. Such a reading calls into question the identification of the subject as Milo II of Bray, since according to what little we know of his life he was not any more preoccupied with virtue than the average nobleman. Still, his political conversion might have been accompanied

111. Line 60, ed. Bresslau, 70.

112. *Carmina minora* 37, "De Anglia," ed. Scott, 24–25.

by a religious one that the present eulogist wanted to acknowledge; and a poet more familiar with monastic virtues than aristocratic ones might well have chosen his laudatory epithets according to his own experience, not necessarily that of his subject.

The Ovidian distichs of all three poems have been enlivened by the liberal application of rhetorical figures of speech and thought. Medieval Latin poets in general displayed a predilection for devices that highlighted repetition and variation. Twelfth-century poets especially favored forms of ornamentation such as anadiplosis (*reduplicatio*), asyndeton, and *annominatio.* Poems 90 through 92 all employ anadiplosis in combination with another variety of iteration, such as anaphora or epistrophe. For example, a phrase that caps the ending of one line may be repeated to begin the next. In one case the repetition is extended by later reusing the same ending:

> Nil gerit utilius *principe terra bono.*
> *Principe terra bono* colitur . . . (90.2–3)
> cum uiret et floret *principe terra bono* (90.10)

Similar constructions appear in 91.106–107 and 91.109 (where the phrase repeated is "maior erit"), and 92.4–5 and 7 ("Milo ruit").

A second rhetorical device in which the poet or poets delight is asyndeton. Sometimes it is restricted to a single hexameter, but in other instances its exuberance cannot be contained and spills over into the next line:

> Pax, pietas, lex, ordo, fides, concordia regnant (90.9)
> . . . bona, bella, salubris,
> deliciosa, potens, fertilis, ampla satis (91.1–2)

Extending plain and simple asyndeton are instances of a more elaborate omission of conjunctions, in which one series of nouns or phrases is matched with another one of verbs. Such an arrangement went in the Middle Ages by the name of *versus rapportati.*[113] Cases in point would be the following:

> Principe terra bono colitur, seruatur, habundat,
> Agricolis, armis, deliciis opibus. (90.3–4)

and

> Lingua, mente, manu clamauit, credidit, egit
> Quod rex, quod ratio, quod pia iura docent. (92.15–16)

113. Curtius, *European Literature and the Latin Middle Ages,* 286–287, and Norberg, *Introduction to the Study of Medieval Latin Versification,* 54–55.

This type of asyndeton may have become a vogue owing to the influence of Hildebert, who resorts to a related form of zeugma often in his poetry. A memorable example is *Carmina minora* 22.3–4.[114] Hildebert's zeugma differs, in that it features different clauses that share the same verb, but it is similar in presenting the other elements in groups of three.

A third favored effect is *annominatio*, which entails the repetition of similar sounds. This device is typical of much Medieval Latin writing. Very often it plays upon a noun and verb with the same root, in which case the ornament is categorized as *figura etymologica*. All three poems apply this technique freely, as the emphasized elements in the following lines from Poem 90 exemplify:

> Martellus *consul* qui talia *consul*it orbi
>   Ut meritis plenis se *prob*et esse *prob*um.
> Qui *patr*ie *patr*ocinium felicibus horis . . . (90.13–15)

Among numerous other instances in the three poems, compare 91.29 ("supplicibus supplicet") and 92.22 ("suscepit suscipientem").

With these general similarities in mind, we can undertake direct comparison of the poems. A closer inspection of Poems 90 and 91 reveals some word choices and ideas that appear in both, but other stylistic mannerisms that differ. To begin with verbal similarities, 90.33 and 91.31 both begin "scit quia continuo" (knows that . . . at once). Both poems use the phrase "morum floribus" (flowers of good morals) in the same metrical position, near the end of each poem, at 90.88 and 91.98. 90.94 has the ending "nobiliumque decus" (ornament of nobles), similar to 91.20 "iusticieque decus" (ornament of justice).

Although the resemblance may reflect the conventions of panegyric rather than common authorship, both Poems 90 and 91 praise their respective subjects in similar terms, For example, they both dwell on the leader's zeal for justice that can become *ferox* (fierce), at 90.32 and 91.23. The concluding lines of both also have much in common: 90.96 "cuius in eternum nobile nomen erit" (his name will be renowned forever) sounds very much like 91.12: "nomen propterea nobile semper erit" (your name will therefore be always renowned). Admittedly, a panegyric that concludes with the notion of immortal fame takes us into the territory of the commonplace, where we linger through the concluding couplets:

> Interea longum ualeat Martellus et omnis
>   Qui pro Martello uota benigna facit (90.99–100)

> *Meanwhile, may Martel long prosper, together with everyone*
>   *who offers kind prayers for Martel.*

---

114. Ed. Scott, 11: "larga Ceres, deus Archadie, Bachusque replebant / horrea, tecta, penum, farre, bidente, mero."

Ergo diu uiuat rex Lodouicus et omnis
  Qui super hoc uerbo uota benigna facit. (91.115–16)

Therefore long live King Louis and everyone
  who after this discourse offers kind prayers.

Yet clichéd or not, the overlap between the lines from "et omnis" to the end is too remarkable to be merely coincidental.

Although these similarities are striking, certain stylistic traits that may not result from conscious effort on the part of the poet seem to differ from Poems 90 to 91. The second poet reuses certain words repeatedly: *satis* occurs six times (2, 11, 15, 17, 27, 69), and *nimium/nimis* four times (5, 26, 37, 111). *Nichil* occurs six times (4, 7, 55 [twice], 62, 65), while *maior* appears seven times in lines 106–110, as well as thrice earlier in the poem (15, 69, 72). Repetition to this extent does not happen in Poem 90, where *satis*, *nimium*, and *maior* each are used only once (67, 81, 90), *nil* and *nichil* a total of four times (2, 42, 70, 81).

The author of Poem 91 is also decidedly fond of *geminatio* (55 "uile nichil, nichil indignum") and the repetition of sounds generally, with some jingling results (13 "atqui... aliis precii tibi ... alti"; 81 "eras eremus"; 91 "proauos abauos atauosque"; 93–103 "Carolum Carolique patrem pater illi / Pipinus ... / Pipinus Carolusque ... / Pipini Carolique"). In particular, the recurrence of *satis* and *nimium/nimis* marks the writer of the second poem in this section as less skilled than that of the first: he seems reliant on nonce words to fill metrical space. The poet of 91 adheres less closely to classical norms of prosody. One useful index is the occurrence of a strong caesura in the fifth foot, which classical poets avoided, although it was more permissible if the fifth foot began with a monosyllable. Poem 90 contains four such caesuras, three with leading monosyllables (45 "et prior instat"; 53 "quot legiones"; 77 "hoc ego plane"). The fourth occurrence is a proper name (85 "Scipione"). In contrast, Poem 91 permits twice as many fifth-foot caesuras, five of them without the mitigating monosyllable (7 "nichil umquam"; also 55, 65, 77, 93). The author of Poem 91 also lengthens short vowels at the pentameter break several times (34, 38)—a common enough practice, but one not shared by the author of Poem 90. Disparities in the prosody of Poems 90 and 91, then, point to two different authors, as do the slight differences in the usage of rhetorical figures, as detailed above. While certainly some expressions are repeated word for word and some ideas recur, the overlaps may well signify imitation rather than identity. Taken together, the differences and coincidences might offer evidence that Poem 91 was composed by a student imitating Poem 90, in a clumsy replication of a model by a teacher.

The similarities and dissimilarities between Poems 90 and 91 are so complex and inconsistent that they make any determination regarding authorship a challenge. In turn, Poem 92 has less in common with either 90 or 91 than 90 and 91 have with each other. Since Poem 92 is an epitaph, whereas 90 and 91 were written in praise of the living, some differences in tone are to be expected. Poems 91 and 92 reveal a few verbal and conceptual parallels, but they share only a single identical phrase, "esse cupit" (91.72 and 92.30 "desires to be"), which is generic enough to be chance.[115]

Reading Poems 90 and 92 together, we find that they share only a single very brief phrase of the sort that might have been deployed by almost any Medieval Latin poet: 90.2 "nil gerit utilius" (begins line: "produces nothing more useful") and 92.38 "nil gerit iste locus" (ends line: "This place contains nothing"). In comparison with the close verbal resemblances between Poems 90 and 91, these correspondences are weak. Just as the composition processes of Poems 90 and 91 were clearly related somehow, it is equally apparent that 92 does not share their origin.

The most striking difference between Poem 92 and its two predecessors in the manuscript is the frequent alliteration used in Poem 92. This trait stands out especially in lines 11–23, which feature ten instances of alliteration, eight of them implicating adjacent words. Cases in point would be "*s*acra *s*acrum fouit *s*apiancia" (13) and "*d*iues, *d*ans *qu*ociens *cu*i *d*aret et *qu*id erat" (18). The most flamboyant is not in lines 11–23 but in a later hexameter: "*s*ic *sus*cepta *s*emel *susc*epit *susc*ipientem" (39). No comparable lines come to the fore in Poems 90 or 91. In those poems alliteration is certainly an occasional adornment, but for the most part an unobtrusive one (an exception would be 91.93–94). The difference is especially noticeable when the poems are spoken aloud. To conclude, the use of alliteration in Poem 92 demonstrates a distinct esthetic sensibility from what is displayed in Poems 90 and 91. Whatever the authorship of Poems 90 and 91, 92 is likelier by another poet (whether a third or a second).

In summary, these three poems provide some piquant examples of literary praise and blame from the twelfth century. Possible identifications of the subjects of the poems reveal interests along an east-west trajectory in northern France, from Anjou through Île de France and Champagne. Also notable is a subtle but persistent expression of enmity toward Bertrada of Montfort and her partisans. [BKB, with JL and PP]

POEM 90. Incipit "Omnibus in rebus quas, mi Philippe, uidemus." Fifty elegiac distichs. Not in Walther. Not in *In principio*.

The subject of Poem 90, named as "Martellus consul" in line 13, is most probably Geoffrey Martel le Jeune, count of Anjou (1103–1106). Stylistic as well

115. Among the tenuous parallels are 91.41 ("cor duplex scriptamque manum, linguamque loquacem") and 92.15 ("lingua, mente, manu clamauit, credidit, egit"); 91.30 ("ipse sibi") and 92.10 ("ipse sui"), and 91.45-46 (mention of Nestor: "reddidit . . . Nestora consilio") and 92.28 ("consilioque potens," the phrase used in *Ilias Latina* 177 to describe Nestor).

as historical considerations make it unlikely that the poem refers to an earlier count Geoffrey of Anjou (1040–1060), who was also known as Martel. The poet's many reminiscences of Ovid, for one, suggest a date of composition after 1050, rather late for the celebration of the first Martel's youth.[116] Moreover, since the elder Geoffrey Martel consolidated and expanded upon the political successes of his father, Fulk Nerra (972–1040, count 987–1040), the contrast implied between the peaceful new regime and the lawless old one (for instance, in lines 69–70) would not be appropriate.[117] A few later Angevin Geoffreys were also on occasion given the cognomen Martel (such as Geoffrey Plantagenet, 1113–1151, and his younger son Geoffrey, 1134–1157) but they too avoided notable conflicts with their fathers, and so can be discounted as subjects.

Geoffrey Martel le Jeune enjoyed a brief but apparently brilliant heyday as coruler of the county of Anjou. His father, Fulk IV "Rechin," had tried to disinherit him in favor of Fulk V the Younger (1095–1143, count 1109–1129, king of Jerusalem 1131–1143). Fulk V the Younger was a son of Bertrada of Montfort, the wife Fulk IV took in 1089. After defeating Fulk IV in the attempted disinheritance, Geoffrey figures in charters from 1103 to 1106 as *comes* (count). The old count had been troubled by rebellious barons throughout his rule, and the resulting battles had devastated the countryside. Orderic Vitalis reports that Fulk rather enjoyed the pillaging and profited from it.[118] Fulk's reputation was thus hardly chivalric, and his disorderly personal life only gave clerical chroniclers more of which to disapprove. Geoffrey's success against his father and subsequently against several of the barons quieted the rebellions and foretold a more peaceful existence for the people of Anjou.[119]

Alas, Martel's promise was sadly short-lived. On May 19, 1106, while besieging Candé, he was struck and killed by an arrow as he made his way to a parley. One chronicler attributed his death to the treachery of his father and Bertrada.[120] Contemporary sources do not speculate further about the forces behind the unknown archer, but they are unanimous in extolling his victim. They describe Martel as "an admirable man, distinguished in justice, a cultivator of the whole of goodness, who was a terror to all his enemies" and as "a subduer and conqueror

116. Ovid's amatory poetry, especially, had little influence on Medieval Latin writers before the mid-eleventh century: see Jean-Yves Tilliette, "Savants et poètes du moyen âge face à Ovide: les débuts de l'*aetas Ovidiana* (v. 1050–v. 1200)," in Michelangelo Picone and Bernhard Zimmermann, eds., *Ovidius redivivus: Von Ovid zu Dante* (Stuttgart, 1994), 67–73.

117. Bernard S. Bachrach, *Fulk Nerra, the Neo-Roman Consul, 978–1040: A Political Biography of the Angevin Count* (Berkeley, 1993), esp. 250–259.

118. *Historia ecclesiastica* 11.16, ed. and trans. Chibnall, 74.

119. See Louis Halphen, *Le comté d'Anjou au XIe siècle* (Paris, 1906), 149–152, 166–174.

120. *Chronica de gestis consulum andegavorum*, ed. Halphen and Poupardin, 66.

of tyrants, protector and defender of churches."[121] The portrait conveyed in Poem 90, then, while conventional, echoes the sentiments of contemporary observers,[122] and Martel's reputation as a "protector of churches" makes it all the likelier that a scholar-cleric would praise him in verse.

Because the poem is emphatically not an epitaph, and because it refers to Martel as "count," it can be dated with some certainty to the years 1103–1106. It was probably written to commemorate some triumph of Martel's, perhaps his power-sharing agreement with his father or his successful cooperation with Renaud of Martigné, bishop of Angers, against Maurice of Craon.

Determining the addressee of the poem is more of a challenge. Poem 90 is introduced as a verse epistle, addressed by the poet to "[his] Philip." The name Philip is rare in France before the birth of Philip I in 1052,[123] and for the next generation or so it is attested primarily in families connected with Anne of Kiev (1024–about 1089), the mother of Philip I.[124] Obvious candidates for the addressee of Poem 90 would then include Philip I himself; his son by Bertrada, Philip of Melun (born 1093); and Philip, bishop of Troyes (1081–1121).

The tone of the poet's address to Philip can help to narrow this field a bit. Poets of the period use the vocative *mi* + a name when writing to someone considered an intimate friend, usually a fellow poet or a former student.[125] Our Philip, then, is either a scholarly contemporary of the poet, perhaps associated with one of the cathedral schools, or perhaps a student—a young literate nobleman—for whom Martel might serve as an example. These circumstances would rule out Philip I, who in 1103 was neither youthful nor particularly connected with the schools.

Identification of the addressee as Bishop Philip is conceivable, especially if we allow that the poet himself might have been a bishop, writing to a colleague, perhaps

121. See *Chronica de gestis consulum andegavorum*, ed. Halphen and Poupardin, 65: "admirabilem virum, justitie insignem, totius boni cultorem, qui terror omnium inimicorum suorum fuit"; and *Annales vindocinenses*, ed. in Halphen, 68: "debellator et expugnator tyrannorum, protector et defensor ecclesiarum."

122. See the descriptions of Angevin counts conveniently collected in C. Stephen Jaeger, *The Origins of Courtliness: Civilizing Trends and the Formation of Courtly Ideals 939–1210* (Philadelphia, 1985), 202.

123. Jean Dunbabin, "What's in a Name? Philip, King of France," *Speculum* 68 (1993): 952.

124. Robert-Henri Bautier, "Anne de Kiev, reine de France, et la politique royale au XIe siècle," *Revue des études slaves* 57 (1985): 564.

125. For example, Baudri writes "mi Marbode" (86.20, ed. Tilliette, 1:82) but does not so address Audebertus (87, ed. Tilliette, 1:83–84), with whom he cannot yet claim friendship. Baudri also uses *mi* in writing to his former student Peter (145.22, in Tilliette, 2:55); Galo, fellow poet and bishop of Léon (193.3, in Tilliette, 2:113); and Odo, cardinal of Ostia (206.2, ed. Tilliette, 2:138). Baudri addresses his "advice to the young" (93, ed. Tilliette, 1:90–92) to Philip, brother of Stephen, the count of Blois; but since Baudri's Philip lived from 1065 to 1100, a poem in praise of a current count Martel could not be directed to him.

to boast about the cooperation achieved with the new count. Taking the rest of the poem's first line into account makes the bishop seem less promising as an addressee, however. "Omnibus in rebus" (in all things) is a sententious phrase, used commonly in both proverbs and the incipits of didactic poems. Its presence warns the reader of a moralizing lesson to follow, in this case about the virtues of a "princeps bonus" (good ruler). This hint of the schoolroom encourages an identification of "mi Philippe" as Philip of Melun, who at the time would have been between ten and thirteen years old, just the right age for reading and construing Latin poetry that conveniently provides a model of political virtue. Whether Bertrada would have approved of her young son's reading a panegyric on her former stepson is impossible to know. Perhaps, as the king and the counts of Anjou continued to make common cause against the Normans, Martel's valor took precedence over Bertrada's personal preferences, and a tutor's Martellian sympathies found expression. An additional piece of evidence possibly bolstering the identification with Philip of Melun is that he held for a time the castle of Montlhéry, the same castle that led to the strangling of Milo II of Bray, who may be the Milo elegized in Poem 92. This overlap between Poems 90 and 92, although minor and conjectural, would tighten the constitution of Group Five as a whole.

One other possible Philip has come to light. The Anglo-Norman writer Philip of Thaon was active as a poet and translator from about 1100 to about 1140. Among the first writers of literary French, he won a name for his translations of current Latin "best-sellers," including a lapidary, a computus, a body-and-soul debate, a bestiary, and, perhaps, the prophecies of the Tiburtine Sibyl (a Latin version of which appears at the end of MS Lat 300).[126] It is not impossible that a poet-friend, perhaps even a former teacher, should have sent this enthusiast of learned literature an example of Angevin panegyric poetry. For the moment, however, the addressee of Poem 90 eludes positive identification.
[BKB]

[8v^{A}] Omnibus in rebus quas, mi Philippe, uidemus,
Nil gerit utilius principe terra bono.
Principe terra bono colitur, seruatur, habundat,
Agricolis, armis, deliciis, opibus.
Cum princeps bonus est, secure terra quiescit
Et procul abcedunt furta, rapina, dolus.
Cum bonus est princeps, si subdita colla repugnant,
Sternuntur facile uiribus ipsa suis.

126. On these writings, see Ruth J. Dean and Maureen B. M. Boulton, *Anglo-Norman Literature: A Guide to Texts and Manuscripts* (London, 1999), 346–348, 355, 383–384, 692–693.

Pax, pietas, lex, ordo, fides, concordia regnant
Cum uiret et floret principe terra bono.
Astat in exemplum consul Martellus, ab ipsis
Partibus inuidie magnificatus homo.
Martellus consul qui talia consulit orbi
Ut meritis plenis se probet esse probum,
Qui patrie patrocinium felicibus horis
Suscepit iuuenis corpore, mente senex.
Hunc tu si uideas ciuilia iura tenentem,
Sublimem dicas et simul egregium.
Circumstant illum populus procerumque senatus
A quibus ut distat corpore, sic animo.
Audit et attandit quid sanciat ille uel ille,
In medium quociens res trutinanda uenit.
Ultima que reliquas omnes sentancia cla*u*dit
Est sua quod nunquam uel titubare potest.
Pauca quidem loquitur sed circumcisa, sed ampla,
Sed que sunt plene pondere fixa suo.
Tamquam de celo, tamquam de uertice ueri
Suscipitur quicquid consulis ore sonat.
Errantes reuocat, miseris miseretur, honorat
Dignos, insequitur crimina, non homines,
Et quem perfecte fecit natura benignum,
[8v^{B}] Peccatis hominum cogitur esse ferox.
Scit quia continuo uicii laxantur habene
Si de iusticie partibus una perit.
Peruigil ad curas alienas, peruigil, inquam,
Ut pius, ut sapiens, ut pater, ut dominus.
Si belli*s* opus est, si tandem tempus in hostem,
Tunc uero quam sit maximus ille docet.
Non uelud ignaui latebras meditatur et umbras,
Non precibus pacem queritat aut spacium,
Sed quasi de sursum uictoria certa paretur,
Nil reputat bello tucius esse sibi.
Conuocat heroes, populos sciet, ordinat agmen,
Instruit, hortatur nomine quemque suo.
Ipse prior rapit arma, prior ferit, et prior instat,
Et reliquis amplas preparat ense uias.
Ut leo quem uisus gladius propulsat in iram
Infremens erigitur, circuit, accelerat,

Sic ubi bellorum Martellus sentit odorem,
Hostibus a facie mox metuendus adest.
Ne*c* prius abscedit quam pulsis omnibus, et pax
Et requies celebris reddita sit patrie.
O quantas acies, quot milia, quot legiones,
Quos animos secum preuius ipse trait.
Illius ad nutum prouincia tota mouetur,
Dum properant omnes bellica signa sequi.
Et nosti que sit nostre constancia gentis,
Quam metuenda manus, quam celeres gladii.
Degenerem uilemque timet se posse probari
Quisquis post primos primus in arma uenit.
Difficile uideas de tot ceruicibus unam
Cui durum sit eo precipiente mori,
Sic ad se populi totos apellat amores
[9r^{A}] Consul, consilii regula magnifici.
Qui tociens uincit quociens ad prelia uenit
Et ui*n*cit quociens resque locus*que* uocat,
Opida que nimium manus et natura tuetur
Non poss*u*nt eius sustinuisse manus.
Iustitiam summis patrie plantauit in horis
Qua cusdode nichil rustica turba timet.
Securos iubet ire boues securus arator,
Securas pascit pastor inermis oues.
Nemo uiatorum timet aduantare latronem,
Nemo latrociniis audet adire uias.
Multiplicare loqui non est opus: omnia paucis,
Pax est conclu*s*a integra, firma, potens.
Dicere quisque potest que sensit; hoc ego plane,
Martello semper debitor *o*rbis erit,
Debitor ut laudet, recolat, miretur, honoret
Et dignum ducat nomine precipuo.
Ergo nichil peccat quisquis maioribus illum
Comparat ac summis patribus an*n*umerat.
In quo complacuit sibi uirtus unica; cuius
Nondum uiderunt tempora nostra parem,
Qua uel in antiquis Paulo, Lelio, Scipione
Qua uel in Augustis Cesaribusque fuit.
O caput excelsum dignum rutilante corona
O animam morum floribus egregiam,

O hominem mira probitatis luce choruscum
Quem laudare satis nulla camena potest.
Cuius honestates sic secula nostra deaurant
Ut mu*n*di possint reddere principio.
[9r^{B}] Hunc ego non metuam celorum pace uocari
Splendorem procerum nobiliumque decus,
Cuius non poterit laudes delere uetustas,
Cuius in eternum nobile nomen erit.
Sit licet ad patres rapiendus legibus eui
Sed meritis eius fama perhennis erit.
Interea longum ualeat Martellus et omnis
Qui pro Martello uota benigna facit.

In all things we see, my dear Philip,
the land produces nothing more useful than a good ruler.
Under a good ruler the land is cultivated by farmers, is preserved by means of arms, and abounds in delight and benefits.
When a ruler is good, the land is at peace without care,
and thefts, pillaging, and fraud depart far away.
When a ruler is good, subjects who throw off the yoke
are easily overwhelmed by his might.
Peace, mercy, law, order, trust, and harmony reign
when the earth burgeons and blooms under a good ruler.
Count Martel stands as an example—
a man esteemed even by the factions that envy him.
Count Martel, who gives such decrees to the world
that by his abundant good deeds he proves his righteousness—
who took up the protection of his fatherland in auspicious times,
young in body, yet mature in mind.
If you should see him maintaining civil laws,
you would say he was both eminent and noteworthy.
Around him stand the people and the senate of nobles,
from whom he differs as much in body as in spirit.
He hears and considers what one side and the other confirms,
whenever a case to be weighed comes before him.
The final decision that caps all others
is his, because it can never even falter.
He speaks few words, and those concise, but sufficient,
and weighted with his full authority.

Just as if from heaven, as if from the height of truth,
whatever sounds forth from the count's mouth is accepted.
He recalls the wandering, pities the lowly, honors
the worthy, hunts down crimes (not men),
and he whom nature made perfectly kind
is compelled by the sins of men to be fierce.
He knows that the reins of vice slacken at once
if a single part of justice perishes.
He is ever watchful of others' interests, watchful, I say,
like a beneficent father, like a wise lord.
If there is need for wars, if at last it is time to proceed against the enemy,
then, truly, he shows how very great he is.
He does not plot subterfuge or pretence, as cowards do,
nor does he seek peace or delay with petitions,
but just as if sure victory might be arranged from on high,
he deems nothing safer for himself than war.
He summons the warriors, rouses the people, draws up an army,
equips it, and exhorts each soldier by name.
He is the first to take up his weapon, he strikes first, charges first,
and opens wide paths for the rest with his sword.
As a lion, propelled to anger upon seeing a sword,
is roused, roaring, circles, and attacks,
just so, when Martel catches the scent of wars,
he is there straightaway, fearsome, facing down the enemy.
Nor does he leave the field before all are defeated, and
its famed peace and repose have been returned to the land.
O how many troops, how many thousands, how many legions,
what courage he brings with him, as he goes in the vanguard!
The entire province responds to his nod,
as all men hasten to follow the battle standards.
And you know how great is the steadfastnesss of our people,
how fearsome the hand, how quick the swords.
Each man fears to be shown unworthy and base
if he first enters the fray after the first onslaught.
You would hardly see one among so many bold men
who thought it hard to die under his command,
to such an extent he summons to himself the people's entire love,
the count, a model of magnificent counsel.
Who conquers as many times as he goes to battle,
and conquers as often as the circumstances and the place demand,

even towns well fortified by nature and by arms
cannot withstand his army.
He has fixed justice at the farthest borders of the land:
under its protection, the peasantry need fear nothing.
Free from care, the plowman bids the oxen go carefree,
the shepherd unarmed grazes his flock in peace.
No traveler fears a brigand's attack:
no one dares to approach the highways for banditry.
There is no need to say more: to state everything in a few words,
the peace reached is complete, solid, and strong.
Everyone can speak his judgment: I myself say clearly,
the world will be forever indebted to Martel,
so let the debtor praise, recall, admire, honor,
and consider him worthy of his eminent name.
So it is no mistake for anyone to compare him with his forefathers
and number him with his greatest ancestors.
In him virtue alone has pleased itself, virtue of which
our times have yet seen no equal,
virtue as it was among the ancients, Aemilius Paulus, Laelius, Scipio,
or among the Caesars Augustus.
O lofty head, worthy of a glittering crown,
O soul, outstanding in its flowers of good morals,
O man, brilliant with the wondrous light of integrity,
whom no muse can praise enough!
His virtues make our age so golden
that they can return us to the beginning of the world.
I won't hesitate to call him—with heaven's permission—
the splendor of princes, the ornament of nobles.
Age will not be able to destroy his praises,
his name will be renowned forever.
Though he must be gathered to his fathers according to the law of time,
his fame for his accomplishments will be everlasting.
Meanwhile, may Martel long prosper, together with everyone
who offers kind prayers for Martel.

Textual Notes

1] *Initial missing.*
2] utilius: ultius *corrected above line.*
6] abcedunt: accedunt *expunged, first* c *corrected to* b *above.*

11] Marcellus: *Marginal dog-headed creature barks, open-mouthed, at this line, calling attention to Martel's name.*
23] sentancia: scantancia *with* sca *expunged, corrected to* se *above*. clau*d*it: cladit.
37] belli*s*: belli *emended for meter and grammar.*
38] docet: dolet *expunged* l *corrected to* c *above.*
51] Ne*c*: Ne *missing final* c.
66] ui*n*cit: uicit *missing abbreviation stroke*. locus*que* uocat: locus uocat.
68] poss*u*nt: possint.
76] Pax est conclu*s*a: Concluda pax est, *with abbreviation stroke through* d.
78] orbis *appears to read* urbis (*with two minims preceding* rbis).
88] a animam s, *with first* a *and final* s *expunged.*
91] deaurent *corrected at line end to* -rant.
92] mu*n*di: mudi *missing abbreviation stroke.*

Commentary

1. **Omnibus in rebus**: This phrase was a common building block of hexameter poetry from the classical period onward. The three words are grouped repeatedly as a metrical unit, always as a line opening. In late antiquity and the Middle Ages the phrase became a common incipit, especially of didactic poems. "Omnibus in rebus" also came to be a convenient beginning for a metrical proverb: the standard compendium boasts seventeen examples, all but two of which are in verse. See Walther, *Proverbia sententiaeque latinitatis medii aevi*, 3:629–630, nos. 20147–20152, and Paul Gerhard Schmidt, *Proverbia sententiaeque Latinitatis medii ac recentis aevi, nova series/Lateinische Sprichwörter und Sentenzen des Mittelalters und der frühen Neuzeit in alphabetischer Anordnung*, 3 additional vols. (Göttingen, 1983), 8:944, nos. 39253c–39255.

2–3. **principe terra bono**: The poet employs a device similar to epanalepsis by beginning a hexameter with the half line with which the preceding couplet ended. In line 10 he repeats the same phrase as a line ending. The repetition emphasizes this phrase, which encapsulates the subject of his poem: under a good ruler the land (thrives). On the matter of epanalepsis, see Carmela Vircillo Franklin, "O sacrata dies: A New Typological Poem in Epanaleptic Elegiacs," *Journal of Medieval Latin* 14 (2004): 69–72. Compare 10.

4. **deliciis, opibus**: A conventional line opening used in a dactylic pentameter by Hildebert, *Querimonia* meter 1. 28, ed. Orth, 73 ("deliciis opibus nomine lactat heram"). Here translated as "delights and benefits," it could also be interpreted as a hendiadys meaning "delightful benefits." The latter approach has the advantage of glossing over the break in symmetry that results from having three verbs followed by four nouns.

5. **princeps bonus**: Prudentius, *Peristephanon* 12.47, ed. Cunningham, 380; Baudri, *Carmina* 211.3, ed. Tilliette, 2:143. **secure terra quiescit**: Compare Ovid, *Fasti* 6.734, ed. Alton, Wormell, and Courtney, 161 (pentameter: "plenaque securae terra quietis erit").

6. **abcedunt** = *abscedunt.* **furta, rapina, dolus**: A certain Guiardinus or Guido, whose poem on the virtues and vices (incipit "Care nepos! tibi quod sequitur mea cura ministrat") appears in a late thirteenth-century manuscript, also uses these words as the ending of a pentameter in line 626: see Jakob Werner, "Guiardinus: Bruchstücke eines lateinischen Tugendspiegels nach der Basler Handschrift," *Romanische Forschungen* 26 (1909): 449. His word choice duplicates Poem 90 in two other passages (see notes on lines 9 and 14 below). A single parallel could be mere happenstance, but three to such a short passage as lines 6–14 raise the distinct possibility that Guiardinus had encountered this poem. Unfortunately, little information about Guiardinus can be gleaned from his text, except that he admired Henry I "le Liberal" (count of Champagne 1152–1181) as a paragon of generosity (lines 141–150), which suggests that the poet lived in northern France in the mid to late twelfth century. Werner hypothesized that Guiardinus might be identical with Guiard of Laon (about 1170–1248), a bishop of Cambrai, but no evidence undergirds such an identification apart from the proximity of the two names.
7. **subdita colla**: The phrase is first attested in Prudentius, *Hamartigenia* 469, ed. Cunningham, CCSL 126:132. In MS Lat 300, Poem 91 praises Louis for similar skill in subduing the obstinate: "Ceruices rigidas et desipiencia corda / Ut fortis reprimit, coripit ut sapiens" (43–44).
8. **uiribus ipsa suis**: A half line of a pentameter common since Ovid, *Remedia amoris* 88, ed. Kenney, 208 ("uiribus aucta suis" ["uiribus ipsa suis" in E]: line ending): compare *Tristia* 4.10.104, ed. Owen ("viribus usa suis": line ending), and *Ex Ponto* 3.5.14, ed., Owen ("viribus illa suis": line opening); also pseudo-Vergil, *Culex* 36, ed. Clausen, 20 ("uiribus apta suis": opening of hexameter).
9. **pax, pietas**: Also a line opening in Guiardinus, line 639, ed. Werner, "Guiardinus," 450.
   concordia regnant: *concordia regn** as a line ending occurs in Venantius Fortunatus, *Carmina* 6.1.141, in Leo, 129; in Reydellet, 2:50 ("concordia regnet"); and in many later poets.
10. **Cum uiret et floret**: Compare Fulk of Beauvais, *De nuptiis Christi et ecclesiae* 3.345, ed. Rousseau, 62 ("dum uiret et floret").
11. **astat in exemplum**: The phrase "in exemplum" appears very frequently in this metrical position. See especially Ovid, *Amores* 1.10.25, ed. Kenney, 25 ("sumite in exemplum": line opening); *Metamorphoses* 8.245, ed. Tarrant, 224 ("traxit in exemplum": line opening); *Fasti* 4.243, ed. Alton, Wormell, and Courtney, 91 ("venit in exemplum": line opening).
14. Play on **prob-**: Compare Baudri, *Carmina* 192.8–9, ed. Tilliette, 2:112; Zurich, Zentralbibliothek, MS C 58, fol. 36, in Werner, *Beiträge*, 78, no. 163, lines 3–4; and Guiardinus, in Werner, "Guiardinus," 459, Anhang II, line 24 ("Et falsum reprobat et probat esse probum").

15–16. The poet's joy at Martel's early accession to power (while his father Fulk is still alive) constitutes an implicit criticism of the old count, who was neither a kindly father to his son (attempting to disinherit him in favor of his younger half-brother) nor a successful ruler (waging war continually with one or another of his vassals). Compare 36.

16. **iuuenis corpore, mente senex**: On the *puer senex* topos, see Ernst Robert Curtius, *European Literature and the Latin Middle Ages,* trans. Willard R. Trask (Princeton, 1990), 98–101.
17. **iura tenentem**: The line ending "iura ten*" is commonplace.
19. **populus procerumque**: First attested in Prudentius, *Contra Symmachum* 2.1104, ed. Cunningham, 249 ("populi procerumque salutem").
21. **Audit et attandit**: Also as a line opening in John of Garland, *Epithalamium beate virginis Marie* 5.614, ed. Saiani, 446. The orthography *attandit* is typical of MS Lat 300.
23. **sentancia claudit**: *sentancia* = *sententia*. For the wording, compare the line ending in Silius Italicus, *Punica* 14.192, ed. Delz, 367 (". . . sententia clausis"). But for the thought, a closer parallel is Warner of Basil (twelfth century), *Paraclitus* 453–454, ed. Hoogterp, 303 ("Quam graue sit telum claudens sententia celum / Sermo Petri docuit").
24. **titubare potest**: Compare Prudentius, *Apotheosis* 1.876, ed. Cunningham, 108.
25. **pauca quidem loquitur**: Ovid, *Ibis* 639 "pauca quidem, fateor" (line opening), ed. Owen. Thereafter "pauca quidem," especially with verbs of speaking, is common. **circumcisa**: Probably the adjective is used mainly in a rhetorical sense, to mean "concise." In the Vulgate, *circumcido* is paired metaphorically with *mentes* (Lv 26:41), *cordes* (Dt 10:16, 30:6, Jer 9:26, Ez 44:7, Acts 7:51, Rom 2:29), and *aures* (Jer 6:10, Acts 7:51); and Moses asks the Lord (Ex 6:12), "Quomodo audiet Pharao, praesertim cum incircumcisus sim labiis?" ("How will Pharao hear me, especially as I am of uncircumcised lips?"). The circumcised tongue is a later monastic image, related to the importance of silence in monastic practice: for example, see Haimo of Auxerre, *Homilia XIV in circumcisione Domini,* in PL 118.96B ("Circumcidenda est lingua a maledictionibus, perjuriis, falsitatibus, murmurationibus et a consuetudine otiosi sermonis") and Bruno of Segni, *Expositio in Genesim* 17, in PL 164.193A ("Lingua circumcisa non loquitur mendacium").
26. **pondere fixa suo**: At the beginning of the line in Lucan, *De bello ciuili* 1.139, ed. Shackleton Bailey, 5, and Alexander Neckam (also spelt Nequam and, less correctly, Neckham), *Laudes diuinae sapientiae* 2.43, ed. Wright, 374. Compare Bernard Silvestris, *Microcosmus* 2.14, ed. Dronke, 123, and Baudri, *Carmina* 99.145, ed. Tilliette, 1:109.
27. **de uertice ueri**: A remarkable metaphor, if written and transcribed correctly. It is not attested elsewhere, although the similar "culmen ueritatis" was used earlier by Alcuin in a comparable context: *Commentaria in s. Joannis evangelium*, 6.37 (at Jn 15.27 "Cum autem venerit paracletus"), in PL 100.949D ("Ipse namque Spiritus corda eorum et ad scientiam veritatis illustravit, et ad docenda quae nossent, culmine veritatis erexit"). Alcuin is not entirely

accurate here in his quotation of Bede, *Homeliarum Euangelii libri II*, no. 16, "Post Ascensionem," ed. Hurst, 291 ("… et scientia ueritatis inlustrauit, et ad docenda quae nossent culmine uirtutis erexit"). "Culmina ueri" appears as a hexameter line ending in the penultimate line of a poem of about 1160 (incipit "Gaudia qui mundi vis spernere vana rotundi") in praise of the Abbey of Clairvaux attributed in PL 185.1563A–1566A to the Cistercian Richard of Grandselve: "Virtutum dotes scrutando culmina veri / quos imitando potes coelum post fata mereri." Possibly our poet preferred *uertex* to *culmen* for the alliteration.

28. **ore sonat**: Pseudo-Ovid, *Consolatio ad Liuiam* 446, ed. Amat, 77 ("si liceat forti verba tot ore sonet").
29. **Errantes reuocat**: Common line opening from the early Middle Ages onward, first in Paulinus of Périgueux, *Vita sancti Martini* 3.244, ed. Petschenig, 72 ("Errantes reuocans"). Hildebert begins a line "Qui sic errantes revocat," in *Carmina minora* 51.21, ed. Scott, 44. The idea involved relates to the Parable of the Lost Sheep in Matthew 18.10–14. **miser* miser***: This pairing is understandably common in Christian Latin poetry.
31. **natura benigna**: Line ending in Juvenal, *Satires* 10.301, ed. Clausen, 131, and in later poets.
32. **cogitur esse ferox**: Ovid, *Ex Ponto* 1.2.121–122, ed. Owen, amid similarly flattering lines that praise the emperor Augustus for his reluctance to anger: "sed piger ad poenas princeps, ad praemia uelox, / quique dolet, quotiens cogitur, esse ferox."
33. **laxantur habene**: As a line ending in Valerius Flaccus, *Argonautica* 2.35, ed. Ehlers, 32. Slackening the reins is a fairly common expression for loss of control, most notably, Vergil, *Aeneid* 7.600, ed. Mynors, 275 ("rerumque reliquit habenas": line ending). The closest contemporary parallel is probably Hildebert (or pseudo-Hildebert), *De sancto Vincentio* 220–221, in PL 171.1306A ("Littora nota tene, ne, si laxentur habenae, / praevaleant undae graviores atque profundae"). Compare Simon Aurea Capra (also known as Simon Chèvre d'Or), *Ylias* (B), line 495, ed. Parrott, 127 ("Si laxare velim Muse diffusus habenas"). This dissertation is available at the University of Toronto, dated 1975, with different pagination: this line is on p. 138.
35. **peruigil ad**: Also a line opening in Maximian, *Elegies* 5.9, ed. Sandquist Öberg, 126, widely read as a school text beginning in the eleventh century.
36. **ut pius ut sapiens ut pater ut dominus**: Compare Simon Aurea Capra, *Ylias* (A) 153, ed. Parrott, 116 [= (1975), 125] ("et pius et sapiens"), and 174, Parrott, 120 [= (1975), 129] ("ut dux, ut dominus, ut pater inter eos").
38. **maximus ille**: Popular since Ovid, *Remedia amoris* 782, ed. Kenney, 236 ("maximus ille fuit": second half of a pentameter).
39. Compare Vergil, *Aeneid* 4.171, ed. Mynors, 181 ("nec iam furtiuum Dido meditatur amorem").

41. **uictoria certa**: Simon Aurea Capra, *Ylias* 119, printed as *Versus de excidio Troiae* in PL 171.1450B; *Ylias* (A text) 127 (apparatus), ed. Parrott, *Ylias*, 100 [= (1975), 109] ("dumque sub incerto pendet Victoria certa" as variant for "Sic dubiis alis pendens Victoria belli").
42. Compare Lucan, *De bello ciuili* 3.371–372, ed. Shackleton Bailey, 63 ("et nihil esse meo discetis tutius aevo / quam duce me bellum"). Ovid betrayed a penchant for using the phrase **tutius esse** with a two-syllable word following to form the second half of a pentameter: see *Heroides* 19.162, ed. Kenney, 64 ("tutius esse fretum"); *Tristia* 5.2.78 (=5.2b.34), ed. Owen ("tutius esse miser"); and *Ex Ponto* 1.1.10, ed. Owen ("tutius esse putant"), and 2.2.58, ed. Owen ("tutius esse puto").
43. **Conuocat heroes**: The same line opening (with the Greek accusative form *heroas*) is found in Odo of Magdeburg, *Ernestus* (second decade of the thirteenth century) 7.68, ed. Klein, 148. **sciet** = *ciet.*
44. **nomine quemque suo**: A tag encountered more often as a line opening, but first as the second half of a pentameter in Ovid, *Tristia*, 3.4.64 (=3.4b.18), ed. Owen ("dicere quos cupiam nomine quemque suo").
45. **ipse prior**: A line opening since Lucan, *De bello ciuili* 4.703, ed. Shackleton Bailey, 100.
46. **preparet ense uias**: Lucan, *De bello ciuili* 4.43, ed. Shackleton Bailey, 78 ("caedunt ense viam").

47-48. Lion similes, often including the words *ira, fremere* (or *frendere*), and *erigere*, verge on being stereotypical in epic battle scenes. For examples, see Lucan, *De bello ciuili* 1.205–207, ed. Shackleton Bailey, 7; Silius Italicus, *Punica* 10.21–22, 11.241–244, 17.41, ed. Delz, 248, 282, 448; and Statius, *Thebaid* 7.670–673, ed. Klotz and Klinnert, 272. The line opening **Ut leo** was made commonplace in epic by Statius, *Thebaid* 2.675, 8.124, 9.739, ed. Klotz and Klinnert, 73, 286, 350, and *Achilleid* 1.858, ed. Dilke, 64.

49. **sentit odorem**: A line ending also in Reginald of Canterbury, *Carmina* 2.34, ed. Wright, 2:261, and Theobald, *Physiologus* 1.3, ed. Eden, 26.
50. **metuendus adest**: Claudian, *De sexto consulatu Honorii* 216, ed. Hall, 272 ("Ipse manu metuendus adest inopinaque cunctis").
54. **preuius ipse**: Hildebert (or pseudo-Hildebert), *Carmen in libros Regum* 4.260, in PL 171.1256D, in the same metrical position.
55. **Illius ad nutum**: Comparable expressions can be found in Baudri, *Carmina* 122.47, ed. Tilliette 1:128 ("ad cuius nutum"), and Marbod, *Carmina* 1.39.9, in PL 171.1670B ("per cuius nutum"). **prouincia tota**: Line ending in Maximian, *Elegies* 1.59, ed. Sandquist Öberg, 96.
56. **bellica signa sequi**: Ovid, *Fasti* 5.550, ed. Alton, Wormell, and Courtney, 131 (pentameter ending: "bellica signa dedit"); *Ex Ponto* 2.8.70 ("signa sequar"); and also several times in Vergil and Statius. "Bellica signa sequi" is found as a line ending in Albert of Stade, *Troilus* 1.498, ed. Merzdorf, 27.

57. **nostrae constancia gentis**: The poet proclaims his partisanship here. For the phrasing, see Lucan, *De bello ciuili* 10.490, ed. Shackleton Bailey, 283 ("tanta est constantia mentis": line ending).
58. **metuenda manus**: Silius Italicus, *Punica* 1.390, ed. Delz, 15 ("O metuenda manus"), and Statius, *Thebaid* 10.812, ed. Klotz and Klinnert, 396 ("haec erat, haec metuenda manus"). Since the transmission of Silius Italicus was very limited in the Middle Ages, Statius is likelier to be the ultimate source of inspiration.
59. **posse probari**: Line ending already in Lucretius, *De rerum natura* 2.499, ed. Bailey. Also in Marbod, *Liber lapidum* 447, ed. Herrera, 105.
60. **primus in arma**: As a line opening already in Vergil, *Aeneid* 10.242, ed. Mynors, 340.
63. **apellat** = *appellat.*
65. **ad prelia uenit**: Vergil, *Georgics* 3.98, ed. Mynors, 67 ("ad proelia uentum": line ending), and *Aeneid* 10.901, ed. Mynors, 362 ("ad proelia ueni": line ending). The most important medieval occurrence may be *Waltharius* 612, in *Die lateinischen Dichter des deutschen Mittelalters: Nachträge zu den Poetae aevi Carolini* 6/1, ed. Karl Strecker (Weimar, 1951), 49 ("ad proelia uenit").
66. **resque locusque**: Compare Ovid, *Amores* 1.4.54, ed. Kenney, 11, and *Tristia* 1.1.92, ed. Owen, "resque locusque dabunt" (both second halves of hexameters).
67. **opida** = *oppida.* **natura tue(tur)**: Serenus, *Liber medicinalis* 661, ed. Pépin, 36 ("natura tuendis"), and Claudian, *Carmina minora* 9.9, ed. Hall, 346 ("natura tueri").
68. **sustinuisse manus**: Similar phrases are found as pentameter endings in Ovid, *Fasti* 5.302, ed. Alton, Wormell, and Courtney, 123 ("sustinuisse manum"); *Amores* 1.14.34, ed. Kinney, 31 ("sustinuisse manu"); and *Ars amatoria* 2.216, ed. Kinney, 150 ("sustinuisse manu").
69. **horis** = *oris.*
70. **cusdode** = *custode.* **rustica turba**: A stock phrase from Ovid, *Metamorphoses* 6.348 (line opening), ed. Tarrant, 165.
72. **pascit . . . oues**: Vergil, *Eclogae* 1.45, ed. Mynors, 2 ("pascite ut ante boues": line opening).
73. **aduantare** = *aduentare.*
74. **adire uias**: A very common line ending.
75. **multiplicare loqui**: The ultimate source is 1 Sm 2:3 ("nolite multiplicare loqui sublimia"). Compare Winrich of Trier, *Conflictus ovis et lini* 30, 60, 92, ed. Haupt, 216–218 ("ulterius noli multiplicare loqui").
77. **Dicere quisque potest**: Marbod, *Liber decem capitulorum* 4.53, in *De ornamentis verborum: Liber decem capitulorum*, ed. Leotta, 42 ("Dicere quisue potest se matrem non habuisse?").
78. **debitor orbis**: Compare the line endings in the *De martyrio Maccabaeorum* (ascribed sometimes to Cyprian of Gaul, Hilary of Poitiers, Hilary of Arles,

or Victorinus), recension A 331 and recensio interpolata 327, in *Cypriani Galli poetae Heptatevchos: Accedunt incertorum De Sodoma et Iona et Ad senatorem carmina et Hilarii quae feruntur In Genesin, De Maccabaeis atque De Euangelio*, ed. Rudolf Peiper (Vienna, 1881), 240–269, at 252 and 267 ("Confiteor, totus cum sit tibi debitor orbis"), and Odo of Magdeburg, *Ernestus* 1.252, ed. Klein, 15 ("debitor orbis").

80–82. **Et dignum nomine . . . maioribus illum comparat**: Following the repetition of his cognomen Martel in line 78, this fomulation is likely a glance back at the count's great-uncle, Geoffrey Martel.

81. **Ergo nichil**: A line opening attested already in Martial, *Epigrams* 3.46.11, ed. Lindsay.

83. **uirtus unica**: Compare Juvenal, *Satires* 8.20, ed. Clausen, 106 ("nobilitas sola est atque unica uirtus").

84. **tempora nostra**: Ovid, *Tristia* 2.484 (as the opening of the second half in a pentameter). **nondum uiderunt** as opposed to *necdum*: Compare Silius Italicus, *Punica* 11.583, ed. Delz, 295 ("cur nondum viderit urbis") and Statius, *Thebaid* 8.67, ed. Klotz and Klinnert, 283 ("quod nondum viderit aether").

85. C. **Laelius** (about 190–after 129), and P. Cornelius **Scipio** Aemilianus Africanus (184/5–129) are often associated in Latin literature on account of their remarkable friendship, most notably in Cicero, *Laelius de amicitia*, ed. Simbeck. L. Aemilius **Paul(l)us** (died 160), the father of Scipio, is an unusual but not problematic addition. A successful military leader who ended the Third Macedonian War at Pydna, he is also an exemplar of virtue. On his virtue, see Cicero, *De officiis* 2.22.76, ed. Atzert, 81, which mentions the integrity of Paulus and his son Scipio—in this context, for declining to keep rich spoils of war.

Since all three figures are known for military successes (Laelius defeated Viriathus of Lusitania: see *De officiis* 2.11.40, ed. Atzert, 68) as well as for personal virtue, they constitute appropriate models for Martel. The three are named, along with others, in a list of virtuous men in Cicero, *Tusculanae disputationes* 1.46.110, ed. Pohlenz, 274, perhaps the poet's immediate source: "Multo autem tardius fama deseret [i.e., their fame outlives them] Curium Fabricium Calatinum, duo Scipiones duo Africanos, Maximum Marcellum Paullum, Catonem Laelium, innumerabiles alios, quorum similitudinem aliquam qui arripuerit, non eam fama populari, sed vera bonorum laude metiens, fidenti animo, si ita res feret, gradietur ad mortem . . ." The threesome also appears in Cicero, *De natura deorum* 2.165, ed. Ax, 116, in a list of particular individuals whom the gods cherish. Relating the ancestry of a thoroughly French noble to heroes of Rome is an instance of the *translatio imperii* ("transfer of rule") motif.

87. **O caput**: Statius, *Thebaid* 8.739, ed. Klotz and Klinnert, 314. **rutilante corona**: Similar line endings are found in Silius Italicus, *Punica* 16.119, ed. Delz, 424 "rutilante coruscum" (see also on line 91); Flodoard of Reims, *De*

Christi triumphis apud Italiam 11.6.33, in PL 135.797C ("rutilante coronam"); and Hrotsvitha of Gandersheim, *Passio sancte Agnetis uirginis et martiris* 420, ed. Berschin, 129 ("rutilante corona").

88. **morum floribus**: Tertullian, *De pudicitia*, ed. Munier, 144, begins "Pudicitia flos morum." Philip of Harvengt (died 1183) uses the phrase *morum floribus* in his commentary on the Song of Songs 2.16, in PL 203.279B.

89. **luce choruscum**: Line ending in Valerius Flaccus, *Argonautica* 1.486, ed. Courtney, 16, and Silius Italicus, *Punica* 1.463, ed. Delz, 18.

90. **Quem laudare satis**: Compare the line opening in Statius, *Thebaid* 7.379, ed. Klotz and Klinnert, 259 ("Nec laudare satis"). In content, this line offers in miniature what Curtius would call an incapacity or inexpressibility topos: *European Literature and the Latin Middle Ages,* 159–162 and 409–412.

91–92. **secula nostra deaurant**: Vergil introduced the idea of a "new" Golden Age, in which a virtuous ruler institutes and presides over a return to the paradisiacal state that existed before Jupiter overthrew Saturn. For example, see *Aeneid* 6.792–793, ed. Mynors, 252 ("Augustus Caesar, diui genus, aurea condet / saecula"). The topos appears often in panegyric thereafter. Our poet offers a clever and unusual variation on this theme, in which Martel's virtues figuratively provide the gilding for the age; his use of the verb *deauro*, which rarely appears in a figurative sense, is also striking. This is not to say that he was unique in associating the reign of Geoffrey Martel le Jeune with the return of the Golden Age, since Baudri resorts to similar terms in one of his epitaphs for the prince: see *Carmina* 211.3, ed. Tilliette 2:143 ("Tempora reddiderat princeps bonus aurea mundo").

94. **nobiliumque decus**: Compare Ovid, *Heroides* 17.54, ed. Kenney, 45 ("Tyndareique decus": pentameter line ending).

95. **delere uetustas**: Ovid, *Metamorphoses* 1.445 (also a line ending), ed. Tarrant, 18.

96. **nobile nomen**: A stock phrase since Silius Italicus, *Punica* 1.273, 16.329, 17.303, 17.452, ed. Delz, 11, 432, 458, 464.

97. **legibus eui**: Lucan, *De bello ciuili* 2.82 (line ending), ed. Shackleton Bailey, 27; Arator, *De actibus apostolorum* 1.308, ed. McKinlay, 30.

98. **fama perhennis**: Ovid, *Amores* 1.10.62, ed. Kenney, 26 ("fama perennis erit": second half of a pentameter).

100. **uota benigna**: Baudri, *Carmina* 62.12, ed. Tilliette, 1:62. [BKB]

POEM 91. Incipit "Francia dulcis, aue, regio bona, bella salubris." Fifty-eight elegiac distichs. Not in Walther. *In principio*, reference 143717.

Subject and Genre

Poem 91 is a panegyric celebrating the accession of Louis VI (1081–1137) to the throne of France. Louis was consecrated king after the death of his father, Philip I, in 1108, and the poem was likely composed around this date, since the poet claims in line 79 that the kingdom was recently ruled by Philip ("Recently you went astray, wretched, under a gray-haired king"). Louis was born in 1081, the son of Philip and Bertha of Holland. Though the records of Louis' childhood are limited, we are fairly well informed when it comes to the decade that preceded his accession. This period, from roughly 1097 to 1108, serves as the historical background of "Francia dulcis, aue." Whether or not the poet drew on actual events for the subject matter of his panegyric, Louis had ample opportunity during the decade preceding his coronation to prove his mettle to any future encomiast.

Louis first demonstrated his skill as a military leader in 1097–1098, when he led a successful campaign in the Vexin against King William Rufus of England.[127] Around this time Louis was armed as a knight by Guy of Ponthieu, and at some point between 1098 and 1100 he was designated as the heir apparent by Philip, in keeping with Capetian tradition.[128] As *rex designatus*, Louis began to play an increasingly active role in the affairs of the kingdom, as evidenced by his participation in a further series of military campaigns.

After 1100 Louis established himself as an energetic defender of ecclesiastical and monastic rights against the encroachments of secular lords. In 1101 he took the side of Adam, the abbot of Saint-Denis (1099–1122) in a dispute over customary rights (*consuetudines*) with Burchard of Montmorency (about 1070–circa 1124). In the end Louis forced Burchard to submit to royal authority.[129] Shortly thereafter Louis led an attack against the castle of Drogo (Dreux) III of Mouchy (born about 1070), an ally of Burchard's who had persecuted the canons of Saint-Pierre of Beauvais.[130] In 1102 Louis warred against Count Ebles II of Roucy (1063–1104),

127. Suger, *Vita Ludovici* 1, in Waquet, 4–15; *Deeds of Louis the Fat*, 24–28. See also Luchaire, 5–6, no. 6.

128. For the early deeds of Louis, see Luchaire, 5–6, nos. 6–8; Dietrich Lohrmann, "Louis VI," in Joachim Ehlers, Heribert Müller, and Bernd Schneidmüller, eds., *Die französischen Könige des Mittelalters von Odo bis Karl VIII* (Munich, 1996), 127–138, esp. 131–133; and Ivan Gobry, *Louis VI: Histoire des rois de France* (Paris, 2003). For the Capetian practice of designating the heir apparent to the throne, see Robert Fawtier, *The Capetian Kings of France*, trans. L. Butler and R. J. Adam (London, 1960), 48–49.

129. *Vita Ludovici* 2, in Waquet, 14–19; *Deeds of Louis the Fat*, 29–30. See also Luchaire, 8–10, no. 16.

130. *Vita Ludovici* 2, in Waquet, 14–19; *Deeds of Louis the Fat*, 29–30. See also Luchaire, 10–11, no. 18. The campaign against Drogo took place in 1101 or 1102.

who had plundered lands belonging to the churches of Reims and Laon.[131] Louis' swift and decisive campaign stood in notable contrast to the previous inaction of his father in punishing Ebles.[132] In 1103 Louis besieged the castle of Léon of Meung (died 1103), an unruly vassal of the bishop of Orléans, and burned it to the ground with the rebel and his unfortunate garrison still inside.[133]

Such forceful actions to protect the rights of the Church made a favorable impression on the French clerics who were responsible for preserving Louis' memory in writing. Suger of Saint-Denis (1081–1151)—Louis' biographer, friend, and advisor, and an invaluable source for our understanding of his reign—notes approvingly that Louis "took care that the churches prospered and zealously sought peace for those who prayed, those who toiled, and the poor, which had not been done for a long while."[134]

Louis' defence of the rights and possessions of the Church may have been motivated by political concerns as much as by personal piety. Bishops were a traditional source of support for the heretofore weak Capetian kings, and Louis was, like his father, intent on pacifying unruly lords and expanding the authority of the monarchy. By curbing the anarchy that had characterized eleventh-century France and in particular by protecting Church property, he won the admiration of many, including Suger and our own poet. Suger's unabashed glorification of Louis makes him a useful basis of comparison with the anonymous author of Poem 91. Though his biography of Louis VI was written some thirty years after Louis' accession (and thus probably after the writing of "Francia dulcis, aue"), it approximates the poem in its tone and in its "legitimizing, myth-making aspect of royal history."[135] Suger's *Vita Ludovici* is a kind of panegyric in its own right and helps in turn to illuminate the thoughts of the poet of "Francia dulcis, aue."

The poet follows conventions in his praise of Louis: he speaks of the new king's physical attractiveness (16); his zeal for justice but moderation in executing it (20–34); his temperance, thrift, and diligence (35–40); and his bravery and wisdom (43–44). Nor does the poet scruple to highlight the virtues of Louis by criticizing his

131. *Vita Ludovici* 5, in Waquet, 24–29; *Deeds of Louis the Fat*, 34–35. See also Luchaire, 12, no. 20.

132. *Vita Ludovici* 5, in Waquet, 24–29; *Deeds of Louis the Fat*, 34–35.

133. *Vita Ludovici* 6, in Waquet, 28–29; *Deeds of Louis the Fat*, 36. See also Luchaire, 15, no. 25.

134. *Vita Ludovici* 2, in Waquet, 14 ("ecclesiarum utilitatibus providebat, oratorum, laboratorum et pauperum, quod diu insolitum fuerat, quieti studebat"); *Deeds of Louis the Fat*, 29.

135. See Gabrielle M. Spiegel, *The Chronicle Tradition of Saint-Denis: A Survey* (Leiden, 1978), 45. Like our poet, Suger "presents the Capetian monarch as the realization of the highest ideals and goals of medieval kingship, as an exemplar to present and future rulers, and as the focal point of French history, carrying on the work of his illustrious ancestors and extending it by his ceaseless labors in behalf of the spiritual aims of medieval society." For Suger's relationship with Louis and their common political vision see Lohrmann, "Louis VI," 130.

father, Philip. The latter is characterized as "a king in name only" (53), foolish (58), and wicked (67), and so he was held to be by many chroniclers of his reign.

Philip I, who was born in 1052 and ruled from 1060 to 1108, rose to power when the fortunes of the royal house were at a low ebb, and he interested himself primarily in increasing the power of the monarchy and enlarging the royal demesne. "Nearly all the enterprises of Philip I," summarizes one historian, "show the same character, at once inglorious and practical."[136] Philip, reluctant to give up the power of appointing bishops, displayed scant sympathy for the ecclesiastical reform movement of the second half of the eleventh century. Nor did he hesitate to appropriate for the royal coffers the income of bishoprics that stood temporarily vacant, or whose bishop was absent.[137] More scandalous even than Philip's overt sale of Church offices was his abduction of, and subsequent marriage to, Bertrada of Montfort, the wife of Fulk Rechin of Anjou, in 1092.[138] Having repudiated his first wife, Bertha of Holland, Philip failed to confirm the legitimacy of his new marriage and was excommunicated in 1095 by Pope Urban II (1088–1099). After promising that he would renounce Bertrada, Philip reneged, and in 1097 Urban not only renewed the excommunication of the king but even placed his entire kingdom under interdict. Philip's quarrel with the papacy dragged on under Urban and his successor, Paschal II (1099–1118), and the affair was resolved only in 1104, when Philip swore once again to give up Bertrada (a vow he did not keep) and was once again absolved by the pope.

Though Philip retained the support of most of his bishops throughout these turbulent times, his quarrels with Rome and his personal conduct garnered for him an unsavory reputation among later chroniclers of his reign. Suger criticizes both Philip's adulterous marriage and his self-indulgent behavior, depicting the king in his last years as given over to the sins of the flesh: "He indulged himself too much and did not take care of either his kingdom or the health of his noble and handsome body."[139] Philip's behavior, in Suger's account, stands in stark contrast to the piety of Louis, a defender of the Church and protector of the poor. Both Suger and our poet were keen to emphasize the disparities between father and son.

136. Louis Halphen, "France in the Eleventh Century," in *The Cambridge Medieval History,* ed. J. B. Bury, H. M. Gwatkin, and J. P. Whitney, vol. 3 (Cambridge, 1922), 111. Fawtier has a similar assessment: "He had no greatness of vision, only a clear eye for the tasks immediately ahead" (*The Capetian Kings of France*, 18).

137. For Philip's relationship with the Church, see Augustin Fliche, *Le règne de Philippe 1er, roi de France* (Paris, 1912; repr., Geneva, 1975), 335–345.

138. Bertrada herself may well have been complicit in the arrangement. Both Orderic Vitalis and William of Malmesbury report that she initiated the liaison with Philip. For a discussion of Philip's marriage to Bertrada, see Fliche, *Le règne de Philippe 1er,*, 40–77.

139. *Vita Ludovici* 13, in Waquet, 82; *Deeds of Louis the Fat*, 61.

The Genre of Panegyric

The poet of "Francia dulcis, aue" need not have concerned himself overly with the historical details of the reigns of Philip and Louis in producing his panegyric. To find suitable material he could have resorted instead to the conventions of praise poetry.[140] Praise poetry in the Middle Ages fell under the antique rhetorical classification of epideictic oratory, known in the Latin handbooks as the *genus demonstrativum*. The *Rhetorica ad Herennium* (first century BCE), now regarded as anonymous but thought in the Middle Ages to be the work of Cicero, sets out a comprehensive inventory of the subjects appropriate for praise (*laus*). Its exposition was particularly important, since this treatise served as one of the most important textbooks of classical rhetorical theory in the medieval period. According to the *Rhetorica ad Herennium* the appropriate topics to be considered in a speech of praise fell into three categories: *res externae* (circumstances, like *genus* [descent], over which the subject had no control), *res corporis* (physical appearance), and *res animi* (qualities of mind, often organized around the four cardinal virtues of prudence, justice, temperance, and fortitude).[141] Thus in "Francia dulcis, aue" we find praise of Louis' ancestors (91–104) and his physical features (16), along with extensive discussion of his bravery (43–44, 47, 50), wisdom (43–44, 46, 109–112), zealous pursuit of justice (19–20, 23–24), and moderation (27–34). The conventions of the genre also dictated that the different periods of the subject's life should be treated separately.[142] Accordingly, our poem makes a division between Louis' present virtues (chiefly at 15–18, 21–50), his youth (19–20), and his future greatness (106–110).

Poem 91 corresponds to a model of panegyric that became increasingly widespread in late eleventh and early twelfth centuries in which praise of a ruler was connected to the land over which he or she ruled.[143] Hildebert of Lavardin's panegyric on Henry I and Matilda of England provides a contemporary analogue.[144] The introduction to Hildebert's poem closely recalls "Francia dulcis, aue" in its praise of the riches and temperate climate of the land:

> Anglia, terra ferax, tibi pax diuturna quietem,
> Multiplicem luxum merx opulenta dedit.

---

140. For medieval panegyric on kings and nobles in general, see Franz Bittner, *Studien zum Herrscherlob in der mitellateinischen Dichtung* (Bamberg, 1962). For a summary of the literary conventions of panegyric, see esp. 161–165.

141. *Rhetorica ad Herennium* 3.6.10, ed. and trans. Caplan, 172–175.

142. See Quintilian, *Institutio oratoria* 3.7.10, ed. and trans. Russell, 2:106–107. Isidore of Seville, *Etymologiae* 2.4, defines the three *tempora* as *ante ipsum, in ipsum,* and *post ipsum.*

143. Annette Georgi, *Das lateinische und deutsche Preisgedicht des Mittelalters* (Berlin, 1969), 88–89, notes the development of this form of praise from an earlier tendency to emphasize the king's associations with divine rule.

144. *Carmina minora* 37.1–4, ed. Scott, 24.

Tu nimio nec stricta gelu, nec sidere fervens,
  Clementi celo temperieque places.

England, fruitful land, a long peace has made you tranquil,
  Your costly wares have given you great wealth.
You, neither bound overmuch with ice nor scorched by the sun,
  Are pleasing through your moderate weather and climate.[145]

The language chosen to characterize Henry and his rule in this poem recalls the praise of Louis in "Francia dulcis, aue." While according to Hildebert, Henry is "not inferior to his grandfathers and his father the king" (14), Louis is here described as being the equal of his Carolingian ancestors: "no less is he, although young and a novice" (105).[146] Under Henry Hildebert predicts that "there will be peace in the Church, reverence for the law, justice for wrongs, and glory in the affairs (of England)" (15–16). Likewise, the poet of "Francia dulcis, aue" details the flowering of peace, justice, and respect for the law under Louis (85–90).

In both of these praise poems the author associates the virtues of the ruler with the natural productivity of the land while avoiding the usage of explicitly Christian language or imagery. We might expect the poet of "Francia dulcis, aue" to thank God for Louis' accession to the throne, but he gives credit instead to *natura*:

Plus satis est quod te natura beavit in illo
  Quam quicquid seclis pluribus ante dedit. (17–18)

It is enough that Nature blessed you in him more
  Than whatever she had granted to many generations before.

Later the poet writes:

Nec dubium cuiquam solers natura relinquet
  Hunc hominem plene complacuisse sibi. (113–114)

Nor will resourceful Nature leave anyone in doubt
  That this man has wholly won her over.

The *natura* topos—the conception that the virtues of a region and its ruler are attributable to Nature—becomes more common in the panegyric of the late eleventh and twelfth centuries.[147] Most of Hildebert's panegyric to *Anglia* and its rulers comes in the guise of a monologue spoken by *natura*, who appoints both Henry and his consort to rule over England:

145. Praise of the land was also treated in the rhetorical handbooks of antiquity. Quintilian, *Institutio oratoria* 3.7.27, ed. and trans. Russell, 2:114–115, briefly mentions the *laus locorum*, noting that both appearance (*species*) and usefulness (*utilitas*) are sources of praise.

146. *Illo* refers either to the glory (*decus*) of Charlemagne and Pepin, or to one of the two kings.

147. See Georgi, *Das lateinische und deutsche Preisgedicht*, 93–94.

Tempus erit, quo sceptra tibi promissa gubernet
  Henricus . . . (13–14)

The time will come for Henry to control the scepter promised to you

Huic sociam dispono thori . . . (19)

I appoint a companion for his bed . . .

His ego principibus sum te factura beatam
  Anglia . . . (33–34)

I am going to make you blessed with these rulers, England.

In making *natura* responsible for blessing the land with such capable rulers, both Hildebert and the poet of "Francia dulcis, aue" steer clear of religious imagery. Our poem, then, does not testify to the incipient development of the French "royal ideology" of the twelfth and thirteenth centuries, an ideology that emphasized the sacred elements of monarchy and that served to consecrate the authority of the king.[148]

In one respect, our poet's glorification of *Francia* diverges noticeably from the praise of *Anglia* in Hildebert's poem: "Francia dulcis, aue" reveals a heightened national pride. During the period of this poem's composition the expansion of the French royal demesne and the consolidation of royal power under the Capetians gave rise to an increasing French pride and national consciousness.[149] This patriotrism manifests itself in the poet's commendation not only of the land for its fertility and bountifulness (1–9) but also of the *Franci* themselves for their independence from foreign control. The second boast is certainly not one that early twelfth-century *Anglia* could make.

As well as disclosing strong nationalistic sentiment, Poem 91 shows how the Capetian kings of the twelfth century strove to impart some of the glory of the Carolingian past to their own dynasty. Our poet compares Louis (91–104) favorably with the illustrious Carolingians Pepin III (died 768) and Charlemagne (742–814), who handed down to future French kings the mantle of empire (99) and undying fame (103–104). While the comparison of a newly crowned Louis VI with the great emperor Charlemagne may strike modern readers as fanciful, the poet was merely articulating a crucial component of Capetian royal ideology.

148. Joseph R. Strayer, "France, the Holy Land, the Chosen People, and the Most Christian King," in *Medieval Statecraft and the Perspectives of History* (Princeton, 1971), 300–314.

149. For a brief discussion of the growth of French national identity, see Bernd Schneidmüller, "Constructing Identities of Medieval France," in *France in the Central Middle Ages 900–1200*, ed. Marcus Bull (Oxford, 2002), 15–42.

Though the earliest Capetians had emphasized their links to the Carolingian kings, initiatives to appropriate some of the glory of Charlemagne grew more overt toward the end of the eleventh century.[150] Even Philip's choice of the name Louis for his eldest son, a name that harked back both to Clovis (about 466–511) and Louis the Pious (778–840), evoked the Merovingian and Carolingian past.[151] Suger makes the bond between Louis and Charlemagne explicit in the first chapter of the *Vita Ludovici*, where he remarks that Louis "followed the ancient custom of Charles the Great and other highborn kings" in his reverence toward Saint-Denis, the royal abbey that functioned as a burial-place of French kings and that furnished an education to both Louis and Suger. Later, when Pope Paschal II visited the abbey of Saint-Denis and sought help from Louis and Philip against the German emperor, Suger reports, "He asked that they follow the established custom of their predecessors, Charles the Great and other kings of the French, and make a bold stand against tyrants, enemies of the Church, and above all the emperor Henry" (*Vita Ludovici,* 10).

We can only speculate about the circumstances surrounding the composition of Poem 91, but conceivably the poem was written in an atmosphere of uncertainty about Louis' accession. Though Louis was pronounced the heir apparent at some stage between 1098 and 1100, he had not yet been crowned when Philip died in 1108. As an unconsecrated heir to the throne, Louis' claim depended on his status as Philip's eldest son, but this relationship could not necessarily guarantee an uncontested succession. Ivo (about 1040–1116), the bishop of Chartres at the time of Philip's death, recognized the potential for powerful magnates to stir up trouble during this uncertain period and arranged for the archbishop of Sens to consecrate Louis at an assembly of bishops in Orléans immediately after Philip's burial. The archbishop of Reims disputed the legitimacy of these hasty proceedings and asserted the unique right of the occupants of his see to crown the king-designate. According to Suger (*Vita Ludovici*, 14), Ivo justified his actions by pointing to the danger from certain "regni perturbatores" (disturbers of the realm). In addition to the possible peril from these fractious nobles, Louis also had to worry about the possibility of a plot to place on the throne his half-brother, Philip of Mantes (living in 1123), son of Philip I and Bertrada. Although the young king soon solidified his control of the monarchy and

150. "From the time of Louis VI at the latest, we find the entourage of the reigning family seeking to exploit for the latter's benefit the legend of the great emperor which, thanks to the epics, flourished in France at that time . . . From this heritage, the Capetians derived above all the high prestige of sacred kingship." Marc Bloch, *Feudal Society*, trans. L. A. Manyon (Chicago, 1961), 388. See also Jean Dunbabin, *France in the Making 843–1180* (Oxford, 1985), 265: "It is inevitable that the kingship of the Louis should be discussed in terms of a return to the past, for this was the way they themselves justified it."

151. Andrew W. Lewis, *Royal Succession in Capetian France: Studies on Familial Order and the State* (Cambridge, Mass., 1981), 47–48.

exercised his authority decisively, "Francia dulcis, aue" could have been written when the prospects of the new ruler seemed to hang in the balance.[152]

Style

The poet of "Francia dulcis, aue" draws on a number of classical authors, such as Ovid, Statius, and probably Vergil, Lucretius, and Silius Italicus. One phrase ("nequid nimis") is ultimately Terentian (*Andria* 61 [1.1.34], ed. Kauer and Lindsay). In several places (3, "inclita bellorum"; 20, "commune bonum"; 32, "meruere mori"; 116, "uota benigna") the poet's language appears to echo the panegyric epic on Louis the Pious by the ninth-century poet and courtier Ermoldus Nigellus.[153] Although a shared indebtedness to Vergil may account for some of the resemblances, the similarities between the poems seem to go beyond such an obvious common source. Ermoldus's poem, which like Poem 91 is written in elegiac couplets, celebrates the deeds of the most famous royal Louis up to the time of our poem, and it could have provided the poet with a worthy stylistic model. Beyond style, the poet could have been drawn to Ermoldus because of resemblances in their circumstances. Ermoldus was in exile when he wrote his epic and was trying to win his way back to court. In addition, the Carolingian poet, like the poet considered here (see lines 79–80), wished to make the young king whose favor he was currying appear good by contrast to his father.

The poet's style and diction recall those of the so-called Loire Valley poets, Marbod of Rennes, Baudri of Bourgueil, and Hildebert. His language resembles that of Baudri and Marbod in several places (for example, 6, "perpetui . . . ueris," and 17, "natura beauit"), and the form of panegyric in which ruler and land are extolled together is also present in Hildebert's poem to Henry and Matilda.[154] Like the Loire Valley poets, the author of Poem 91 employs a classicizing style. He eschews explicit mention of God or the saints, highlighting Louis VI's virtues with reference to a catalogue of classical figures: Aeneas, Cato, Socrates, Nestor, Ajax, Ulysses, Paris, and Hector. The indiscriminate mingling of historical and mythical figures reminds us that the story of Troy and Vergil's *Aeneid* were treated as history, not myth, in the Middle Ages.

The poet manifests a predisposition for lists (1–3, 36–40, 45–48), in which he often employs asyndeton (1–2, "regio bona, bella, salubris, / deliciosa, potens, fertilis, ampla satis"), and evidences a fondness for tricola (as in 7, 36, 41, 85–86, 91) and isocola in general (5, 7, 16, 20, 43, 66, 77, 90, 102). Still more incessant is his use of various types of repetition, including anadiplosis (55, "uile nichil, nichil

152. For details concerning the accession of Louis VI, see Lewis, *Royal Succession in Capetian France*, 52–54; Lohrmann, "Louis VI," 132–133; and Luchaire, 30–31, no. 57.

153. *Carmen in honorem Hludowici Christianissimi Caesaris Augusti*, ed. Dümmler; ed. and trans. Faral (with different line numbering).

154. *Carmina minora* 37, ed. Scott, 24–25.

indignum"; 110, "consilio maior, maior et ingenio"), anaphora (63, "de corde fero, de pleno corde uenenis"; 77, "solet esse, solet reperiri"; 79/81, "nuper oberrabas . . . nuper eras eremus,"; 91/93, "respicit ad proauos . . . respicit ad Carolum"; 109, "maior erit sensu, maior probitatis amore"), polyptoton (93–94, "Respicit ad . . . patrem; pater illi / Pipinus"; 97, "reges in regibus ambo"; 107, "maior erit, quoniam longe maiora parabit"), *derivatio* (27, "pro tempore temperat iram"; 28 "iusticie iustior"; 30, "supplicibus supplicet"; 97, "patres patrie"; 100, "milia mille"; 103, "manet decus atque manebit"), and chiasmus (44, "ut fortis reprimit, coripit ut sapiens"; 59–60, "sepe decorus / de male distorto palmite flos oritur").[155] Alliteration is evident but not obtrusive. In sixteen instances two consecutive words alliterate, while in six cases three words in the same line do so. [JL]

[9r^{B}] *F*rancia dulcis, aue, regio bona, bella, salubris,
   Deliciosa, potens, fertilis, ampla satis,
Inclita bellorum titulis populoque feroci,
   Qui nichil indomitum contremuisse potest.
Te nimium nec stringit hiems nec cauma resoluit,
   Sic prope perpetui gaudia ueris habes.
Non portenta creas, non monstra seris, nichil umquam
   Horrendum uisu uel generare soles.
Innumeras horientis opes uel in hoc superasti,
   Quod numquam superat gens aliena tuam.
Sed, fateor, sunt ista satis preciosa tuumque
   Nomen propterea nobile semper erit.
Atqui plus aliis precii tibi uandicat alti
   Quod Lodouicus rex tua ceptra gerit.
Quem dignum maiore satis defandit honore
   Tunc celebris facies, tunc probitatis amor.
Plus satis est quod te natura beauit in illo
   Quam quicquid seclis pluribus ante dedit.
Qui regni curam teneris suscepit in annis
   Ad commune bonum iusticieque decus,
[9v^{A}] Mirus homo uitas hominum mortesque tueri,
   Et cum momentis pondera discutere.
Iusticie studiis asper similisque feroci,
   Et radice tenus crimina tota secans,
Scit quia non prestat plenam medicina salutem,
   Que non ad nimium uulnera persequitur.

155. The distinctions among these terms follow Heinrich Lausberg, *Handbook of Literary Rhetoric*, ed. D. E. Orton and R. D. Anderson, trans. M. T. Bliss, A. Jansen, D. E. Orton (Leiden, 1998), 274–298, § 608–664, except in the case of chiasmus, which Lausberg treats as a variant of isocolon; see 322, § 723n2.

Sepe tamen pro re, pro tempore temperat iram;
Parcit iusticie iustior ipse satis.
Obuius et facilis precibus lacrimisque reorum
Ut pro supplicibus supplicet ipse sibi.
Scit quia continuo bona pars nudabitur orbis
Si pereant omnes qui meruere mori.
Sic igitur iustus, sic clemens optat haberi,
Ut uirtus neutra destruat alterutram.
Natus amare bonos, hic culpas odisse malorum,
Pacem ferre, sequi iura, tenere modum,
Dapsilis et parcus ne quid nimis, ocia semper
Detestans, aliquid utile semper amans,
Non inconsultus, non lubricus aut uiolentus
Non ex a*b*rupto quelibet accipiens,
Cor duplex scriptamque manum linguamque loquacem
Causas pestiferi criminis esse putat.
Ceruices rigidas et desipiencia corda
Ut fortis reprimit, coripit ut sapiens.
Reddidit Eneam pietate, rigore Catonem,
Ingenio Socratem, Nestora consilio,
[9v[B]] Aiacem factis, dictis imitatur Ulixem.
In uultu Paris est, Hectora mente gerit,
Hectora non qualem post currum traxit Achilles,
Sed qualis Danaas terruit igne rates.
Certe non talem se prebuit ante Philipus,
Qui pater est huius sanguine, non meritis.
Ille tuus non rex, quoniam rex nomine solo
In manibus gladii teque tuosque dedit.
Hic quia uile nichil, nichil indignum meditatur,
Omnino rex est nomine reque tuus.
Vere non semper sapiunt quicumque patris sunt;
Est aliquid stultos dissimulare patres.
Exemplum natura dedit, quod sepe decorus
De male distorto palmite flos oritur.
Sepe per alueolum deformem fons preciosus
Oritur et uicii contrait inde nichil,
Et de corde fero, de pleno corde uenenis
Multociens uerbum dulce piumque sonat.
Unde nichil mirum si consimili ratione
Delituit nequam, surgit honestus homo.

Degenerat non qui peruersum non imitatur,
Sed qui post iustum despicit ire patrem.
Immo satis maior laus illi surgit in euum
Qui uirtute sua se trait in precium.
Sicut in extremum miser est qui primus in evum,
Maiori sempe*r* pessimus, esse cupit,
[10r^A] Sic, cum sunt nati precii, defenditur omnis
Qui generis speculum nititur esse sui.
H*oc* Lodouicus plene fecisse probatur
Et faciet, quoniam sic placet ipse sibi.
Sensus in antiquis solet esse, solet reperiri;
Nunc aliud quiddam tampora nostra can*un*t.
Nuper oberrabas cano sub rege misella;
Nunc iuuenis ducit te meliore uia.
Nuper eras eremus, predatio uasta latronum,
Quantus ut irriguis nunc tua claustra uirent,
Et quasi post hiemem uernans tibi redditur aestas,
Dum post tristitias gaudia plena tenes.
Undique bella silent et per castella, per urbes,
Per uicos legum sancio sancta uiget.
Rex tuus iste tui sic te facit esse potentem,
Ut iam nemo tuis obuiet imperiis.
Ille tibi pacem rigidam firmamque parauit,
Quam seruare salus, quam uiolare mori.
Respicit ad proauos abauos atauosque parentum
Qui te reg*n*orum constituere caput.
Respicit ad Carolum Carolique patrem; pater illi
Pipinus, nanus corpore, mente gigas.
Pipinus Carolusque uelud duo lumina mundi
Omnibus exemplum grande fuere boni.
Ambo patres patrie, reges in regibus ambo
Depicti morum floribus et radiis.
Sub quibus imperii multum creuisse decorem
Argumentorum milia m*ille* probant.
Unde sue fame titulos emere perhennes,
Quos memorare pium, quos numerare labor.
[10r^B] Pipini Carolique manet decus atque manebit,
Quippe perhennat eos nescia fama mori.
Non minor hic illo, quamuis tener atque nouellus;
Immo, si liceat uiuere, maior erit.

Maior erit, quoniam longe maiora parabit,
  Temporis ut nostri multiplicetur honos.
Maior erit sensu, maior probitatis amore,
  Consilio maior, maior et ingenio.
S*ensus* alta nimis uirtus requieuit in illo,
  Que se continuo proferet in medium.
Nec dubium cuiquam solers natura relinquet
  Hunc hominem plene complacuisse sibi.
Ergo diu uiuat rex Lodouicus et omnis
  Qui super hoc uerbo uota benigna facit.

Hail, sweet France, fortunate region, beautiful, wholesome,
  delightful, powerful, fruitful, very spacious,
renowned for distinctions in war and for a fierce people,
  who are not capable of fearing anything unvanquished.
Winter does not bind you overmuch, nor heat melt you;
  thus you have the joys of an almost everlasting spring.
You do not create monsters; you beget no monstrosities; nor are
  you accustomed even to produce anything frightful to see.
In this you have surpassed the countless riches of the Orient,
  that a foreign race never overcomes yours.
But, I admit, these are very precious things, and your
  name will therefore be always renowned,
and yet that King Louis bears your scepter lays claim
  for you to high praise in greater quantity than the other things;
both a famous physical appearance and a love of prowess
  protect him, well enough worthy of greater honor.
It is enough that Nature blessed you in him more
  than whatever she had granted to many generations before.
He, while in tender years, undertook responsibility for ruling
  for the common good and ornament of justice,
a marvelous man to watch over the lives and deaths of men,
  and to examine burdens upon the scales.
Harsh and almost fierce in his zeal for justice,
  and cutting off all crimes at the root,
he knows that the medicine does not provide complete health
  that does not deeply penetrate wounds.
Often, nevertheless, he moderates his anger in accordance with the time and situation;
  he himself, quite just, refrains from doing damage to justice.

He is accessible and accommodating to the prayers and tears of the guilty,
so that he himself entreats on behalf of his suppliants.
He knows that a good part of the world will be laid bare at once
if all should perish who deserved to die.
Therefore he wishes to be considered just in this way, merciful in this way,
so that neither virtue destroys the other.
This man was born to love the good, hate the faults of the wicked,
bring forth peace, follow the law, and keep moderation,
abundant and thrifty, lest anything be excessive, always hating leisure,
always loving something useful,
not incautious, not deceitful or violent,
not dealing with anything precipitately,
he deems a twofold heart, a written hand, a chattering tongue
to be the causes of deadly crime.
Stiff necks and foolish hearts
as he is brave, he subdues, as he is wise, he chides.
In his devotion he has made Aeneas live again; in his strictness, Cato;
in his intellect, Socrates; in his wisdom, Nestor.
In deeds he imitates Ajax, in words Ulysses.
In appearance he is Paris; in his mind he acts as Hector,
not the kind of Hector whom Achilles dragged behind the chariot,
but the one who terrified the Danaean ships with fire.
Surely Philip did not show himself as such a one earlier,
who is the father of this man in blood, but not in deserts.
That one is not your king, since, a king in name only,
he gave you and your people into the hands of the sword.
Since this man thinks nothing cheap, nothing unworthy,
he is fully your king, in both name and reality.
Truly, anyone who is a father is not always wise;
it is something to disregard foolish fathers.
Nature has provided the example, that often a lovely flower
is born from a badly twisted vine.
A precious fountain often springs up through an ugly channel
and acquires no flaw from it,
and from a savage heart, from a heart full of venom,
many times sweet and pious speech rings out.
For this reason it is nothing marvelous if, by a similar principle,
the wicked man has vanished, the noble comes forth.
He does not slip who does not imitate a wicked father,
but rather he who scorns to follow a just one.

Instead, greater praise is won in perpetuity for him
who by his own virtue advances himself toward reward.
Just as he is wretched to the end who desires to be first in perpetuity,
ever most wicked to his forebear,
so, when there are children of value, each one is protected
who strives to be the model of his kin.
Louis is confirmed to have done this fully,
and he will do it, since in that way he pleases himself.
Understanding usually exists, usually is found in olden times;
now our times sing of something else.
Recently you went astray, wretched, under a gray-haired king;
now a young man leads you along a better path.
Recently you were a desert, the empty spoil of robbers,
to the same degree as your cloisters are now green with waterings,
and, as if after winter, the warmth of spring returns to you,
while after sorrows you are full of joy.
On all sides wars are silent, and throughout castles, throughout cities,
throughout towns the holy sanction of law flourishes.
Thus this king of yours makes you powerful over yourself,
so that now no one opposes your commands.
He has compacted a strong and steady peace for you,
which it is safety to preserve and death to violate.
He looks back to the great-grandfathers of his kinsfolk, and their fathers and grandfathers
who have made you the head of kingdoms.
He looks back to Charles and the father of Charles; this man's father was
Pepin, a dwarf in stature, but a giant in mind.
Pepin and Charles, like two lights of the world,
were a great example of goodness to all.
Both were fathers of the fatherland, both kings among kings,
adorned by the flowers and radiance of their good morals.
Under them a thousand thousands of proofs confirm
that the distinction of the empire grew greatly,
whence they procured the everlasting claims to their fame,
which it is righteous to recall, but laborious to count.
The glory of Pepin and Charles remains and will remain,
since a fame that cannot die immortalizes them.
No less is he, although young and a novice, than that man;
rather, if it should be granted him to live, he will be greater.

He will be greater, since he will accomplish things greater by far,
so that the distinction of our age will be multiplied.
He will be greater in understanding, greater in the love of what is right,
greater in wisdom, greater too in intelligence.
In him has come to rest an exceedingly profound strength of understanding,
which will soon become widely known.
Nor will resourceful Nature leave anyone in doubt
that this man has wholly won her over.
Therefore long live King Louis and everyone
who after this discourse offers kind prayers.

Textual Notes

1] *Initial missing.*
13] alii*s*: alii.
15] deffandit, *with first* f *expunged.*
35] Natus amare bonos, hic: Hic Natus amare bonos (*to be emended* metri causa *and because the scribe's use of a second large initial indicates his awareness that he had put the wrong word first*).
38] amans: *After* amans *is written* agens, *which is here omitted (for rhyme and meter).*
44] ut fortis *written over two-word erasure.*
46] *Below the last line of* 9v^{A} *is a drawing of, from left to right, a goat, ram, and lion, labeled:* caper, aries, leo.
58] disimulare, *with* si *added supralinearly with ligature to* s*: extra minim disregarded.*
65] si de consimili, *with* de *monogram expunged.*
72] semper: sepe, *with oddly formed* p *and* m *added supralinearly.*
75] H*o*c: Hic.
78] can*unt*: can̄t.
79] oberrabas *glossed supralinearly* id est francia.
86] per vicos *written above* per vicos.
87] rex tuus iste viget te facit esse potentem, *corrected supralinearly to* rex tuus iste sic. potentem *expunged, with* potentem *written again supralinearly.*
91] abauos ad atauosque, *with* ad *expunged.*
92] reg*n*orum: regorum.
102] memorare: mememorare (*with dittography*).
111] *Sensus*: S.

Commentary

1. **Francia**: The exact geographical area designated by this term depends on context, since the definition of *Francia* changed over time and was employed differently even by writers of the same period. In the Carolingian era (about 750–900) *Francia* referred to a region extending from the Loire to the

lower Rhine and upper Maine.[156] In the tenth century, *Francia* designated the zone between Lotharingia and the Seine, or, more commonly, between Lotharingia and the Loire; it was not used to denote the whole kingdom of West Francia.[157] This area, *Francia* writ large, comprehended regions (the most significant being Normandy, Gascony, Britanny, Septimania, Catalonia, Burgundy, and Aquitaine) that maintained high degrees of autonomy throughout the tenth and early eleventh centuries, and, in some cases, for longer. The correspondence between the term *Francia* and the whole West Frankish kingdom was established decisively only in the second half of the twelfth century, and even then the modifier *tota* was usually supplied to express the idea of the whole kingdom.[158] Suger of Saint-Denis, for example, in the *Vita Ludovici*, still employs *Francia* to designate the royal demesne centered on the Île de France.[159] One contemporary poet who uses the term *Francia* seems to have excluded Aquitaine from its territories. Baudri of Bourgueil's poem on the death of Gerhard of Corbie, the founder and first abbot of the monastery of La Sauve-Majeure in Aquitaine, mentions that Gerhard left *Francia* to come to Bordeaux:

Francia natalis sibi sorduit hancque reliquit
  Silvestres saltus Burdegalae veniens (79.7–8).

His native France grew dreary and he left her,
  Coming to the wooded glades of Bordeaux.[160]

Yet, in certain contexts *Francia* might be interpreted more generally, even in the first half of the twelfth century.[161] In a panegyric, *Francia* might well have been meant in its broadest sense in order to enhance Louis' prestige.

Francia dulcis: Compare Baudri, *Carmina* 82.7, ed. Tilliette, 1:78 and 1:195n5. **dulcis . . . bella**: In French the description of France as sweet (*douce*) and beautiful (*belle*) became standard after the appearance of the first *chansons de geste* at the beginning of the twelfth century. *Douce France* occurs for the first time in the *Song of Roland*, called to mind by a dying Roland.[162]

---

156. See Schneidmüller, "Constructing Identities of Medieval France," 24.

157. See Dunbabin, *France in the Making,* 4–5.

158. See Margret Lugge, *"Gallia" und "Francia" im Mittelalter: Untersuchungen über den Zusammenhang zwischen geographisch-historischer Terminologie und politischem Denken vom 6.–15. Jahrhundert* (Bonn, 1960), 171–172.

159. Charles T. Wood, "*Regnum Francie*: A Problem in Capetian Administrative Usage," *Traditio* 23 (1976): 117–118.

160. Baudri, *Carmina* 79.7–8, ed. Tilliette, 1:77.

161. Colette Beaune, *The Birth of an Ideology: Myths and Symbols of Nation in Late-Medieval France,* trans. Susan Ross Huston, ed. Frederic L. Cheyette (Berkeley, 1991), 284.

162. Beaune, *The Birth of an Ideology,* 285.

3. **inclita bellorum**: Perhaps recalling Vergil, *Aeneid* 2.241–242, ed. Mynors, 134 ("o patria, o diuum domus Ilium et incluta bello / moenia Dardanidum!"). Compare also Alcuin, *Carmina* 9.67, ed. Dümmler, 230 ("Hesperiae populus, quondam gens inclita bello"), and Ermoldus Nigellus, *Carmen in honorem Hludowici* 1.337, ed. Dümmler, 15 ("nam quemcumque suo congressa est inclita bello"), ed. Faral, 32 (as 1.372).
   populoque feroci: The ferocity of the Franks was proverbial, at least among French authors. According to the *Chronicle* of Fredegar, the Franks were originally a group of Trojan refugees who derived their name from their leader, a certain Francio: see *Chronicarum libri IV*, 2.5 and 3.2, ed. Krusch, 46 and 93. However, a parallel etymology also held that *Franci* derived from *feritas* ("ferocity").[163] The poet likely draws on this latter tradition in his reference to the "fierce people" of Francia.

   A passage in Ermoldus Nigellus may also resonate in our poet's use of the *feritas* etymology. Early in Book 1 of the *Carmen in honorem Hludowici*, Zado, the Moorish ruler of Barcelona, prepares to defend his city against the Frankish army, led by Louis the Pious. When he hears from one of his men that Louis is leading the Frankish host, Zado breaks out in a despairing monologue, ed. Dümmler, 1:15–16 (as 1.364–383), ed. Faral, 32 (as 1.329–348) in which he touches upon the well-known ferocity of the Franks, ed. Dümmler, 1:15 (as 1.378–379), ed. Faral, 32 (as 1.343–344): "Namque ipsum nomen Francorum horresco recensens: / Francus habet nomen a feritate sua" (I shudder to recall the name of the Franks: 'Frank' takes its name from their ferocity). Included in Zado's speech is the phrase *inclita bello*, which our poet uses to describe the people of *Francia* in line 3.
5. **cauma**: A borrowing from Greek, *cauma* denotes a burning heat, especially that of the sun. The more common *aestas* means both "summer" and "summer heat," and would seem to offer a closer parallel to *hiems*. As a spondee, however, *aestas* would not scan before *resoluit*. *Cauma* is postclassical; it appears in the Vulgate (Job 30.30) and frequently in patristic authors like Jerome. Compare also Aldhelm, *Aenigmata* 100.73, in *Collectiones aenigmatum Merovingicae aetatis*, vol. 2, *Tatuini opera omnia; Variae collectiones aenigmatum Merovingicae aetatis; Anonymus de dubiis nominibus*, ed. F. Glorie (Turnhout, 1968), 539 ("Siccior aestivo torrentis caumate solis"); and *Carmen de virginitate* 1192, in *Aldhelmi opera*, ed. Ehwald, 403 ("torrida flammantis laturum caumata solis").
6. **perpetui . . . ueris**: Baudri of Bourgueil draws upon Ovid (*Metamorphoses* 5.391, ed. Tarrant, 140: line opening) for the phrase "perpetuum uer" in two of his poems: *Carmina* 7.217, ed. Tilliette, 1:21 ("aut mixtum speres autumno perpetuum ver"), and 129.12, ed. Tilliette, 1:138 ("ne semper desit mihi perpetuum ver"). **gaudia ueris**: For the line ending, compare Poeta Saxo,

163. Compare Isidore of Seville, *Etymologiae* 9.2.101, ed. Lindsay, where both accounts of the origin of "Frank" are given. See also Beaune, *The Birth of an Ideology*, 284–288.

Annales de gestis Karoli Magni imperatoris 4.380, ed. von Winterfeld, 55 ("ora madent lacrimis falsa inter gaudia veris").

7. **portenta . . . monstra . . . horrendum uisu**: The idea that France alone was free from monsters derives from Jerome, *Contra Vigilantium*, in PL 23.339A [= 355A, in other printings] ("Sola Gallia monstra non habuit, sed viris semper fortibus, et eloquentissimis abundavit"). For the phrasing, see Lucretius, *De rerum natura* 5.837, ed. Bailey ("multaque tum tellus etiam portenta creare"), and 5.845, ed. Bailey ("cetera de genere hoc monstra ac portenta creabat").
8. **horrendum uisu**: Compare Statius, *Thebaid* 6.939, ed. Klotz and Klinnert, 238 ("horrendum visu per quas modo fugerat auras").
9. **horientis** = *orientis.*
13. **Atqui plus alii*s* precii tibi uendicat alti**: *Alii* makes no sense without emendation, since it cannot fit logically as either a dative singular (neither "to another . . . for you" nor "to another you" signifies) or a nominative plural. The minimalist approach is to supply a final *s* so that it may be construed as an ablative of comparison, with reference to all the preceding advantages that France is said to possess: Louis surpasses them all.

    If the line underwent more than one change between its composition and the text as it is presented in the Houghton manuscript, the last word of the line may also need attention. The phrase *uindicat acta* is found as a line ending in pseudo-Vergil, *Culex* 276, ed. Clausen, 30. Even closer is the line ending "sibi vendicat actus" in Hildebert, *Querimonia* meter 4.1, ed. Orth, 91, which Migne prints as "sibi vindicat actus" when he supplies another version of this metrum in Hildebert's *Carmina miscellanea* 127.1, in PL 171.1437B. But to accommodate either of these constructions would require substantial reworking of the line, which produces adequate sense with the addition of the single *s.*
14. **ceptra** = *sceptra.*
16. **probitatis amor**: Compare Purchard of Reichenau, *Gesta Witigowonis* 198, ed. Strecker, 269 ("Purchardus, ductor, summae probitatis amator")
17. **natura beauit**: This phrase occurs most often as a hexameter ending. For instance, see Marbod, *Carmina* 24.21, in PL 171.1660D ("praestat habere palam, quo te natura beavit"); the anonymous *Rapularius* 2, line 81, ed. Gatti, 6:340 ("Materno dum me gremio natura beavit"); and Robert Partes, incipit "Ut quid lingua silet," line 99, in "The Poems of Robert Partes," ed. Cornog, 230 ("his exornavit, his te natura beavit"). Guiardinus uses this phrase in his poem on the virtues and vices, line 875, in Werner, "Guiardinus," 457 ("te licet innumeris felix natura beavit").
19. **qui regni curam teneris suscepit in annis**: At the age of sixteen Louis had been assigned a military command by Philip, who was becoming increasingly physically infirm. Louis was named *rex designatus* between 1098 and 1100. The phrase "teneris . . . in annis" is attested routinely from antiquity

on in this metrical position. The pairing "regni cura," although medieval rather than classical in origin, is also common.

20. **commune bonum**: Used in the same metrical position by Ermoldus Nigellus, *Carmen in honorem Hludowici* 2.293, ed. Dümmler, 2:33 ("Hoc commune bonum suscipite unanimes"), and Faral, 74 (as line 942).

22. **cum momentis pondera discutere**: The rare expression *pondera discutere* derives from Gregory the Great's *Moralia in Job* 28.10, ed. Adriaen, 3:1413: "alius in una lingua quam novit sermonum pondera interpretando prudenter discutit, et tamen reliquis bonis quae non habet patienter caret" ("Another, in a language that he knows, skillfully weighs the values of words through interpretation, and yet he patiently does without the rest of the goods, which he lacks"). Gregory uses the phrase *pondera discutere* figuratively to refer to the evaluation of the "weight" of words.

Since in this section of "Francia dulcis, aue" the author praises Louis' marvelous ability to dispense justice, it makes sense to understand *pondera discutere* as referring to legal decisions of some sort. While *discutere* clearly means "to assess" or "value," the precise meaning of *pondera* is more difficult to determine. It may refer to a balance, or set of scales: see the *OLD* 1400, *pondus* 3b. The *momenta*, in this interpretation, would be the weights in the scales, and hence to "examine the scales with their weights" would be to evaluate judicial claims of some sort, perhaps to weigh justice against mercy or to decide between life and death. Cicero uses "rationis momenta" to mean the weight(s) of an argument at *De natura deorum* 1.5.10, ed. Dyck, 25. He also employs "momenta rationum" similarly at *Academica* 1.12.45, ed. Plasberg, 19.

Alternatively, *momenta* and *pondera* could be taken as synonyms that refer to the value of a person or a claim, or to "weighty matters" in general. In Classical Latin, *pondus* typically denoted the weight or bulk of an object and *momentum* its downward force, but the distinction between these terms is often blurred in late antique and medieval authors. Compare Venantius Fortunatus, *Carmina* 7.12.5, ed. Leo, 165, ed. Reydellet, 2:103 ("cuncta mouens secum momenta et pondera rerum"); and Andrew of Saint-Victor, *Expositiones historicae in libros Salomonis: Expositio historica in Ecclesiasten* 1446–1447, ed. Lohr and Berndt.

23. **Iusticie studiis**: Compare Paulinus of Nola, *Carminum appendix* 3.139, ed. Hartel, 353 ("iustitiae studium").

25. **medicina salutem**: *Medicina* followed by an oblique form of *salus* occurs routinely at the end of hexameters, from Ovid, *Tristia* 2.269, ed. Owen ("eripit interdum, modo dat medicina salutem").

27. **temperat iram**: Compare *Aeneid* 1.56–57, ed. Mynors, 105 (". . . celsa sedet Aeolus arce / sceptra tenens mollitque animos et temperat iras"), and Dracontius, *Satisfactio* 209, ed. Speranza, 25 ("rex, qui dat veniam subiecto et temperat iras").

29. **facilis precibus**: Compare Priscian, *Carmen in laudem Anastasii Imperatoris* 183, ed. Chauvot, 63 ("et faciles precibus populorum praebuit aures").
32. **meruere mori**: This phrase occurs at the same position in Ermoldus Nigellus, *Carmen in honorem Hludowici* 4.228, ed. Dümmler, 2:64, and Faral, 160 (as line 2109) ("perculit ut pueros qui meruere mori").
37. **dapsilis et parcus**: Compare Plautus, *Pseudolus* 1266 (5.1.21), ed. Lindsay ("dari dapsilis, non enim parce promi").
37. **nequid nimis**: Compare Terence, *Andria* 60–61 (1.1.33–34), ed. Kauer and Lindsay ("nam id arbitror / adprime in vita esse utile, ut nequid nimis").
38. **amans**: The manuscript presents *agens*, which makes the line hypermetric and violates the rhyme scheme. Although neither participle has been expunged, *agens* is omitted here. The scribe may have added it to explain the following line of adjectives that are attached to no participle, but its presence is not necessary for sense.
41. **linguamque loquacem**: Compare Ovid, *Metamorphoses*, 2.540, ed. Tarrant, 51 ("lingua fuit damno; lingua faciente loquaci"). The thought expressed in the line may be that a twofold heart reveals itself by writing one thing but saying another.
43. **ceruices rigidas et desipiencia corda**: For the first phrase see Ovid, *Tristia* 1.4.14, ed. Owen ("cervicis rigidae frena remittit equo"). Suger remarks (*Vita Ludovici* 8) that during his period as king-designate Louis "subdued the disobedient and either seized troublesome castles or made them submissive by any means possible."
44. **fortis**: Suger provides several instances of the king's personal bravery. For instance (*Vita Ludovici* 2), Louis fights his way into the middle of Drogo of Mouchy's castle and wins glory in battle as a "brave champion" (*fortissimus palestrita*) and a "marvelous swordsman" (*spectabilis gladiator*). In a later engagement (*Vita Ludovici* 12) with the forces of Humbald, lord of the castle of Sainte-Sévère, the king-designate proves himself to be singularly courageous.

    The main thrust of the couplet is to confirm that Louis embodies the combination of *sapientia* and *fortitudo*, the two greatest desiderata in a king. For a recent study that refers to earlier scholarship on this platitude, see Thomas D. Hill, "The Crowning of Alfred and the Topos of *Sapientia et Fortitudo* in Asser's Life of King Alfred," *Neophilologus* 86 (2002): 471–476.

    coripit = *corripit*
46. **Nestora consilio**: Compare *Ilias Latina* 176–177, in *The Latin Iliad: Introduction, Text, Translation, and Notes*, ed. George A. Kennedy (Fort Collins, Colo, 1998), 21: "quos iuxta fidus sollerti pectore Nestor / consilioque potens." For a similar catalogue of virtues and the classical archetypal figures who personified them, see Stephen of Rouen, incipit "Flos comitum, decus imperii, vis maxima belli" (a poem in praise of Count Waleran de Mellento), lines 25–28, in the appendix to the *Draco Normannicus*, ed. Howlett, 2:767:

"Hic Paris in facie, statura Nestor, Ulixes / consilio, belli viribus Hector erat: / Croesus divitiis, in causis Quintilianus, / eloquio Cicero, versibus ipse Maro."

48–50. The comparisons with Paris and Hector here may well relate to the prestige of Trojan origins, to which Capetian monarchs began to lay claim. For instance, the epitaph of Philip I declares him as arising "ex genere Priami" (from the race of Priam).

53. **nomine solo**: A stock line ending as early as Silius Italicus, *Punica* 1.329, ed. Delz, 13 ("heu priscis numen populis, at nomine solo").

54. **in manibus gladii teque tuosque dedit**: The expression *manus gladii* ("hands of the sword") is biblical. Compare Job 5.20, Ps 62.11, Isa 18.21, and Ezek 35.5. Both the ablative *manibus* and the accusative *manus* are attested after *in* with a verb of motion in the Vulgate (for the rarer ablative form, see Judges 2.14 and 2.23). Presumably the poet uses the ablative *manibus* here for metrical reasons, since the phrasing "in manus gladii" cannot be accommodated in dactylic poetry.

57. **patris** = *patres.*

58. **stultos dissimulare patres**: Although the poet emphasizes that, as king, Louis did not follow the example set by Philip, the son seems to have avoided alienating his father while the latter remained alive. Suger of Saint-Denis remarks (*Vita Ludovici* 13) that Louis "had taken care never to displease his father in any way while he lived. Nor had he upset his father's lordship over the kingdom by any sort of plot, as other young men customarily do." He also describes how, at Philip's funeral, Louis wept with "appropriate filial affection."

79. **oberrabas**: A scribe glossed the word with the explanation "that is, France" to clarify that the verb in the second person was addressed to the personification of France.

83. **et quasi post hiemem**: Compare Reiner of Liège, *De conflictu duorum ducum et animarum* 1.131–132, in PL 204.83D ("nunc quasi post hiemem verno redeunte sereno / post adversa, secunda deo radiante redibunt").

85. **bella silent**: Louis waged war frequently during the period of time between his acquisition of a military command (1097–1098) and his coronation (1108). For the wording, see Silius Italicus, *Punica* 5.461–462, ed. Delz, 129 (". . . Murranum ille eminus hasta / perculerat, quo non alius, cum bella silerent").

86. **legum sancio**: Compare Gunther of Pairis, *Ligurinus* 2.204 and 3.381, ed. Assmann, 208 and 252.

93. **Carolum Carolique patrem**: Charlemagne (742–814) and his father, Pepin III (714–768).

94. **Pipinus, nanus corpore, mente gigas**: Pepin III was surnamed "The Short." An excursus on his small size but great courage is provided in Notker the Stammerer (Notkerus Balbulus), *Gesta Karoli* 2.15, ed. Haefele, 78–80. Compare Aegidius of Paris, *Karolinus* 1.352, ed. Colker, 252 ("mente gigas et vi fuit auctior ille Pipinus").

95. **lumina mundi**: A common hexameter ending.

98. **depicti morum floribus et radiis**: Compare Poem 90.88 "morum floribus" (see commentary). For *radii morum* see Walther, *Proverbia sententiaeque*, 1:53, no. 450 ("ad radios morum laxatur hiems animorum"). For *flores morum* see Walther, 5: 373, no. 31674 ("tu morum flores cape virtutumque decores, laude decorari si gliscas et decorari").
101. **fame titulos**: Compare Dracontius, *Satisfactio* 298 ("titulos famae").
104. **perhennat** = *perennat*
111. **requieuit in illo**: This hexameter ending originated in Ovid, *Metamorphoses* 4.662, ed. Tarrant, 118.
112. **proferet in medium**: Compare Statius, *Thebaid* 2.553–554, ed. Klotz and Klinnert, 66, and Stephen of Rouen, *Draco Normannicus* 1.1544, ed. Howlett, 2:650 ("profert in medium").
113. **solers natura**: Compare Avienus, *Aratea* 1835, ed. Breysig.
116. **uota benigna**: The phrase is found in Ermoldus Nigellus, *Carmen in honorem Hludowici* 4.74, in *Poetae Latini aevi Carolini* 2:60; and *Ermold le Noir*, 148, as line 1955; and in Florus of Lyon, *Carmina*, 24.37–38, ed. Dümmler, 552. [JL]

POEM 92. Incipit "Flete senes, plorate uiri, iuuenes lacrimentur." Twenty-five elegiac distichs. Not in Walther. *In principio*, reference 142098.

Poem 92, a eulogy for a certain Milo, has elicited at least two guesses as to whom its subject might be. In the description of MS Lat 300 provided to the Houghton Library by bookseller Nicolaus Rauch, and produced apparently by André Vernet, the Milo in question is identified as Cardinal Bishop Milo of Palestrina.[164] Created a cardinal by Pope Urban II, Bishop Milo was sent to France as a papal legate with the special charge of addressing the issue of simony. His activities as legate in France stretched at least between the years 1095 and 1103, and he is believed to have died in 1112.[165] In an apparently earlier discussion of the poem, however, Vernet states that its subject is "without doubt" Milo II of Bray, the seneschal of the castle of Montlhéry assassinated by his cousin Hugh of Crécy in October of 1116 or 1117.[166] The career of this Milo, as far as it intersects the political considerations that seem to underlie the collocation of poems in Houghton MS Lat 300, has already been sketched out in some detail above, in the discussion of the contents of Group Five.

The conventionality of form and heavy reliance on cliché generally evident in poems of the *planctus* genre can often pose difficulties for extracting from a poem

164. Ziolkowski, "A Bouquet of Wisdom and Invective," 26n35. The bookseller's description of the manuscript accompanied it upon its sale to the Houghton library in 1965.

165. *Histoire littéraire de la France*, vol. 10 (Paris, 1756), 19–20. On Bishop Milo's activities in 1103, including his intervention in a conflict between the bishop of Autun and the abbot of Cluny, see also Theodor Schieffer, *Die päpstlichen Legaten in Frankreich vom Vertrage von Meersen (870) bis zum Schisma von 1130* (Berlin, 1935), 169.

166. Vernet, "Séance du 16 avril," 53.

of this type trustworthy biographical details about the subject of its eulogistic praise. Milo is described, for example, as having been pious (13, 45–46), morally upright (9–12, 31–32), and generous (17–18). His modesty is marked out for special mention (19–20, 33–40), with a personified Modesty even taking up her residence in the vessel of himself that Milo provided. As has already been noted, the singling out of such qualities might reasonably incline one to seek the poem's subject in the ranks of ecclesiastical rather than secular society. Yet while one would not wish to cast doubt on the sincerity of the panegyrist, there is little in this catalog of praises—as much a "mass of goodnesses" (43) as Milo himself is said to have been—that might not conceivably have found a place in the eulogy of almost any lay or ecclesiastical magnate of the time. Even if the poet's description of "his holy breast . . . nurtured by holy wisdom" (13) might perhaps be seen as excessive were it meant to be applied to a worldly figure of primarily secular influence, still such conventional laudations as these afford little help in the struggle to establish or confirm the identity of the poem's subject.

However, Poem 92 contains a number of more specific indications as to the position and activities of the person whose demise it laments. The poet lays particular stress on Milo's "great burden of public affairs" (4), saying that the deceased was celebrated as "the glory of public affairs" (5). Milo's activities obviously entailed involvement in the administration of justice. Alongside the general statement that he was "the renown of justice" (6), for example, it is asserted that his death will have compromised the very stability of "public laws, which through his agency had stood for a long time" (8).

That such remarks are more than just the stock-in-trade of eulogy is confirmed by the detailing of Milo's generosity. Although he is qualified as being wealthy himself and as bestowing his wealth upon others (18), it is stated even more specifically that among his benefactions was the lavishing upon the needy of "the wealth of the condemned" (17). Such a statement can only imply a figure actively engaged in the legal system, with the power to distribute as he saw fit the financial proceeds that accrued from the assessment of judicial penalties.

It would be difficult to reconcile such a description with a claim that Poem 92 was composed upon the death of Cardinal Bishop Milo of Palestrina. While "righteous laws" (16) are listed among Milo's guiding forces, little in the poem conjures up the issues of canon law with which Bishop Milo's papal commission would surely have preoccupied him, whereas the mention of "public laws" (8) would seem to imply far more the laws of the *res publica* than the laws of the Church. A eulogy for Cardinal Milo by Bishop Marbod of Rennes includes, alongside declarations of holiness that border upon sanctification, much about the campaign of the papal legate against simoniacs:[167]

---

167. This poem (incipit "Roma beata nimis, que sic excrevit ab imis"), composed in rhyming

> Roma . . .
> Cernens Ecclesiam turbari per simoniam,
> Misit legatum per Gallica regna probatum,
> Contra Simonem iussit pugnare Milonem. (1, 6–8)
>
> *Rome . . .*
> *discerning the Church to be troubled by simony,*
> *sent a proven legate throughout the Gallic realms,*
> *ordered Milo to fight against Simon*

Or again:

> Sed fidei pilo penetrauit ad intima Milo . . .
> Emptores uidi uerbi mucrone recidi,
> Et Simon immundus sibi succubuit pudibundus. (40, 43–44)
>
> *But with the spear of faith Milo pierced through to the heart . . .*
> *Purchasers I saw cut back by the blade of the word,*
> *and impure Simon yielded to him shamefaced.*

Milo's combat against simony was clearly perceived to form the central and most important facet of his work in France, and to find no mention of simony in Poem 92, or indeed no explicit reference at all to service to the Church, argues against equating the poem's Milo with Bishop Milo. Similarly, the assertion that Milo "proclaimed, believed, did / what king . . . instructed" (15–16) indicates a man whose duty lay first and foremost with the secular power. This is in sharp contrast with the man who, as Marbod's eulogy points out, had been sent to France by, and was thus directly answerable to, the papal administration in Rome.

Of the two persons nominated as its possible subjects, the portrait drawn in the poem finds a much better match in the person of Milo II of Bray.[168] This

hexameters, is edited by Walther Bulst, in "Studien zu Marbods *Carmina varia* und *Liber decem capitulorum*," *Nachrichten von der Akademie der Wissenschaften in Göttingen* (1939): 205–206. For brief discussions, see *Histoire littéraire de la France*, 10:20, and Manitius, *Geschichte*, 3:56 and 644. For its praise of Milo's holiness, consider lines 49–51: "Nunc capis in coelis tua praemia, serue fidelis. / Nunc super astra situs, diademate nunc redimitus, / nostros oratus audi" (Now you receive your rewards in heaven, faithful servant. / Set now above the stars, crowned now with a diadem, / hear our prayers).

168. The biographical details that follow concerning Milo II of Bray are drawn from Abbot Suger's biography of King Louis VI, *Vita Ludovici* chaps. 8, 18, 19, 20, 21, and 23. An epitaph for Milo II appears in a manuscript of Saint-Amand (Paris, Bibliothèque nationale, MS lat. 5129, fol. 103r) that is best known for its dossier of texts on the Crusades. Though the epitaph names a date in May, the month could refer not to when Milo died but instead to when he was interred at the Cluniac priory of Longpont-sur-Orge (not far east of Montlhéry), which took place most likely in the "premiers mois" of 1118 (Mirot, *La Chronique de Morigny*, 23n4; see also Cusimano, *A Translation of the Chronicle of the Abbey of Morigny*, 184n16).

Milo's engagement in the political affairs of the realm cannot be doubted, and as viscount of Troyes and, later, seneschal of Montlhéry he would certainly have been a man who, like the poem's addressee, played a part in the rendering of public justice on the estates under his control. As seneschal, holding Montlhéry at least in theory at the will of Louis VI, he would also obviously have been in a position to receive instruction from the king. Milo II's career as a king's man was, however, far from unblemished. The castle of Montlhéry had been ceded to the crown in 1104 by Milo's elder brother Guy II Trousseau (died 1109), and in 1105 Milo, claiming ancestral right, endeavored to wrest control of the castle from Philip I's seneschal Guy I, count of Rochefort (about 1055–1108). Milo's siege of Montlhéry was broken, however, and Milo himself constrained to flee in despair, by the actual arrival of forces under the command of Guy of Rochefort and the feared approach of additional troops under the command of the future Louis VI, whose fiancée had been trapped within the castle by the besiegers. In 1109 Louis, by then on the throne, bestowed the seneschalship of Montlhéry upon Milo. This was largely, however, an act of expediency, to counter attempts by the king's enemies (including Louis' half-brother Philip of Melun) to confer possession of the strategically important castle on their partisan, and Milo's cousin, Hugh of Crécy (died 1147).

Although Milo swore fealty and allegiance to the king at that time, the years 1111 to 1113 found Milo, along with Hugh of Crécy, allied with Count Thibaud IV of Blois (1093–1151) and Henry I of England (about 1068–1135) in their wars against Louis. At the conclusion of those wars Milo was humbled through the forced annulment of his marriage to Count Thibaud's sister, but he retained possession of Montlhéry and does not seem to have opposed Louis in any significant way between then and the time of his death. Indeed, the sorrow expressed by Louis at the interment of Milo II of Bray, and his subsequent vengeance on Milo's murderer, Hugh of Crécy, are both recorded in the *Chronicle of Morigny*.[169] If Milo II is in fact the subject of Poem 92, then his characterization as one who "did / what king . . . instructed" (15–16) may well represent the state of affairs at the time of his death, overlooking conveniently a string of less fortunate episodes from his earlier career.

The assassination of Milo II in October of 1116 or 1117 also agrees with the single bit of absolutely firm biographical information in Poem 92, the poet's statement that "the first day of his death and the last of his life was / the first day following the tenth of October" (49–50). Ironically, however, it is also the circumstances surrounding Milo II's death that would perhaps bring most seriously into question

169. On the circumstances of Milo's murder, and the treachery ascribed to Hugh of Crécy, see Mirot, *La Chronique de Morigny*, 22–24 and Cusimano, *Chronicle of Morigny*, 46–51. Milo, who would appear to have been in his early thirties at the time of his death, is there described as "optime indolis et strenuissimum in armis juvenem" (a young man of highest inborn quality and a most valiant warrior).

his identification as the subject of the poem. Seeing that he was murdered in the course of a power struggle with his own cousin, it is hard to imagine that a lament for the death of Milo II would not draw upon the emotional force of these events, emphasizing the untimeliness of his demise, its violent nature, or the treachery of his own kin in bringing it about. In fact, the poet placed at the literal center of his fifty-line poem the assertion that Milo "chose sooner to perish / than to forsake the sure ways of right" (25–26). Yet whereas this statement does hint at a death brought about by taking the side of right in some unnamed conflict, as the only allusion in the poem to the assassination of Milo II it would represent an example of severe understatement, in a genre where such was not necessarily either goal or commonplace. Similarly, it might be seen as somewhat curious that no direct reference is made in the poem to military prowess, if indeed the death it laments is that of a man whose career was marked, as was Milo's, by a number of significant martial episodes. Perhaps, given Milo's unfortunate choice of allegiance and pronounced lack of success in several of these conflicts, it was thought most politic to avoid mention of such subjects in the lament. There would obviously have been additional impetus for such omission were the poem originally intended to be recited at Milo's interment, where Louis VI, as we have seen above, was in attendance.

Some doubt must obviously remain as to the precise addressee of the poem. The Milo whose death is lamented may be neither the cardinal bishop nor the viscount of Troyes, but rather some as yet unidentified namesake of both. If this is the case, then the evidence of the poem might very well lead the would-be seeker to search among the ranks of chronologically eligible bishops and abbots for a Milo of sacred inclination yet bearing some secular authority, the details of whose life and death accord with those found in the poem. Yet while allowing for this possibility, it must also be admitted that no person likelier than Milo II of Bray has yet been proposed for identification as the addressee of Poem 92. His biography corresponds reasonably well with the content and likely date of the poem, and the thematic threads that appear to interweave the placement and ordering of Poems 90 through 92 in MS Lat 300 add further weight of logical probability to his candidacy. It is certainly imaginable that the poet may have had some practical or political motivation for playing down the circumstances of Milo II's assassination, or that those circumstances may have been so well known to a contemporary audience as to obviate the need for anything more than the oblique mention with which we are presented. Or perhaps in the face of a violent and unfortunate death the poet chose to focus on the celebration of a life and its achievements.

One further piece of evidence may tie Poem 92 to Milo II of Bray. Describing Milo's attempt to capture Montlhéry in 1105,[170] Abbot Suger tells how the men of Montlhéry, despite their more recent oaths of allegiance, are willing to accept

170. Waquet, 40.

Milo as their lord in recognition of his familial ties to the castle. To this observation he prefixes the following quotation from Horace: "Quo semel est imbuta recens servabit odorem / testa diu" (A jar will keep for a long time the fragrance with which it was once imbued when new).[171] Although Suger's biography of Louis VI was written twenty or more years after the death of Milo II of Bray, is it possible that his employment of this Horatian tag, introducing the most substantial appearance by Milo in the *Vita*, was influenced by a familiarity with our Poem 92, and its description of its subject as a "new vessel, and one without dregs" (35)? Or, given the ubiquity of such citations of Horace in medieval literary culture, might the attempt to see such a resonance across decades be a concession to a misty romanticism more appropriate for a poetical composer of panegyric than for a hard-nosed critic of literature? [PP]

[10r[B]] Flete senes, plorate uiri, iuuenes lacrimentur
Cum pueris, doleat sexus uterque simul.
Ille uir egregius, toto uenerabilis orbe,
Cum magno rerum pondere Milo ruit.
Milo ruit, qui forma boni, qui gloria rerum,
Qui laus iustitie, qui fauor orbis erat.
Milo ruit, cum quo longas traxere ruinas
Que per eum steterant publica iura diu.
Qui certum uiciis se restens moribus hostem
Deuicit mundum uictor et ipse sui.
Cuius facta modum, mores tenuere decorem;
Cuius sermo frequens de probitate fuit,
Cuius sacra sacrum fouit sapiancia pectus,
Assistens docili digna magistra uiro.
Lingua, mente, manu clamauit, credidit, egit
[10v[A]] Quod rex, quod ratio, quod pia iura docent.
Sparsit opes dampnatorum sibi pauper egenis,
Diues, dans quociens cui daret et quid erat.
Incola terrarum, celorum ciuis, honorem
Quem peperit probitas grande putauit onus.
Assertor ueri falsos et falsa repressit,
Firmus et ex uoto que retenenda tenens.
Non timor hunc, non spes certo de tramite torsit,
Non fauor euicit, non uiolauit amor.
Iusticiam siciens elegerat ante perire
Quam certas equi deseruisse uias.

171. Horace, *Epistles* 1.2.69–70, ed. Shackleton Bailey, 257.

Tristibus, iratis reuocauit gaudia, pacem,
Eloquio placidus consilioque potens
Et quo pene nichil ualet artius esse, negauit
Se sibi dum reliquis utilis esse cupit.
Cauit amicicias inhonestas cultor honesti;
Cauit ab immundis uiuere mundus amans.
Viuere mundus amans luxum ferit, omnia spreuit
Seque pudicicie prebuit hospicium,
Que mirata nouum uas et sine fetibus inquit,
"Ad mores certe nec facit iste modos.
Non est migrandum de sedibus his. Maneamus!
Oppositum nobis nil gerit iste locus."
Sic suscepta semel suscepit suscipientem,
Indiuisa comes et sine fine manens.
O uere felix et celo teste beatus,
Qui bona que docuit fecit et ipse prior.
[10vB] Non fuit hic aliquid nisi quedam massa bonorum,
Natus nature, nobile principium,
Quem fouit pietas, spes iuuit, pax adamauit,
Gloria nutriuit sustinuitque fides.
Mercibus his plenus nostra de ualle recessit
Ad superos, carnis uellere deposito.
Prima fuit mortis illius et ultima uite
Octobris decimam prima secunda dies.

Weep, elders! Lament, men! Let young men shed tears
along with boys, let both sexes grieve together!
That outstanding man, honored throughout the entire world,
Milo, has fallen, with his great burden of public affairs!
Milo has fallen, who was the image of goodness, the glory of public affairs,
the renown of justice, the favor of the world!
Milo has fallen, and with him the public laws (which through his agency
had stood for a long time) have collapsed into vast ruins.
Holding himself out as a sure enemy against vices through his morals,
he overcame the world, a victor even over himself.
His deeds held to moderation, his morals to seemliness;
his conversation was often of goodness;
His holy breast was nurtured by holy wisdom,
worthy mistress standing by a man ready to learn.

With tongue, with mind, with hand, he proclaimed, believed, did
what king, what reason, what righteous laws instructed.
A poor man to himself, he spread about the wealth of the condemned to those in need,
a wealthy man in giving whenever there was someone to whom and something to give.
Earthly inhabitant, heavenly citizen, the honor
that goodness produced he reckoned a great burden.
Defender of truth, he checked false men and false things,
firm and holding by desire to those things that should be held fast.
Fear did not, hope did not wrench him from the unerring path,
favor did not overcome him, passion did not harm him.
Thirsting for justice, he chose sooner to perish
than to forsake the sure ways of right.
He restored joys to the sad, peace to the wrathful,
gentle in eloquence and capable in counsel.
And, than which almost nothing can be more difficult, he denied
himself to himself as he desired to be useful to others.
A devotee of decency, he was on guard against indecent friendships;
desiring to live purely, he was on guard against impure men.
Desiring to live purely, he smote down extravagance, spurned everything,
and showed himself to be a haven for Modesty,
who, having marvelled at her new vessel, and one without dregs, said:
"Surely this man does not place limits on morals.
One must not depart from these abodes. Let us stay!
This place contains nothing antagonistic to us."
Having been once received in this way, Modesty received him who received her,
a companion inseparable and remaining without end.
O truly happy and—with heaven as witness—blessed one,
who himself was first to do the good things he taught!
This man was nothing if not, as it were, a mass of goodnesses,
born of nature, a noble beginning,
whom righteousness cherished, hope aided, peace longed for,
glory nourished, and faith sustained.
Filled with these assets, he has departed from our valley
to those dwelling in heaven, having laid aside the fleece of the flesh.
The first day of his death and the last of his life was
the first day following the tenth of October.

Textual Notes

1] *Initial missing;* l *expunged after* viri.

4] pondere: ponde *with correction* dere *added above line.*

8] publica fac diu *with* iura *written above* fac diu.

11] facta: fata.

14] magistra: magiistra, *with a supralinear* i *above the* g, *followed by an* i *on the line with a ligatured supralinear* s.

23] torsit *appears at the end of the line above* traxit. *The first syllable of* tramite *probably led the scribe to write* traxit.

28] placidus: pladus *with correction* ci *written above line.*

30] dum: ddum, *without indicated deletion of the additional* d.

33] ferit: frit.

42] fecit: feget *corrected above the line to* fecit

47] ualle *written with a smudged second letter, apparently an* a, *expunged and with a clear* a *added above the line.*

48] ad superos *written twice, with the first occurrence struck out by a stroke through the words.*

49] mortis *written supralinearly with a line to mark the place of insertion.*

50] secunda *is a correction (by the original scribe, in the right margin) for a word that begins* sed. [PP]

Commentary

1. **Flete senes**: This incipit may well reflect knowledge of Peter Riga, *Floridus aspectus* (composed about 1162), "De venditione Joseph," lines 154, 156, 158, and 160 (all of which all end with this phrase), in PL 171.1386CD. This poem was later incorporated into Peter Riga, *Aurora*, "Liber Genesis," lines 1206, 1208, 1210, 1212, and 1214. See *Aurora: Petri Rigae Biblia versificata*, ed. Paul E. Beichner, 2 vols. (Notre Dame, 1965), 1:74. The juxtaposition of **iuuen*** and **lacrim*** in dactylic poetry was established by Statius, *Thebaid* 9.36, ed. Klotz and Klinnert, 318, and Silius Italicus, *Punica* 6.545 and 13.868, ed. Delz, 158 and 358.
2. **sexus uterque**, a cliché in dactylic poetry, appears in this same metrical position in both Hildebert, *Carmina minora* 26.14, ed. Scott, 17, and Baudri, *Carmina* 99.186, ed. Tilliette, 1:110; the latter also uses it elsewhere: 97.45 and 98.64, ed. Tilliette, 1:97 and 101.
3. **uir egregius** is found occasionally in this metrical position. **toto uenerabilis orbe**: The rest of the line is almost a formula that goes back to Venantius Fortunatus, *Carmina* 8.16.3, in Leo, 198; in Reydellet, 2:158; and *Vita sancti Martini* 3.175, in Leo, 336.
5. **forma bon*** is a common pairing. Even more so is the line ending **gloria rerum**, especially in Hildebert (*Carmen in libros Regum* 1, prologue 1; *Vita*

beate Marie Egiptiace 2, ed. Larsen, 231; and *Carmina miscellanea* 7.11 and 50.1, in PL 171.1388D and 1402B).

7. The line ending **traxere ruinas** dates to Vergil, *Aeneid* 8.192, ed. Mynors, 288 ("scopuli ingentem traxere ruinam"). *Trahere ruinam* or *-s*, like the more common *dare ruinam* or *-s*, meant "to collapse" (OLD, 1666, *ruina*, 1b, 2b, and especially 3c). See Vergil, *Aeneid* 2.465–466, ed. Mynors, 141 ("ea [turris] lapsa repente ruinam / cum sonitu trahit").
8. **publica iura** is a cliché.
9. **restens**: The spelling may speak to the same influences of pronunciation as do the more frequent cases in which an *-en* in standard Latin is spelled *-an* in MS Lat 300. The line ending **moribus hostem** may be indebted or related to Baudri, *Carmina* 87.19–21, ed. Tilliette, 1:84 ("Denuo dixisti quoniam tria moribus obsint, / Quae tria, si superent, ducunt in perditionem: / Femina, census, honos, ferales moribus hostes").
10. **uictor et ipse**: Common in this metrical position, as in Baudri, *Carmina* 94.24, ed. Tilliette, 1:93.
    probitate: An exceedingly difficult word to translate since its meanings cover a range from "moral worth" to "prowess."
13. **sapiancia** = *sapientia*.
15. **Lingua, mente, manu**: A line opening attested from Alcuin, *Carmina* 88.2.6 (a pentameter), ed. Dümmler, 1:309, and Rabanus Maurus, *Carmina* 9.11 (a hexameter), ed. Dümmler, 2:171.
16. **pia iura**: Stock in this metrical position.
22. **retenenda** = *retinenda*.
23. **certo de tramite**: In this metrical position in Horace, *Satires* 2.3.49, ed. Shackleton Bailey, 218.
25. **iustitia* siti*** occur now and then in conjunction, most notably as a line ending in Hildebert, *De operibus sex dierum* 3.4. Ultimately the image of the "thirst for justice" derives from the Beatitudes (Mt 5:6 "Beati, qui esuriunt et sitiunt iustitiam").
26. **deseruisse uias**: Compare the line ending of Prosper of Aquitaine, *Epigrammatum ex sententiis s. Augustini liber unus* 97.10, in PL 51.528C ("deseruisse viam").
28. **consilioque potens**: A line opening already in *Ilias Latina* 177.

32–33. **mundus amans**: Ever so slight a wrinkle on the cliché *mundus amat*.

33. **omnia spreuit**: A line ending in *Waltharius* 853, ed. Strecker, 59, and Hildebert or pseudo-Hildebert, *Inventio sanctae crucis* 143, in PL 171.1317D.
35. **fetibus** = *fecibus*. In this sort of instance it can be impossible to ascertain whether the manuscript presents a variant spelling or a copyist's slip.
38. **iste locus**: A stock pentameter ending from Ovid, *Heroides* 16.192, ed. Kenney, 37.
41. **sine fine mane***: Cliché.
42. **ipse prior**: Cliché.

43. **quedam**: Translated here "as it were": see *OLD* 1551, *quidam*[1] 3b.
massa bonorum: In this challenging phrase the first noun could refer to a lump of raw material, which would accord well with the nearby characterization of Milo as a "beginning."
44. **nobile principium**: Compare William of Conches, *Glosae super Boetium,* In Consolationem III metrum 6, ed. Nauta, 137 ("omnium est nobile principium, sed mali degenerant ab eo per vitium, et ita sunt ignobiles"). [JL]

POEM 93. Incipit "Flos, decus, exemplum iuuenum, patrie, probitatis." Three elegiac distichs. Not in Walther. Not in *In principio*.

[10v^{B}] *F*los, decus, exemplum iuuenum, patrie, probitatis,
Occidit heu multis Frodo ruina bonis.
Alter Aristotiles, Paris alter, et alter Homerus
Ingenio, forma, carmine Frodo fuit.
Martis prima dies, Egipto teste, nefanda
Frodonis uitam clausit aitque uale.

Flower of youths, grace of the fatherland, model of goodness,
Frodo has perished, alas! a disaster for many good men.
Frodo was in talent another Aristotle, in appearance another Paris,
in poetry another Homer.
The first day of March, unspeakable (as Egypt can attest),
concluded Frodo's life and said "Farewell."

Textual Note

1] *Initial missing.*

Commentary

1. **Flos, decus**: A cliché for opening hexameters. **Flos . . . iuuenum**: In an epitaph by Baudri for a canon of Tours named Alexander, the deceased is characterized as being the "flos iuuenum" (*Carmina* 41.4, ed. Tilliette 1:53). **exemplum iuuenum**: In the same metrical position there appears in pseudo-Ovid, *Consolatio ad Liuiam* 13, ed. Amat, 60: "Occidit exemplum iuuenis uenerabile morum" (especially interesting since the line contains the verb *occidit*, with which line 2 in Poem 93 begins).
2. **Frodo**: Baudri left three eulogies in distichs (*Carmina* 28–30, ed. Tilliette, 1:46–48) for a scholar named Frodo who left Anjou to seek his fortune in England, where he died or at least was buried (*Carmina* 29.2, ed. Tilliette, 1:47). **Occidit, heu**: Found in a few poems as a line opening, with the first being Ennodius, *Carmina* 2.1.9, ed. Vogel, 46.

3. **Alter Aristotiles**: Baudri also refers to Frodo as an "Aristotle." **Paris alter**: In Vergil, *Aeneid* 7.321 (line ending), ed. Mynors, 266, and Baudri, *Carmina* 10.18, ed. Tilliette, 1:35. **et alter Homerus**: Line ending in Horace, *Epistles* 2.1.50, ed. Shackleton Bailey, 293. "Alter Homerus" is also a line ending in Baudri, *Carmina* 201.31, ed. Tilliette, 2:131, and a line opening in an anonymous poem (with the incipit "Viribus, arte, minis, Danaum clara Troia ruinis") that was printed erroneously as a continuation of Simon Aurea Capra, *Ylias* 235, the composite poem being entitled *Versus de excidio Troiae*, in PL 171.1452C. For the origin of the error, see Parrott (1975), 70; for a discussion of the relationship between the anonymous poem and Simon's, see 67–71. The preferred edition of "Viribus, arte, minis" is in *Poésies populaires latines antérieures au douzième siècle*, edited by Edélestand du Méril (Paris, 1843; reprint, Bologna, 1969), 400–405. The poem, attested in more than a dozen manuscripts, has been attributed to Peter of Saintes (who flourished about 1145), among others: see Faral, "Le manuscrit 511 du 'Hunterian Museum' de Glasgow," 47.
4. **Ingenio, forma**: Compare the line opening "Ingenio formae" in pseudo-Ovid, *Heroides* 15.32 (Epistula Sapphus ad Phaonem), ed. Knox, 79.
5. **Martis prima dies, Egipto teste, nefanda**: This verse assumes an unusually close familiarity with a poem, probably from the eight or ninth century, that has the incipit "Bis deni binique dies scribuntur in anno." See *Anthologia Latina*, no. 680a (previously no. 736), ed. Buecheler and Riese, 156–157. Interestingly, the same tradition recorded there is also handled in Zurich, Zentralbibliothek, MS C 58, fol. 7, in Werner, *Beiträge*, 34–35, no. 79. The first two lines of the eighth- or ninth-century poem refer to twenty days of the year in which one hour is to be feared by mortals. Lines 5–6 explain the association with Egypt: "Si tenebrae Aegyptus Graeco sermone uocantur, / Inde dies mortis tenebrosos iure uocamus." Last but not least, line 9 of the poem begins "Martis prima necat, cuius sub cuspide quarta est."

   The poem gives voice to a belief held for more than a millennium in the unluckiness of certain days at certain hours. These days were sometimes marked in calendars as "dies Aegyptiaci" (Egyptian days), so-called because the Egyptians were associated with expertise in the calendar and astrology. See Bonnie Blackburn and Leofranc Holford-Strevens, *The Oxford Companion to the Year* (Oxford, 1999), 590–591.

POEM 94. "*R*eddere sufficerent plures, Iuliane, beatos." Three elegiac distichs. Not in Walther. Not in *In principio*.

[10v[B]] *R*eddere sufficerent plures, Iuliane, beatos
  Que simul intulerant se satis ampla tibi;
Sed quam fragili pendebant omnia filo!

Ecce iacent casus pondera lapsa tui.
Nunc te suscipiat uernans et amena uoluntas
Et foueant animam pax requiesque tuam.

Julian, the things that once presented themselves to you in much abundance
would have been enough to make many people happy;
but how frail was the thread on which everything was hanging!
Look now, the weights of your fall lie collapsed.
Now may a delightful and flourishing goodwill bear you up,
and may peace and repose cherish your soul.

Textual Note

1] *Initial missing.*

Commentary

1. The Julian in the first line is a puzzle. The notion that the poet could be alluding to a place such as Saint-Julien, the Benedictine abbey in Tours, is ruled out by the closing mention of a soul. Who could be meant? In this instance the Loire Valley poets, who sometimes afford clues about personages named in poems in MS Lat 300, offer no help. The poetry of Baudri makes no reference to any Julian. Whereas Hildebert names Julian several times, but always Julian the Apostate, and Rodulfus Tortarius mentions only the saint named Julian, Poem 94 seems to refer to a contemporary.
2. **satis ampl***: A stock phrase in hexameter poetry.
3. **fragili**: Normally the first two syllables of the adjective are short, but here all three must be scanned long. If this violation of prosody signals a textual corruption rather than authorial incompetence, what remedies are possible? Although *filum* is often found modified by the adjective *tenuis*, replacing *fragili* with *tenui* does not improve the meter here. The word that could replace *fragili* to save the scansion would be *subtili*, used in conjunction with *filo* since Lucretius, *De rerum natura* 4.88, ed. Bailey ("Quae vulgo volitant subtili praedita filo"). The phrase "subtili filo" appears in the same metrical position as here in Fulk of Beauvais, *De nuptiis Christi et ecclesiae* 5.340, ed. Rousseau, *Fulcoii Beluacensis Utriusque De nuptiis Christi et ecclesiae libri septem*, 100 (also numbered 182).
4. The image seems to be of the weights on a balance-scale, which has tipped so that Julian's situation is no longer in the balance but has fallen. Compare Poem 91.22.
6. **pax requiesque**: This wording appears twice in this metrical position in Ermoldus Nigellus, *Carmen in honorem Hludowici* 1.154 and 3.498, in *Poetae Latini aevi Carolini* 2:9 and 55; and *Ermold le Noir*, 18 and 132, as lines 189 and 1751.

POEM 95. Incipit "*M*auricius locuples ui*uan*di lege peracta." Two elegiac distichs. Not in Walther. Not in *In principio*.

[10v[B]] *M*auricius locuples ui*uan*di lege peracta
Mortuus est, sed non hec sua culpa fuit:
Si licuisset ei precio corrumpere fata,
Nequaquam uiuos deseruisset adhuc.

Rich Maurice died when the law of life was finished,
but through no fault of his own:
if he had been allowed to tamper with fate by bribery,
he would by no means yet have left the living.

Textual Notes

1. *Initial missing*. ui*uan*di: uuiadi.

Commentary

1. These two elegiac distichs are an epigram or epitaph for a dead man named Maurice. The orthography *uiuandi* for *uiuendi* is typical of this manuscript.
2. **Mortuus est**: A line opening frequent from Paulinus of Nola, *Carmina* 31.554, ed. Hartel, 327.
culpa fuit: A common cliché in dactylic poetry. Two interesting incidences are in an epitaph by Marbod, *Carmina* 2.19.3–4, in PL 171.1721A ("Se tibi culpa fuit, quod nullum laedere velles, / Quale tuum meritum cum bona culpa fuit").
3. **corrumpere fata**: This pairing rings a slight change on the ending "rumpere fata," stock since Lucan, *De bello ciuili* 2.107, ed. Shackleton Bailey, 28. [PP and JZ]

Group Six: Prophecy of the Tiburtine Sibyl

MS Lat 300 presents its readers one final surprise by ending with a text unexpected in a poetic anthology. The only prose piece in the collection, on fol. 11r–v, is a version of one of the all-time "best-sellers" of the Latin Middle Ages—the prophecy of the Tiburtine Sibyl (*Sibylla Tiburtina*). The Greeks had identified nine of these prophetesses: the Persian, Libyan, Delphic, Cimmerian, Eythraean, Samian, Cumaean, Hellespontine, and Phrygian. To these the Romans added a tenth, the Tiburtine Sibyl. As with the rest, she is named after her location, in this case the Etruscan town of Tibur (known today as Tivoli). A recent survey found 112 extant manuscripts of the Latin text of the prophecy, dating from the eleventh to the sixteenth centuries.[172]

Although the exact wording of the Tiburtina, as the text is customarily designated, varies greatly from one version to the next, the contents are more or less stable. The Tiburtina begins with a presentation of the background and character of the Sibyl and proceeds to describe her encounter with a group of Roman senators, who ask her to interpret their shared dream-vision of nine suns appearing. The Sibyl's prophecy, whose wording often echoes that of the apocalyptic discourse in the synoptic Gospels (Matthew 24, Mark 13, Luke 21), describes each of the nine successive "generations" of humanity that correspond to these suns. The fourth generation includes a retelling of the life of Christ that is often referred to as the "Sibylline Gospel," and the later generations contain a species of political prophecy known as "prophecy after the fact" (*uaticinium ex euentu*). In this case the prophecy after the fact focuses on rulers from various periods of history, who are for the most part identified by their initials, including Roman emperors, Charlemagne, and Lombard, Ottonian, and sometimes French rulers, depending on when and where a particular version of the Tiburtina was written. The text concludes with an apocalyptic vision of the last emperor, the advent and defeat of Antichrist, and the triumph of Christ and the saints.

With almost none of the Sibylline Gospel and very little historical prophecy, the version in MS Lat 300 is shorter than most of the others. It mentions only a few rulers and no contemporary ones. The redactor of this version was clearly more interested in the vision of the end of the world than in remarking on the contemporary political scene, but even the apocalypse is somewhat abbreviated. The abridgment is so severe in some passages that the text becomes cryptic. For example,

172. Anke Holdenried, *The Sibyl and her Scribes: Manuscripts and Interpretation of the Latin Sibylla Tiburtina c. 1050–1250* (Aldershot, Hants., England, 2006), 173; "Conspectus of Extant Manuscripts," 177–197. MS Lat 300 is not included.

in the Gospel section, the appearance of the priests of the Hebrews is sudden and unexplained. A few lines later is the "inicium quale non fuit ab inicio mundi" (a beginning such as there has not been from the beginning of the world), which is nonsense until compared with fuller versions of the text, which have "initium dolorum quale non fuit" (a beginning of suffering, such as there has not been).

The text that circulated as the prophecy of the Tiburtine Sibyl developed in stages over a long period of time. A Greek version appeared in the fourth century, and the first version of the Latin from which the text in MS Lat 300 descends was probably written around 1000.[173] Many variants of the text are extant, and it is a major scholarly task to separate the strands from one another to determine what was written when and by whom. A text that originated about 1030, edited by Ernst Sackur in the late nineteenth century, is now held to be the second of at least four Medieval Latin versions.[174] A variant of this version from about 1190 is known as the "Bedan recension" because it was printed in *Patrologia Latina* 90 with works of Bede, although Migne ascribed the Tiburtina to "auctor incertus" (an unknown author).[175] Bernard McGinn published an edition of the fourth version, which dates from about 1100, based on Chicago, Newberry Library, MS f.6 (early twelfth century).[176] McGinn's edition is the one that has most in common with the text in MS Lat 300. Among the known manuscripts of the Tiburtina, Wrocław, Biblioteka Uniwersytecka, MS R. 436 (s. XI–XII?), fols. 143–146v, in particular has many verbal and structural similarities to the Houghton text, although it contains the usual elaborations of political prophecy, and so is about three times as long.[177]

Why was the Tiburtina included on the last folio here? Recalling that the

---

173. For a fuller account, see Bernard McGinn, "*Teste David cum Sibylla*: The Significance of the Sibylline Tradition in the Middle Ages," in *Women of the Medieval World: Essays in Honor of John H. Mundy*, ed. Julius Kirshner and Suzanne F. Wemple (Oxford, 1985), 7–35. An edition and translation of the Greek Tiburtina can be found in Paul J. Alexander, *The Oracle of Baalbek: The Tiburtine Sibyl in Greek Dress* (Washington, D.C., 1967), 9–22.

174. Ernst Sackur, *Sibyllinische Texte und Forschungen* (Halle an der Saale, 1898; repr., Turin, 1963), 177–187. On the relationship of this text to others, see "The Bedan Recension of the *Sibylla Tiburtina*: New Manuscript Evidence and its Implications," in *Latin Culture in the Eleventh Century*, ed. Michael W. Herren, Christopher J. McDonough, and Ross G. Arthur (Turnhout, 2002), 410–443, at 412.

175. The Bedan recension, PL 90.1181–1186, also appears in Godfrey of Viterbo, *Pantheon*, ed. Pertz, 145–147. All dates derive from Holdenreid's very useful stemma, "Bedan Recension," 440–441.

176. Bernard McGinn, "Oracular Transformations: The 'Sibylla Tiburtina' in the Middle Ages (With Particular Reference to the Newberry Library Version)," in *Sibille e linguaggi oracolari: mito storia tradizione: Atti del convegno Macerata-Norcia, settembre 1994*, ed. Ileana Chirassi Colombo and Tullio Seppilli (Pisa, 1998), 636–644.

177. Anke Holdenried deserves thanks for having drawn attention to this manuscript in an e-mail of December 19, 2005. Although the Wrocław MS reveals many similarities to MS Lat 300, enough small differences remain (in the form of words added, different orthographical quirks, and small changes in word order) to make unlikely a direct dependency of either on the other.

poems were arranged so that some thematic relationship links each one to another near it, we might try to find some similar connection between the Tiburtina and the occasional poems that precede it. The historical flavor of Poems 90 through 95 contains a piquant note of *memento mori* beginning with the formulaic lines near the close of Poem 90, "though he must be gathered to his fathers according to the law of time, / his fame for his accomplishments will be everlasting." The lament for Milo in Poem 92 situates panegyric in the context of death, and the short epitaphs that follow bring the first of the four last things—death, judgment, heaven, and hell—into ever sharper focus. The climactic passage of the Tiburtina, its breathless catalogue of the events that will end the world, occurs here as a natural consequence of musing about death.

The arrangement of the entire manuscript also reveals a development of perspective that culminates in apocalyptic vision. From the solipsistic concerns about sickness and love, the poets' vision has become ever broader, encompassing the scriptural knowledge and book learning that are embodied in the biblical epigrams; contemporary politics and history; death, which is of course universal; and, finally, in the Tiburtina, the end of the world, which too is universal for the living, the dead, and for Christ and Antichrist as well. Rulers, their triumphs and failures, and the sufferings they impose on the population, will come and go through successive generations, but in the end, Christ will triumph with the saints and rule forever. As the scribe concludes the anthology with this blissful image of the inevitable end of history, it is no wonder he feels compelled to end his text with the word "Amen" writ large. [BKB]

fol. 11r

*D*ecem Sibille fuerunt que a doctis auctoribus celebrantur. Sibille uero grece, prophet*e* Latine, Hebraice / uates dicuntur. Haec autem erat nobili prole orta: filia Manasse quarta etate Dauid fuisse narratur. Grece cognomen / eius Tiburtina, Latine Haburnea. Ipsa per angelum nunciata nacitura in uirginitate permansit; procedente / uero tempore cum circuisset Asiam, Macedoniam, Postatiam, Agatuldeam, Ciliciam, Pontum, Phamphiliam, Galaciam, peruenit / Egiptum, Ethiopiam, Bagadam, Babiloniam, Africam, et prophetauit, dicens: a malis malum, a [5] bonis bonum.

Quo audito principes Romanorum nunciauerunt regi suo. Ecce deprecati sunt ut eam manda- / ret; et fecit sic. Que cum uenisset Romam, omnes Romani intanderunt in eam. Pulcritudinem eius admirabantur. / Capilli eius sicut aurum fulgebant, cilia eius super oculos nigra, caro eius et gula sicut lac candida. / Tunc dixerunt: O magistra et domina, quam decorosum est corpus tuum! Volumus te interrogare super som- / nium nostrum; audiuimus enim famam nominis tui et sapienciam tuam. Que respondens inquit: exeamus de loco isto stercoris, et ascendamus in montem Auantinum, et ibi reuelabo somnium uestrum. *Huc* / cum uenissent, ait: Nunc uos centum seniores somnium uestrum dicite. Qui dixerunt: Vidimus vii so- / les splandentes super omn*e*m terram. Primus erat fulgens nimis et magnus. Secundus splendidior et / clarior. Tercius sanguineus igneus et terribilis ac splendens multum. Quartus totus sanguineus. Quintus / tenebrosus ferens quasi tonitrua. Sextus tenebrosus nimis, habens aculeos acutos quasi scor- piones. Septimus terribilis sanguineum habens colorem. Octauus fulgens et sanguineus totus. / Nonus nimis tenebrosus unum radium tamen lucidum habens.

Tunc regina: Nouem inquit soles / ix generationes sunt. Primus namque sol prima generatio est, in qua erunt simplices homines clari, amantes / libertatem ueram, mansueti, benigni, amantes consolationem pauperum, sapientes. Secundus sol secunda / generatione est in qua erunt homines crescentes splandide, iuuentutes deum colentes, sine malicia conuersantes in terra. Tertius sol tertia generatio est cum exsurget gens contra gentem. Quartus sol quarta generatione est in qua uirgo ab horiente ueniens / concipiet filium nomine Ihesum. Tunc exsurget Cesar Augustus et subiciet sibi omnem terram; et postea / conuenient omnes sacerdotes Hebreorum. Et erit ciuitas magna et habitabunt in ipsa populi mul- / ti, .l. et due lingue. Post haec exsurget rex de propria tribu uota uouens et faciens holocausta: ecce / continuo occidetur. Postea uero exsurgent alii reges quorum unus ab inimicis igni comburetur. Postea exsurget rex per .C. ha- bens nomen. Hic erit fortis in prelio, iudicans iuste, et destruet templa idolorum. In diebus illis erunt templa sancta in nomine Domini / et edificabuntur ecclesie in honore apostolorum et martirum. In octaua autem generatione exsurget Salicus de Frantia per / .K. nomen habens et ipse erit pius, magnus, nobilissimus atque potentissimus, misericors, faciens ius- / titiam pauperibus. Postea ueniet alius rex qui inuadet Romam et captiuabit eam. Post haec *alius* de genere Longobardorum / regnabit usque ad annum centum. Tunc erit inicium quale non fuit ab inicio mundi. Erunt mul- te tribulationes, sanguinis effusio, terre motus per regiones, multe ciuitates captiuabuntur / et non erit qui resistat, quia Dominus erit iratus in populum. Erunt autem rapaces cupidi tiranni /

fol. 11v

odientes pauperes. Post haec exsurget rex Romanorum habens aspectum decorum / et splandidum nimis, statum grandem, membra candida, oculos sicut / stellam matucinam; et regnabit annis decem. Tunc erunt diuicie / et habundentia per huniuersum orbem. Disperdet templa idolorum; omnes / ad baptismum conuertet. Ecce omnes ciuitates altaribus et crucibus [5] honorabuntur. Post haec exsurget princeps de tribu Dan, filius per- / ditionis qui omnia subuertet. Tunc exsurget princeps ab septentrione cum ex- / ercitu inumerabili qua Alexander inclusit Gog et Magog. Cum hoc / uiderit rex Romanorum, uadet ad domum Domini in ipsum montem / Caluarie, et tollet coronam de capite suo et tradet regnum [10] Christianorum Deo. Et assumetur crux sancta in celum cum corona regis. / Et cum uenerit Dominus iudicare seculum per ignem apparebit / signum filii hominis in celo, id est crux sancta. tunc Elias / et Enoch preliabuntur cum Antichristo et percucientur ab eo. Et ueniet / Dominus et interficiet filium perdicionis spiritu oris sui et iudicabit [15] seculum per ignem. Hic est finis seculi et dies iudicii: beati qui / parati sunt in illa hora. Eritque regnum sanctorum in eternum / et cum Christo regnabunt in eternum. Amen. [18]

There were ten Sibyls, who are made famous by learned authors. They are called Sibyls in Greek, prophets in Latin, vates in Hebrew. This Sibyl came from a noble family: she is said to have been the daughter of Manasses during the fourth age, the age of David. In Greek she is called Tiburtina; in Latin, Haburnea. Her birth was announced by an angel, and she lived as a virgin. With the passage of time, after she had made the circuit of Asia, Macedonia, Postatia, Agatuldea, Cilicia, Pontus, Pamphilia, and Galacia, she traversed Egypt, Ethiopia, Baghdad, Babylonia, and Africa, and prophesied, saying: "Evil comes from evil men, and [5] good from good."

The Roman nobility, when they heard this, announced it to their king. Lo and behold, they beseeched him to summon her; and he did so. When she came to Rome, all of the Romans gazed at her. They wondered at her beauty. Her hair glistened like gold, her brows were black above her eyes, her flesh and throat were milk-white. Then they said, "O mistress and lady, how comely is your appearance! We wish to question you about our dream, for we have heard the report of your name and your wisdom." In answer, she said, "Let us depart [10] from this place of dung, and go up to the Aventine Hill, and there I will explain your dream." When they arrived there, she said, "Now, you hundred elders, tell me your dream." They said, "We saw seven suns shining over all the earth. The first was very bright, and large. The second, more brilliant and clearer. The third, bloody, fiery, and very brilliant. The fourth, entirely bloody. The fifth, dark, as if containing thunder. The sixth, very dark, with sharp points like scorpions. The seventh, with a terrible bloody color. The eighth, all brilliant and bloody. The ninth, very dark but with one bright ray."

Then the queen replied, "The nine suns are nine generations. The first sun is the first generation, in which there will be simple, honorable men, loving true liberty, gentle, kind, loving the consolation of the poor, and wise. The second sun is the second generation, in which there will be men growing brilliantly, youth worshipping God, living without malice in the earth. The third sun is the third generation, when nation will rise against nation. The fourth sun is the fourth generation, in which a virgin coming from the East will conceive a son named Jesus. Then Caesar Augustus will arise and will subject all the earth; and afterward all the priests of the Hebrews will convene. And there will be a great city, and many people will live in it, and fifty-two languages. After this will arise a king from his own tribe, vowing vows and making burnt offerings. Lo and behold, he will be killed immediately. Afterward other kings will arise, one of whom his enemies will kill by fire. Afterward a king will arise having a name beginning with C. He will be strong in battle, judging justly, and he will destroy the temples of idols. In those days there will be holy temples in the name of the Lord, and churches will be constructed in honor of the apostles and martyrs. In the eighth generation, then, a Salian from Francia will arise having a name beginning with K, and he will be pious, great, most noble, powerful, and merciful, dealing justice to the poor. Afterward will come another king who will invade Rome and capture it. After this, another from the race of the Lombards will rule for a hundred years.

Then there will be a beginning such as there has not been since the beginning of the world. There will be much suffering, shedding of blood, earthquakes in different regions. Many cities will be captured, and there will be none to resist, since the Lord will be angered against the people. There will be plunderers, grasping men, tyrants,

fol. 11v

and those who hate the poor. After this will arise the king of the Romans with a beautiful and brilliant appearance, tall in stature, with shining limbs and eyes like the morning star; and he will reign for ten years. Then there will be wealth and abundance throughout all the earth. He will destroy the temples of the idols; he will convert everyone to baptism. Behold, all cities will be adorned with altars and crucifixes. After this will arise a prince from the tribe of Dan, a son of destruction, who will overturn everything. Then a prince from the *north will arise with an army beyond number where Alexander has enclosed Gog and Magog. And when the king of the Romans sees this, he will go to the house of the Lord on Mount Calvary itself, and he will take the crown from his head, and he will hand over the kingdom [10] of the Christians to God. And the holy cross will be taken up to heaven with the crown of the king. And when the Lord comes to judge the world in fire, a sign of the son of man will appear in the sky, that is, the holy cross; then Elijah and Enoch will battle with Antichrist, and will be beaten by him. And the Lord will come, and will kill the son of destruction with the breath of his mouth, and will judge [15] the world in fire. This is the end of the world and the day of judgment. Happy are they who have prepared for this hour. And there will be a kingdom of saints unto eternity; and they will reign with Christ unto eternity. Amen." [18]*

Textual Notes

fol. 11r

1] *Initial* D *missing.* propheta (*as if from a neuter* *prophetum) *emended to* prophete.
4] agaltuldeam *first* l *expunged.*
10] nostrum *m blotted and corrected above line*; audimus *supralinear correction to* audiuimus; sapiaciae, a *and* ae *expunged and corrected to* en *and* em *above line;* inquit *supplied above line*; exemus *added* a *above line.*
13] omnem: omnium *H*, omnem *Sackur, McGinn.*
18] gnentones *second* n *expunged,* re *supplied above.*
29] post haec *alius* de genere: post haec de genere *H.*

fol. 11v

Possibly different scribe: larger ductus, long i, *and two-stroke* s.

1] ex . . . . rex r . . . . orum *text abraded and smudged. McGinn*: unde erit rex Romanorum; *Sackur*: rex grecorum.
6] prinpceps *second* p *expunged.*
8] quia *later corrected to* qua.
11] *Huc*: *Apparently* Huc *became* Uc, *which in turn became* Ut (*the manuscript reading*).
17] sanctorum et in: et *expunged.*

Commentary

fol. 11r

1–2. **prophete latine, hebraice uates**: The etymologies here combine information from Isidore of Seville and Rabanus Maurus: Isidore, *Etymologiae* 7.8.1, ed. Lindsay ("Quos gentilitas vates appellant, hos nostri prophetas vocant, quasi praefatores"), and Rabanus Maurus, *De uniuerso* 15.3, in PL 111.420B ("Sibyllae generaliter dicuntur omnes feminae vates lingua graeca . . . Decem autem Sibyllae a doctissimis auctoribus fuisse traduntur"). The curious assignment of *uates* to Hebrew and *propheta* to Latin stems from the author's understanding of Isidore's *gentilitas* not as "pagans" but as "Jews," speakers of Hebrew, in contrast to "our" people, who, in the mind of the author, must be Christian Latin-speakers. This etymological invention does not appear in other editions of the Tiburtina.

2. **filia Manasse**: In Sackur and PL 90 the Sibyl is the daughter of Priam and Hecuba. The Newberry MS names Manasses and Papilia as her parents. Manasses was the eldest son of Joseph and Aseneth (Genesis 41:50–51; 46:20). **quarta etate Dauid**: That is to say, during the fourth of the six ages of the world. According to a scheme outlined by Augustine, the fourth age runs from King David to the Babylonian Captivity: see *De catechizandis rudibus* 22.39, ed. I. B. Bauer, 163–164. Bede, *De temporibus* 20, ed. Jones, 605, lines 19–20, informs us that Manasses ruled for 55 years during the fourth age.

   The Newberry text begins with a summary of the ages of the world, placing the Sibyl in the age of David: see McGinn, "Oracular Transformations," 616 and 636.

3–4. Most of the places are listed occur in the same order in the printed editions. "Postatiam" appears elsewhere as Erostachiam, Erastochiam, Heresteciam (Sackur variants, PL 90) and Perhostiam (McGinn). Agatuldeam is seen as Agaguldeam (Sackur, McGinn), Agagalleam, Agagusdeam (Sackur, PL 90), and Agagul (Sackur). Pontus is an addition not printed elsewhere.

   The second part of the list in MS Lat 300, from Egypt onward, contains only the first five of the nine or more place names that appear elsewhere. The list has some similarities with the nationalities enumerated in Acts 2:9–11. Just as the Galilean disciples of Jesus, "filled with the Holy Spirit," miraculously speak so that people of various nations and languages can understand what they say, the divinely inspired Sibyl also communicates with people in a number of different nations.

3. **tiburtina, haburnea**: Here, as though they are alternative names. Lactantius transmits Varro's list of ten Sibyls, in which Albunea is the name of the Tiburtine Sibyl: see *Divinae institutiones* 1.6.12, ed. Brandt and von Laubmann, 1:22, lines 15–16. **Ipsa per angelum . . . in uirginitate permansit**: These details, present in the Newberry version, are here greatly condensed: compare McGinn, "Oracular Transformations," 637.

6–7. The beauty of the Sibyl is proverbial, but the features that are singled out for comment here—golden hair, dark brows, white skin—differ from those elsewhere. In Sackur, the Sibyl's appearance is recounted after the narrator tells the dream of the senators, and she is "venusto vultu, aspectu decoro, eloquens in verbis atque omnis pulcritudine satis composita" (with a charming countenance and comely appearance, articulate in words and altogether well put together in beauty); the Bedan recension is similar. The Newberry text has an extensive description of the Sibyl's appearance in the sentence before her parentage is given: "erat autem vultus eius multum splendidus, capilli eius sicut purpura, oculi eius sicut stella matutina fulgentes, corpus eius gracile, statura eius equalis, caro eius et gula candida sicut lac" (furthermore, her countenance was very brilliant, her hair like purple cloth, her eyes flashing like the morning star, her body slim, her height average, her skin and throat bright white like milk).

The detail about the Sibyl's eyebrows, which is peculiar to the Houghton version, conforms to a well-established ideal of attractiveness in the twelfth century, according to which a blond person would have dark brows. Alice M. Colby, *The Portrait in Twelfth-Century French Literature* (Geneva, 1965), 68–69, summarizes the components of male and female beauty, which include blond hair, white skin, sparkling eyes, and dark brows. She lists seven instances of fine dark eyebrows on blond heroes or heroines, noting that when the color of eyebrows is mentioned at all, it is brown or black (p. 38).

9. **O magistra**: The dialogue between the senators and the Sibyl occurs in different places in different versions of the text. In MS Lat 300, as in the Newberry version, the senators narrate their dream directly, whereas in Sackur and the Bedan recension, the narrator relates it in the third person, before the dialogue begins. In this, the Houghton/Newberry version agrees with the Greek text: see McGinn, "Oracular Transformations," 618.

12. **vii**: This first mention of the vision of multiple suns has seven; hereafter, there are nine, the usual number. Sackur notes that a Syrian version of the Sibyl's interpretation of the hundred Romans' vision of multiple suns has seven.[178] Whoever originated this variant might have been thinking of the seven planets, or the seven stars of the Pleiades; or perhaps he was simply not very skilled with Roman numerals (see note on line 24, below.)

21–22. The section that refers to Christ, sometimes called the Sibylline Gospel, is only a shadow of its usual length. Apparently it is also unusual in that the virgin and her son come from the East ("ab horiente") and not from the South: see McGinn, "Oracular Transformations," 618–619 and 639. (In Sackur, no geography is mentioned—only "de stirpe Ebreorum.")

24. **.l. et due**: Fifty-two rather than the traditional seventy-two languages of the world. Hans Sauer notes that in texts that mention the number of world languages, sixty-two is an occasional variant in England.[179] But here scribal error appears to be at work, not least because of the odd way of writing the number: why not express the entire number in Roman numerals? Instead, we have an odd combination of a numeral, a Tironian "et" that may well have taken the place of the missing "xx," and "due" written out in full. At the same time, it is conceivable that the redactor of this text made the change from

178. Sackur, *Sibyllinische Texte und Forschungen*, 143, no. 453. The transmission to Syria must have occurred during Roman imperial rule, which Sackur takes as convincing evidence that the Sibylla Tiburtina has its basis in an ancient sibylline text. Why seven in Syria? Sackur (p. 144) associates them with the seven Babylonian planetary gods.

179. Hans Sauer, "Die 72 Völker und Sprachen der Welt: Einige Ergänzungen," *Anglia: Zeitschrift für englische Philologie* 107 (1989): 61–64, no. 884.

seventy-two (or sixty-two) deliberately, since fifty-two, being the number of weeks in a year, had its own special significance.

25. **unus . . . ab inimicis igni comburetur**: The unfortunate Roman emperor Valens, supposedly burned to death in a peasant's hut in 378: see Alexander, *Oracle of Baalbek*, 33n98. **rex per .C. habens nomen:** Constantine. The Tiburtina regularly refers to rulers as kings, whether or not they used that title.

27. **salicus de Frantia per .K. nomen habens**: Charlemagne, that is, Karolus Magnus. The old scholarly distinction between Salian and Ripuarian Franks has been shown to be invalid: the Merovingian *Lex salica* is simply "civil law," and the substantive *salicus*, which developed from the adjective, designates someone who is subject to this code rather than to Roman law.[180] In the twelfth century, Otto of Freising asserted that the word referred to "nobilissime Francorum," the most noble among the Franks.[181] Hereafter, the association of the word with a subset of the Franks took hold. Our author may or may not be using the word in Otto's sense; in any case, he is not distinguishing between two Frankish groups, but between the Roman king in the preceding generation and the Frankish king named here.

29–30. **de genere Longobardorum regnabit**: The reading in the manuscript provides no subject for the verb. To specify the subject of *regnabit* and make the sentence less cryptic, options for words that could be supplied include *rex*, *unus*, *quidam*, and what has been conjectured here: *alius*. Compare Sackur, 184, ("de ipso B procedunt XII B et erit genere Langobardus et regnabit usque ad annos centum"). **inicium**: Compare Sackur, 184 ("inicium dolorum").

fol. 11v

4. **habundantia, huniuersum**: Generous use of *h*. See also **horiente**, fol. 11r, line 21.

12. **cum uenerit dominus iudicare seculum per ignem** recalls the responsory from the burial service ("Libera me"), whose second versicle concludes "dum ueneris iudicare saeculum per ignem."

18. The final line is written in large irregular uncial, and "**Amen**" extends beyond the writing frame to the right edge of the page. Several lines, not part of the Sibylline text, have been effaced below this. [BKB]

180. See Matthias Springer, "Gab es ein Volk der Salier?" in *Nomen et gens: Zur historischen Aussagekraft frühmittelalterlicher Personennamen*, ed. Dieter Geuenich, Wolfgang Haubrichs, and Jörg Jarnut (Berlin, 1997), 58–83.

181. Otto of Freising, *Chronica* 4.32, ed. Hofmeister, 224.

Appendix: Cento of Moral Aphorisms

Although the main texts in MS Lat 300 were written in France in the second half, probably in the final third, of the twelfth century, the manuscript contains a few additions that were made later in the twelfth and thirteenth centuries. Added in the bottom margin on fol. 8r, running across the breadth of the folio side, is a short cento of moralizing observations in prose. The hand belongs to the second half of the thirteenth century and reveals features similar to English hands of that period. The text presented is a pastiche of quotations or paraphrases that relate to the Bible, Seneca the Younger, and Gregory the Great's *Moralia in Job*. The contents relate loosely to *De paupere ingrato* (Poem 89 in Group Four), which is based on Seneca the Elder's *Controversia* 5.1,[182] but there is no need to assume that the prose cento was written in response to the verse.

> Eccl. xi. In uestibus ne glorieris unquam. Ier[onymus] qui sordido erubescit ornatu numquam gloriabitur pretioso. Illum facit humana derisio deo proximum quem a prauitate uite innocentia fecit alienum. Cum omnis fortuna sit timenda, magis timenda est prospera quam aduersa, quia sepe bonum quod non tollit aduersitas premens, tollit adulatio mulcens.
>
> *Ecclesiasticus 11: "Glory not in apparel at any time." Jerome: "A man who blushes at shabby garb will not ever glory in expensive garb." "The mockery of people makes next to God that man whom blamelessness of life has rendered unfamiliar with wickedness of life." "Though all fortune is to be feared, more to be feared is good than bad, in that often what oppressive adversity does not take away, caressing flattery does."*

Commentary

Eccl. xi: Ecclesiasticus (Sirach) 11:4 ("in uestitu ne glorieris umquam"). **Ier[onymus]**: Although labeled as being from Jerome, this saying is a variation of Seneca the Younger, *Epistulae morales* 87.4, ed. Reynolds, 1:303, lines 25–26 ("Qui sordido vehiculo erubescit pretioso gloriabitur"). The Houghton text recalls Peter the Chanter, *Verbum abbreuiatum (textus conflatus)*, ed. Boutry, 1.8.183, p. 61, who ascribes a paraphrase of the Senecan anecdote to a *philosophus*, concluding, "Qui enim sordido erubescit et precioso nonnumquam gloriabitur." Our scribe's *nunquam* seems to indicate that he understood "glorying in expensive garb" as a symbolic reward to which the

182. Edwards, "Poetic Invention," 211–213.

truly humble might look forward in the next life, rather than, as Seneca and Peter imply, an manifestation of vanity that is just as blameworthy as blushing on account of shabbiness.

Illum facit: Compare Gregory the Great, *Moralia in Job* 10.28, ed. Adriaen, 570, lines 33–35 ("quia illum facit humana derisio Deo proximum, quem ab humanis prauitatibus uitae innocentia seruat alienum").

Cum omnis fortuna: Compare Peter of Blois, *De duodecim utilitatibus tribulationis*, in PL 207.989C ("Unde dicit Gregorius: 'Etsi omnis fortuna timenda est, magis tamen timenda est prospera quam adversa'").

prospera quam aduersa: The core of the sentence derives ultimately from Gregory the Great, *Moralia in Job* 5.1, ed. Adriaen, 219, lines 34–36 ("Vnde fit ut sancti uiri magis in hoc mundo prospera quam aduersa formident").

The phrase *aduersitas premens* appears in Peter Comestor, *Sermo* 14 "In hebdomada media vel dominica Laetare," in PL 198.1763D, within a passage that examines the dangers of adversity and prosperity. An earlier passage that contains the phrase *aduersa premunt* and that is likewise beholden to Gregory is Odo of Cluny, *Collationes* 3, in PL 133.617D ("Sancti ergo viri magis in hoc mundo prospera quam adversa formidant. Sciunt enim, quod adversa dum premunt, ad coelestia concupiscenda, quo plena requies est, mente eos impellunt"). [BKB]

Bibliography

EDITIONS AND TRANSLATIONS

Aegidius of Paris. *Karolinus.* In "The 'Karolinus' of Egidius Parisiensis," edited by Marvin L. Colker. *Traditio* 29 (1973): 199–325.

Albert of Stade. *Troilus.* Edited by Theodor Merzdorf. Bibliotheca scriptorum medii aevi Teubneriana. Leipzig: Teubner, 1875.

Alcuin. *Carmina.* In *Poetae Latini aevi Carolini* 1, edited by Ernst Dümmler, 160–351. MGH, Poetae Latini medii aevi. Berlin: Weidmann, 1881.

———. *Commentaria in s. Joannis evangelium.* PL 100.733–1008.

Aldhelm. *Aenigmata.* In *Collectiones aenigmatum Merovingicae aetatis*, vol. 2, *Tatuini opera omnia; Variae collectiones aenigmatum Merovingicae aetatis; Anonymus de dubiis nominibus*, edited by F. Glorie, 367–540. CCSL 133A. Turnhout: Brepols, 1968.

———. *Carmen de virginitate.* In *Aldhelmi opera*, edited by Rudolf Ehwald, 350–471. MGH Auctores antiquissimi 15. Berlin: Weidmann, 1919.

Alexander Neckam (Nequam/Neckham). *Laudes diuinae sapientiae.* Edited by Thomas Wright. Rolls Series 34. London: Public Record Office, 1863.

Alexander, Paul J. *The Oracle of Baalbek: The Tiburtine Sibyl in Greek Dress.* Washington, D.C.: Dumbarton Oaks Center for Byzantine Studies, 1967.

Andrew of Saint-Victor. *Expositiones historicae in libros Salomonis: Expositio historica in Ecclesiasten.* Edited by Charles Lohr and Reiner Berndt. CCCM 143B. Turnhout: Brepols, 1986.

Annales vindocinenses. In *Recueil d'annales angevines et vendômoises*, edited by Louis Halphen, 50–79. Collection de textes pour servir à l'étude et à l'enseignement de l'histoire 37. Paris: A. Picard, 1903.

Anthologia Latina, Pars I: Carmina in codicibus scripta, fasc. 1; Libri salmasiani aliorumque carmina. Edited by D. R. Shackleton Bailey. Bibliotheca scriptorum Graecorum et Romanorum Teubneriana. Stuttgart: Teubner, 1982.

Anthologia Latina: sive poesis Latinae supplementum. Edited by Franz Buecheler and Alexander Riese. Bibliotheca scriptorum Graecorum et Romanorum Teubneriana. Leipzig: B. G. Teubner, 1894–1926.

Arator. *De actibus apostolorum.* Edited Arthur Patch McKinlay. CSEL 72. Vienna: Hoelder-Pichler-Tempsky, 1951.

Arnulf of Orléans. *Miles gloriosus*. In *Commedie latine del XII e XIII secolo*, vol. 4, 11–93, edited by Silvana Pareto. Università di Genova, Facoltà di lettere, Pubblicazioni dell'Istituto di filologia classica e medievale 79. Genova: Istituto di filologia classica e medievale, 1983.

Augustine of Hippo. *De catechizandis rudibus*. In *Avrelii Avgvstini opera*, vol. 13, part 2, edited by I. B. Bauer, 121–178. CCSL 46. Turnhout: Brepols, 1969.

———. *De ciuitate Dei*. Edited by Bernhard Dombart and Alfons Kalb. 2 vols. 5th ed. Bibliotheca scriptorum Graecorum et Romanorum Teubneriana. Stuttgart: B. G. Teubner, 1981.

Ausonius, pseudo-. *Septem sapientum sententiae septenis versibus explicatae*. In *D. Magni Ausonii opuscula*, edited by Karl Schenkl, 246–250. MGH Auctores antiquissimi 5/2. Berlin: Weidmann, 1883.

Avienus. *Aratea*. Edited by Alfred Breysig. Bibliotheca scriptorum graecorum et romanorum Teubneriana. Leipzig: Teubner, 1882.

Bartholomaeus Anglicus (Bartholomew the Englishman). *De genuinis rerum coelestium, terrestrium et inferarum proprietatibus libri XVIII*. Frankfurt am Main: W. Richter, 1601. Reprint. Frankfurt am Main: Minerva, 1964.

Baudri of Bourgeuil. *Poèmes*. Edited and translated by Jean-Yves Tilliette. 2 vols. Paris: Les Belles Lettres, 1998–2002.

Bede. *De temporibus*. In *Opera didascalica*, vol. 3, edited by Charles W. Jones, 585–611. CCSL 123C. Turnhout: Brepols, 1980.

———. *Homeliarum Evangelii libri II*. Edited by David Hurst. In *Opera homiletica: Opera rhythmica*, ed. David Hurst and J. Fraipont, 1–378. CCSL 122. Turnhout: Brepols, 1955.

Berchorius, Petrus (Pierre Bersuire). *Metamorphosis Ouidiana moraliter a magistro Thoma Walleys anglico de professione predicatorum sub sanctissimo patre Dominico: explanata*. Venundatur in aedibus Ascensianis & sub pelicano in vico sancti Iacobi Parisijs, 1509.

———. *Reductorium morale, Liber XV, cap. ii–xv: "Ovidius moralizatus" naar de Parijse druk van 1509*. Utrecht: Instituut voor Laat Latijn der Rijksuniversiteit, 1962.

———. "The *Ovidius moralizatus* of Petrus Berchorius: An Introduction and Translation." Translated by William Donald Reynolds. PhD dissertation, University of Illinois at Urbana–Champaign, 1971.

Bernardus Silvestris. *Commentum quod dicitur Bernardi Silvestris super sex libros Eneidos Virgilii: Commentary on the First Six Books of the "Aeneid" of Vergil*. Edited by Julian Ward Jones and Elizabeth Frances Jones. Lincoln: University of Nebraska Press, 1977.

———. *Commentary on the First Six Books of the "Aeneid" of Vergil*. Translated by Earl G. Schreiber and Thomas E. Maresca. Lincoln: University of Nebraska Press, 1979.

———. *Cosmographia*. Edited by Peter Dronke. Textus minores 53. Leiden: E. J. Brill, 1978.

Bible. Latin Vulgate. *Biblia sacra iuxta Vulgatam versionem*. Edited by Robert Weber. Revised by Roger Gryson. 4th ed. Stuttgart: Deutsche Bibelgesellschaft, 1994.

———. Translated into English. *The Holy Bible: Douay Rheims Version*. Baltimore, Md.: John Murphy Company, 1899.

Bode, Georg Heinrich, ed. *Scriptores rerum mythicarum Latini tres Romae nuper reperti*. 2 vols. Celle, 1834. Reprint, Hildesheim: G. Olms, 1968.

Bruno of Segni. *Expositio in Pentateuchum*. PL 164.147–550.

Carmina Burana. Edited by Alfons Hilka, Otto Schumann, and Bernhard Bischoff. Band 1, vols. 1–3, Band 2, vol. 1. Heidelberg: Carl Winter, 1930–1970.

———. Edited by J. A. Schmeller. Stuttgart: Bibliothek des litterarischen Vereins, 1847.

Catullus (Gaius Valerius Catullus). *Carmina*. Edited by R. A. B. Mynors. Oxford: Clarendon Press, 1958.

Chaucer, Geoffrey. *The Works of Geoffrey Chaucer*. Edited by F. N. Robinson. 2nd ed. Boston: Houghton Mifflin, 1957.

Chronica de gestis consulum andegavorum. In *Chroniques des comtes d'Anjou et des seigneurs d'Amboise*, edited by Louis Halphen and René Poupardin, 25–73. Paris: A. Picard, 1913.

Chronicon Mauriniacense. In *La Chronique de Morigny (1095–1152)*. Edited by Léon Mirot. 2nd ed. Collection de textes pour servir à l'étude et à l'enseignement de l'histoire 41. Paris: A. Picard, 1912.

———. *A Translation of the Chronicle of the Abbey of Morigny, France, c. 1100–1150*. Translated by Richard Cusimano. Mediaeval Studies 22. Lewiston, N.Y.: Edwin Mellen Press, 2003.

Cicero (Marcus Tullius Cicero). *Academicorum reliquae cum Lucullo*. Edited by O. Plasberg. M. Tulli Ciceronis Scripta quae manserunt omnia 42. Bibliotheca scriptorum Graecorum et Romanorum Teubneriana. Stuttgart: Teubner, 1922.

———. *De natura deorum*. Edited by Wilhelm Ax. 2nd ed. M. Tulli Ciceronis Scripta quae manserunt omnia 45. Bibliotheca scriptorum Graecorum et Romanorum Teubneriana. Stuttgart: B. G. Teubner, 1933.

———. *De natura deorum: Book 1.* Edited by Andrew R. Dyck. Cambridge: Cambridge University Press, 2003.

———. *De officiis.* Edited by Karl Atzert. 3rd ed. M. Tulli Ciceronis Scripta quae manserunt omnia 48. Bibliotheca scriptorum Graecorum et Romanorum Teubneriana. Leipzig: B. G. Teubner, 1963.

———. *Epistulae ad Quintum fratrem, Epistulae ad M. Brutum: Accedunt commentariolum petitionis, fragmenta epistularum.* Edited by D. R. Shackleton Bailey. Bibliotheca scriptorum Graecorum et Romanorum Teubneriana. Stuttgart: B. G. Teubner, 1988.

———. *Laelius de amicitia.* Edited by K. Simbeck. In *Cato maior; Laelius,* edited by K. Simbeck and Otto Plasberg, 44–86. M. Tulli Ciceronis Scripta quae manserunt omnia 47. Bibliotheca scriptorum Graecorum et Romanorum Teubneriana. Leipzig: Teubner, 1917.

———. *Tusculanae disputationes.* Edited by Max Pohlenz. M. Tulli Ciceronis Scripta quae manserunt omnia 44. Bibliotheca scriptorum Graecorum et Romanorum Teubneriana. Stuttgart: B. G. Teubner, 1918.

Cicero, pseudo-. *Rhetorica ad Herennium.* Edited and translated by Harry Caplan. Loeb Classical Library 403. Cambridge, Mass.: Harvard University Press, 1954.

Claudian. *De sexto consulatu Honorii.* In *Carmina minora,* edited by J. B. Hall, 263–288. Bibliotheca scriptorum Graecorum et Romanorum Teubneriana. Leipzig: B. G. Teubner, 1985.

Commentum Cornuti in Persium. Edited by Wendell V. Clausen and James E. G. Zetzel. Bibliotheca scriptorum Graecorum et Romanorum Teubneriana. Munich: K. G. Saur, 2004.

Cyprian of Gaul. *Heptateuchos.* In *Cypriani Galli poetae Heptatevchos,* 1–208.

Cyprian of Gaul, pseudo-. *De martyrio Maccabaeorum.* In *Cypriani Galli poetae Heptatevchos,* 240–269.

Cypriani Galli poetae Heptatevchos: Accedunt incertorum De Sodoma et Iona et Ad senatorem carmina et Hilarii quae feruntur In Genesin, De Maccabaeis atque De Euangelio. Edited by Rudolf Peiper. CSEL 23. Vienna: F. Tempsky, 1881.

Declamationes XIX maiores Quintiliano falso ascriptae. Edited by Lennart Håkanson. Bibliotheca scriptorum Graecorum et Romanorum Teubneriana. Stuttgart: B. G. Teubner, 1982.

Dracontius, Blossius Aemilius. *Satisfactio.* Edited by Feliciano Speranza. Biblioteca di Helikon, Testi e studi 9. Rome: L'Erma di Bretschneider, 1978.

Dufour, Jean. *Recueil des actes de Louis VI, roi de France (1108–1137).* 4 vols. Chartes et diplômes relatifs à l'histoire de France. Paris: Diffusion de Bocard, 1992–1994.

Embrico of Mainz. *Embricon de Mayence: La Vie de Mahomet.* Edited by Guy Cambier. Collection Latomus 52. Brussels: Latomus, 1961.

Ennodius (Magnus Felix Ennodius). *Opera.* Edited by Friedrich Vogel. MGH Auctores antiquissimi 7. Berlin: Weidmann, 1885.

Ermoldus Nigellus. *Carmen in honorem Hludowici Christianissimi Caesaris Augusti.* In *Poetae Latini aevi Carolini* 2, edited by Ernst Dümmler, 4–79. MGH Poetae Latini medii aevi. Berlin: Weidmann, 1884.

———. *Ermold le Noir: Poème sur Louis le Pieux et Épîtres au roi Pépin.* Edited and translated by Edmond Faral. Les classiques de l'histoire de France au moyen âge 14. Paris: H. Champion, 1932.

Flodoard of Reims. *De Christi triumphis apud Italiam.* PL 135.595–885.

Florus of Lyon. *Carmina.* In *Poetae Latini aevi Carolini* 2, edited by Ernst Dümmler, 507–566. MGH Poetae Latini medii aevi. Munich: Weidmann 1884.

Fortunatus, Venantius Honorius Clementianus. *Carmina.* In *Venanti Honori Clementiani Fortunati presbyteri Italici opera poetica,* edited by Friedrich Leo, 7–270. MGH Auctores antiquissimi 4/1. Berlin: Weidmann, 1881.

———. *Poèmes.* Edited by Marc Reydellet. 3 vols. Paris: Les Belles Lettres, 1994–2004.

———. *Vita s. Martini.* In *Venanti Honori Clementiani Fortunati presbyteri Italici opera poetica,* edited by Friedrich Leo, 203–370. MGH Auctores antiquissimi 4/1. Berlin: Weidmann, 1881.

Fredegar. *Chronicarum Libri IV.* In *Fredegarii et aliorum Chronica: Vitae sanctorum,* edited by Bruno Krusch, 1–193. MGH Scriptores rerum Merovingicarum 2. Hanover: Hahn, 1888.

Frontinus, Sextus Iulius. *Strategemata.* Edited by Robert I. Ireland. Bibliotheca scriptorum Graecorum et Romanorum Teubneriana. Leipzig : B. G. Teubner, 1990.

Fulk of Beauvais. *Fulcoii Beluacensis Utriusque De nuptiis Christi et ecclesiae libri septem.* Edited by Mary Isaac Jogues Rousseau. Catholic University of America Studies in Medieval and Renaissance Latin Language and Literature 22. Washington, D.C.: Catholic University of America, 1960.

Galo. *Inuectio in monachos.* In *The Anglo-Latin Satirical Poets and Epigrammatists of the Twelfth Century,* edited by Thomas Wright. Vol. 2, 201–207. Rolls Series. London: Longman, 1872.

Gerald of Wales. *Giraldi Cambrensis opera.* Vol. 2, *Gemma ecclesiastica*, edited by J. S. Brewer. Rolls Series 21. London: Longman, 1862.

Godfrey of Viterbo. *Pantheon.* Edited by Georg Heinrich Pertz. MGH Scriptores (in Folio) 22, 145–147. Hanover: Hahn, 1872.

Gregory the Great. *Moralia in Job.* Edited by Marc Adriaen. 3 vols. CCSL 143–143B. Turnhout: Brepols, 1979–1985.

Guiardinus. "Guiardinus: Bruchstücke eines lateinischen Tugendspiegels nach der Basler Handschrift." Edited by Jakob Werner. *Romanische Forschungen* 26 (1909): 417–461.

Gunther of Pairis. *Ligurinus.* Edited by Erwin Assmann. MGH Scriptores rerum Germanicarum in usum scholarum separatim editi 63. Hanover: Hahn, 1987.

Haimo of Auxerre. *Homilia XIV in circumcisione Domini.* PL 118.9–816.

Hildebert of Lavardin. *Carmina minora.* Edited by A. Brian Scott, 2nd ed. Bibliotheca scriptorum Graecorum et Romanorum Teubneriana. Munich: K. G. Saur, 2001.

———. *Carmina miscellanea.* PL 171:1381–1440.

———. *De mysterio missae* 194. PL 171.1177–1196.

———. *De querimonia.* In *Hildeberts Prosimetrum De querimonia und die Gedichte eines Anonymus*, edited by Peter Orth, 69–95. Wiener Studien, Beiheft 26, Arbeiten zur mittel- und neulateinischen Philologie 6. Vienna: Österreichische Akademie der Wissenschaften, 2000.

———. *De sancto Vincentio.* PL 171.1301–1308.

———. *Inventio sanctae crucis.* PL 171.1315–1322.

———. *Vita beate Marie Egiptiace.* Edited by Norbert Klaus Larsen. CCCM 209. Turnhout: Brepols, 2004.

Hildebert of Lavardin, pseudo-. *Carmen in libros regum.* PL 171.1239–1264.

Horace (Quintus Horatius Flaccus). *Opera.* Edited by D. R. Shackleton Bailey. Bibliotheca scriptorum Graecorum et Romanorum Teubneriana. Stuttgart: B. G. Teubner, 1985.

Hrotsvitha of Gandersheim. *Passio sancte Agnetis virginis et martiris.* In *Opera omnia*, edited by Walter Berschin, 114–130. Bibliotheca scriptorum Graecorum et Romanorum Teubneriana. Munich: K. G. Saur, 2001.

Hugh of Mâcon. *Die "Gesta militum" des Hugo von Mâcon.* 2 vols. Edited by Ewald Könsgen. Mittellateinische Studien und Texte 18.1–2. Leiden: E. J. Brill, 1990.

Hugh Primas. *Oxford Poems*. In *The Oxford Poems of Hugh Primas and the Arundel Lyrics*, edited by C. J. McDonough, 27–72. Toronto Medieval Latin Texts 15. Toronto, 1984.

Ilias Latina. In *The Latin Iliad: Introduction, Text, Translation, and Notes*, edited by George A. Kennedy. Fort Collins, Colo.: G. A. Kennedy, 1998.

Isidore of Seville. *Isidori Hispalensis Episcopi Etymologiarum sive originum libri XX*. Edited by W. M. Lindsay. Oxford: Clarendon Press, 1911.

Jerome. *Contra vigilantium*. PL 23.337–352 [23.353–368].

John of Garland. *Epithalamium beate virginis Marie*. Edited by Antonio Saiani. Accademia toscana di scienze e lettere "La Colombaria," Studi 139. Florence: L. S. Olschki, 1995.

———. *Integumenta Ovidii: Poemetto inedito del secolo XIII*. Edited by Fausto Ghisalberti. Testi e documenti inediti o rari 2. Messina and Milan: Casa editrice Giuseppe Principato, 1933.

Juvenal. *Satires*. Edited by W. V. Clausen. Oxford: Clarendon Press, 1992.

Lactantius. *Divinae institutiones*. In *L. Caeli Firmiani Lactanti Opera omnia*, edited by Samuel Brandt and Georg von Laubmann, vol. 1. CSEL 19. Vienna: F. Tempsky, 1890.

Lucan. *De bello civili*. Ed. D. R. Shackleton Bailey. Bibliotheca scriptorum Graecorum et Romanorum Teubneriana. Stuttgart: B. G. Teubner, 1988.

Luchaire, Achille, ed. *Louis VI le Gros: Annales de sa vie et de son règne (1081–1137)*. Paris, 1890. Reprint, Brussels: Culture et Civilisation, 1964.

Lucretius. *De rerum natura libri sex*. Edited by Cyril Bailey. 2nd ed. Oxford: Clarendon Press, 1922. Unpaginated.

Lynn, Inez T. P. A. "A Critical Edition of Latin poems from Oxford, Bodleian Library MS. Rawlinson G.109." M. Litt. thesis, University of Oxford, 2001.

Marbod of Rennes. *Carmina*. PL 171.1647–1686, 171.1717–1736.

———. *De ornamentis verborum: Liber decem capitulorum*. Edited by Rosario Leotta. Tavarnuzze: SISMEL, 1998.

———. *Historia Theophili*. PL 171.1593–1604.

———. *Liber lapidum*. Edited by María Esthera Herrera. Paris: Les Belles Lettres, 2005.

———. *Versus de sancto Laurentio*. PL 171.1607–1614.

Martial. *Epigrammata*. Edited by W. M. Lindsay. 2nd edition. Oxford: Clarendon Press, 1929. Unpaginated.

Maximian. *Versus Maximiani*. Edited by Christina Sandquist Öberg. Acta Universitatis Stockholmiensis: Studia Latina Stockholmiensia 43. Stockholm: Almqvist & Wiksell, 1999.

Milo of St. Amand. *Vita Amandi*. In *Poetae Latini aevi Carolini* 3, edited by Ludwig Traube, 561–609. MGH Poetae Latini medii aevi. Berlin: Weidmann, 1896.

Mythographi Vaticani I et II. Edited by Péter Kulcsár. CCSL 91C. Turnhout: Brepols, 1987.

Nigel of Canterbury. *Miracles of the Virgin Mary, in Verse: Miracula sancte Dei genitricis Marie, uersifice*. Edited by Jan [M.] Ziolkowski. Toronto Medieval Latin Texts 17. Toronto: Pontifical Institute of Mediaeval Studies, for the Centre for Medieval Studies, 1986.

Notker the Stammerer (Notkerus Balbulus). *Gesta Karoli*. Ed. Hans F. Haefele. MGH Scriptores rerum Germanicarum, n.s., 12. Berlin: Weidmann, 1959.

Odo of Cluny. *Collationum libri tres*. PL 133.517–638.

Odo of Magdeburg. *Ernestus.* Edited by Thomas A.-P. Klein. Spolia Berolinensia 18. Hildesheim: Weidmann, 2000.

Optatianus Porfyrius. *Carmina*. Edited by Giovanni Polara. Turin: Unione Tipografico-Editrice Torinese, 2004.

Orderic Vitalis. *The Ecclesiastical History of Orderic Vitalis*. Edited and translated by Marjorie Chibnall. 6 vols. Oxford: Clarendon Press, 1969–1980.

Osbern of Canterbury. *Vita et miracula S. Dunstani*. In *Memorials of Saint Dunstan, Archbishop of Canterbury*, edited by William Stubbs, 69–151. Rolls Series 63. London: Longman, 1874.

Otto of Freising. *Chronica*. Edited by Adolf Hofmeister. MGH Scriptores rerum Germanicarum in usum scholarum separatim editi 45. Hanover: Hahn, 1912.

Ovid (Publius Ovidius Naso). *Amores, Medicamina faciei femineae, Ars amatoria, Remedia amoris*. Edited by E. J. Kenney. Oxford: Clarendon, 1961.

———. *Epistulae Heroidum*. Edited by Henricus Dörrie. Texte und Kommentare: Eine altertumswissenschaftliche Reihe 6. Berlin: Walter de Gruyter, 1971.

———. *Fastorum libri sex*. Edited by E. H. Alton, D. E. W. Wormell, and E. Courtney. Bibliotheca scriptorum Graecorum et Romanorum Teubneriana. Leipzig: B. G. Teubner, 1978.

———. *Heroides, XVI–XXI*. Edited by E. J. Kenney. Cambridge: Cambridge University Press, 1996.

———. *Heroides: Select Epistles.* Edited by Peter E. Knox. Cambridge: Cambridge University Press, 1995.

———. *Metamorphoses.* Edited by R. J. Tarrant. Oxford: Clarendon Press, 2004.

———. *Tristium libri quinque, Ibis, Ex Ponto libri quattuor, Halieutica, Fragmenta.* Edited by S. G. Owen. Oxford: Clarendon Press, 1915. Unpaginated.

Ovid, pseudo-. *Consolatio ad Liuiam.* In *Consolation à Livie, Élégies à Mécène, Bucoliques d'Einsiedeln,* edited by Jacqueline Amat, 60–78. Collection des Universités de France, Série Latine 342. Paris: Les Belles Lettres, 1997.

———. *De Piramo.* In *Pseudo-Antike Literatur des Mittelalters,* edited by Paul Lehmann, 46–51. Darmstadt: Wissenschaftliche Buchgesellschaft, 1964.

Pamphilus de amore. Edited by L[isardo] Rubio and Tomás González Rolán. Barcelona: Bosch, 1977.

Paulinus of Aquileia. *L'œuvre poétique de Paulin d'Aquilée.* Edited by Dag Norberg. Kungl. Vitterhets historie och antikvitets akademiens handlingar: Filologisk-filosofiska serien 18. Stockholm: Almqvist & Wiksell International, 1979.

Paulinus of Périgueux. *Vita sancti Martini.* Edited by Michael Petschenig. CSEL 16. Vienna: F. Tempsky, 1888.

Peter of Blois. *De duodecim utilitatibus tribulationis.* PL 207.989A–1006B.

Peter the Chanter. *Verbum abbreviatum.* PL 205:21–370.

———. *Verbum abbreuiatum (textus conflatus).* Edited by Monique Boutry. CCCM 196. Turnhout: Brepols, 2004.

Peter Comestor, *Sermones.* PL 198.1721–1844.

Peter Riga. *Aurora: Petri Rigae Biblia versificata.* Edited by Paul E. Beichner. 2 vols. Publications in Mediaeval Studies 19. Notre Dame, Ind.: University of Notre Dame Press, 1965.

Philip of Harvengt. *Commentaria in cantica canticorum.* PL 203.181–490.

Plautus (Titus Maccius Plautus). *Comoediae.* Edited by W. M. Lindsay. 2 vols. Oxford: Clarendon Press, 1904–1905.

Plutarch. *Sertorius: A Historical Commentary.* Edited by C. F. Konrad, 1-28. Chapel Hill: University of North Carolina Press, 1994.

Poeta Saxo. *Annales de gestis Karoli Magni imperatoris.* In *Poetae Latini aevi Carolini* 4/1, edited by Paul von Winterfeld, 7–71. MGH Poetae Latini medii aevi. Berlin: Weidmann, 1964.

Priscian. *Carmen in laudem Anastasii Imperatoris.* In *Procope de Gaza, Priscien de Césarée: Panegyriques de l'empereur Anastase 1er,* edited by A. Chauvot, 56–68. Abhandlungen zur Alten Geschichte 35. Bonn: Rudolf Habelt, 1986.

Propertius, Sextus. *Carmina.* Edited by E. A. Barber. 2nd ed. Oxford: Clarendon Press, 1960.

Prosper of Aquitaine. *Epigrammatum ex sententiis s. Augustini liber unus.* In *PL* 51.497–532B.

Prudentius. *Aurelii Prudentii Clementis Carmina.* Edited by Maurice P. Cunningham. CCSL 126. Turnhout: Brepols, 1966.

———. *Contra Symmachum.* In *Aurelii Prudentii Clementis Carmina,* 182–250.

———. *Hamartigenia.* In *Aurelii Prudentii Clementis Carmina,* 116–148.

———. *Peristephanon.* In *Aurelii Prudentii Clementis Carmina,* 251–389.

Purchard of Reichenau. *Gesta Witigowonis.* In *Die lateinischen Dichter des deutschen Mittelalters* 5/1, *Die Ottonenzeit,* edited by Karl Strecker, 260–279. MGH Poetae Latini medii aevi. Leipzig: Karl W. Hiersemann, 1937.

Quintilian. *The Orator's Education.* Edited and translated by Donald A. Russell. 5 vols. Loeb Classical Library 124–127 and 494. Cambridge, Mass.: Harvard University Press, 2001.

Quintilian, pseudo-. *Declamatio* 8. In *I gemelli malati: Un caso di vivisezione (Declamazioni maggiori, 8),* ed. Antonio Stramaglia. Cassino: Università degli studi di Cassino, 1999.

Rabanus Maurus. *De uniuerso (De rerum naturis).* PL 111:9–614.

———. *Enarrationes super Deuteronomium.* PL 108.837–998.

Rapularius 2. In *Commedie latine del XII e XIII secolo,* vol. 6, 319–378, edited by Paolo Gatti. Pubblicazioni del D.Ar.Fi.Cl.Et., n.s., 176. Genoa: Dipartimento di Archeologia, Filologia classica e loro Tradizioni, 1998.

Reginald of Canterbury. *Carmina.* In *The Anglo-Latin Satirical Poets and Epigrammatists of the Twelfth Century,* edited by Thomas Wright, vol. 2, 259–267. Rolls Series. London: Longman, 1872.

Reiner of Liège. *De conflictu duorum ducum et animarum.* PL 204.79–90.

Richard of Grandselve. *Carmen de laude Clarevallis et de religiosa ibidem disciplina.* PL 185.1563–1566.

Robert Partes. "The Poems of Robert Partes." Edited by William H. Cornog. *Speculum* 12 (1937): 215–250.

Rodulfus Tortarius. *Rodulfi Tortarii Carmina.* Edited by Marbury B. Ogle and Dorothy M. Schullian. Papers and Monographs of the American Academy in Rome 8. Rome: American Academy in Rome, 1933.

Sackur, Ernst. *Sibyllinische Texte und Forschungen.* Halle an der Saale, 1898. Reprint, Turin: Bottega d'Erasmo, 1963.

Seneca the Elder (Lucius Annaeus Seneca). *Declamations*. Edited and translated by Michael Winterbottom. 2 vols. Loeb Classical Library 463–464. Cambridge, Mass.: Harvard University Press, 1974.

Seneca the Younger (Lucius Annaeus Seneca). *Ad Lucilium epistulae morales*. Edited by L. D. Reynolds. 2 vols. Oxford: Clarendon Press, 1965.

———. *Tragoediae*. Edited by Otto Zwierlein. Oxford: Clarendon Press, 1986.

Serenus. *Liber Medicinalis*. Edited by R. Pépin. Paris: Presses Universitaires de France, 1949.

Sibylla Tiburtina. In Bernard McGinn. "Oracular Transformations: The 'Sibylla Tiburtina' in the Middle Ages (With Particular Reference to the Newberry Library Version)." In *Sibille e linguaggi oracolari: Mito storia tradizione; Atti del convegno Macerata-Norcia, settembre 1994*, edited by Ileana Chirassi Colombo and Tullio Seppilli, 636–644. Pisa: Istituti Editoriali e Poligrafici Internazionali, 1998.

Sibyllinorum verborum interpretatio [Bedan recension]. PL 90.1181–1186.

Silius Italicus, Tiberius Catius. *Punica*. Edited by Josef Delz. Bibliotheca scriptorum Graecorum et Romanorum Teubneriana. Stuttgart: B. G. Teubner, 1987.

Simon Aurea Capra. *Versus de excidio Troiae*. PL 171.1447–1453.

———. "The *Ylias* of Simon Aurea Capra: A Critical Edition." Edited by M. M. Parrott. PhD dissertation, University of Toronto, 1976.

Statius (Publius Papinius Statius). *Achilleid*. Edited by O. A. W. Dilke. Cambridge: Cambridge University Press, 1954.

———. *Silvae*. Edited by E. Courtney. Oxford: Clarendon Press, 1990.

———. *Thebais*. Edited by Alfred Klotz. 2nd ed. Edited by Thomas C. Klinnert. Bibliotheca scriptorum Graecorum et Romanorum Teubneriana. Leipzig: B.G. Teubner, 1973.

Stephen of Rouen. *Draco Normannicus*. In *Chronicles of the Reigns of Stephen, Henry II, and Richard I*, edited by Richard Howlett, vol 2, 585–757. Rolls Series 82. London: Longman, 1885.

Stevens, John Stevens, ed. *The Later Cambridge Songs*. Oxford: Oxford University Press, 2005.

Suger, Abbot of Saint Denis. *Vita Ludovici. The Deeds of Louis the Fat*. Translated by Richard Cusimano and John Moorhead. Washington, D.C.: Catholic University of America Press, 1992.

———. *Vita Ludovici. Vie de Louis VI le Gros*. Edited and translated by Henri Waquet. Les classiques de l'histoire de France au moyen âge 11. Paris: H. Champion, 1929.

Terence (Publius Terentius Afer). *Comoediae*. Edited by Robert Kauer and Wallace M. Lindsay. Oxford: Clarendon Press, 1926.

Tertullian. *De patientia, De carnis resurrectione, Adversus Hermogenem, Adversus Valentinianos, Adversus omnes haereses, Adversus Praxean, Adversus Marcionem*. Edited by Emil Kroymann. *Qvinti Septimi Florentis Tertvlliani Opera,* part 3. CSEL 47. Vienna: F. Tempsky, 1906.

———. *De pudicitia*. Edited by Charles Munier. Sources Chrétiennes 394. Paris: Éditions du Cerf, 1993.

Theobald. *Physiologus*. Edited by P. T. Eden. Mittellateinische Studien und Texte 6. Leiden: E. J. Brill, 1972.

Valerius Flaccus (Gaius Valerius Flaccus Setinus Balbus). *Argonauticon libri octo*. Edited by Widu-Wolfgang Ehlers. Bibliotheca scriptorum Graecorum et Romanorum Teubneriana. Stuttgart: B. G. Teubner, 1980.

Valerius Maximus. *Factorum et dictorum memorabilium libri novem*. Edited by Karl Kempf. 2nd ed. Bibliotheca scriptorum Graecorum et Romanorum Teubneriana. Stuttgart: Teubner, 1982.

Vergil. *Opera*. Edited by R.A.B. Mynors. Oxford: Clarendon Press, 1969.

Vergil, pseudo-. *Culex*. Ed. W. V. Clausen. In *Appendix Vergiliana*, edited by W. V. Clausen, F. R.D. Goodyear, E. J. Kenney, and J. A. Richmond, 19–36. Oxford: Clarendon Press, 1966.

Victorius, Claudius Marius. *Alethia*. Edited by P. F. Hovingh. In *Commodiani carmina*, ed. Joseph Martin, 115–193. CCSL 128. Turnhout: Brepols, 1960.

"Viribus, arte, minis, Danaum clara Troia ruinis" (incipit). In PL 171:1451–1453.

———. In *Poésies populaires latines antérieures au douzième siècle*, edited by Edélestand du Méril, 400–405. Paris, 1843. Reprint, Bibliotheca musica Bononiensis 2. Bologna: Forni, 1969.

Waltharius. In *Die lateinischen Dichter des deutschen Mittelalters: Nachträge zu den Poetae aevi Carolini* 6/1, edited by Karl Strecker, 1–85. MGH Poetae Latini medii aevi. Weimar: H. Böhlaus Nachfolger, 1951.

Warner of Basil. *Paraclitus*. In "Warnerii Basiliensis Paraclitus et Synodus," ed. Pierre-W. Hoogterp. *Archives d'histoire doctrinale et littéraire du Moyen Age* 8 (1933): 284–319.

William of Conches. *Glosae super Boetium*. Edited by Lodi Nauta. CCCM 158. Turnhout: Brepols, 1999.

Winrich of Trier. *Conflictus ovis et lini*. Edited by Moriz Haupt. *Zeitschrift für deutsches Alterthum* 11 (1859): 215–238.

Wipo. "*Proverbia*." In *Die Werke Wipos*, 3rd ed., edited by Harry Bresslau, 66–74. MGH Scriptores rerum Germanicarum in usum scholarum separatim editi 61. Hanover: Hahn, 1915.

STUDIES

Antonelli, Roberto, ed. "L'antologia poetica." Special issue, *Critica del testo* 2/1 (1999).

Bachrach, Bernard S. *Fulk Nerra, the Neo-Roman Consul, 978–1040: A Political Biography of the Angevin Count.* Berkeley: University of California Press, 1993.

Bautier, Robert-Henri. "Anne de Kiev, reine de France, et la politique royale au XIe siècle." *Revue des études slaves* 57 (1985): 539–564.

Beaune, Colette. *The Birth of an Ideology: Myths and Symbols of Nation in Late-Medieval France.* Translated by Susan Ross Huston. Edited by Frederic L. Cheyette. Berkeley: University of California Press, 1991.

Becker, Alfons. *Studien zum Investiturproblem in Frankreich: Papsttum, Königtum und Episkopat im Zeitalter der gregorianischen Kirchenreform (1049–1119).* Saarbrücken: West-Ost-Verlag, 1955.

Bédier, Joseph. *Les légendes épiques: recherches sur la formation des chansons de geste.* Vol. 4. 2nd ed. Paris: H. Champion, 1921.

Beikircher, Hugo. *Kommentar zur VI. Satire des A. Persius Flaccus.* Wiener Studien: Zeitschrift für klassische Philologie und Patristik 1. Vienna: Hermann Böhlaus, 1969.

Benzinger, Josef. *Invectiva in Romam: Romkritik im Mittelalter vom 9. bis zum 12. Jahrhundert.* Historische Studien 404. Lübeck and Hamburg: Matthiesen, 1968.

Bittner, Franz. *Studien zum Herrscherlob in der mitellateinischen Dichtung.* Bamberg: Volkach, 1962.

Blackburn, Bonnie, and Leofranc Holford-Strevens. *The Oxford Companion to the Year.* Oxford: Oxford University Press, 1999.

Blatt, Franz. *Novum glossarium mediae Latinitatis ab anno DCCC usque ad annum MCC.* Copenhagen: Munksgaard, 1969–.

Bloch, Marc. *Feudal Society.* Translated by L. A. Manyon. Chicago: University of Chicago Press, 1961.

Bond, Gerald A. *The Loving Subject: Desire, Eloquence, and Power in Romanesque France.* Philadelphia: University of Pennsylvania Press, 1995.

Bourgain, Pascale. "Les chansonniers lyriques latins." In *Lyrique romane médiévale: La tradition des chansonniers; Actes du Colloque de Liège, 1989,* edited by Madeleine Tyssens, 61–84. Bibliothèque de la Faculté de Philosophie et Lettres de l'Université de Liège 257. Liège, 1991.

———. "La poésie lyrique médiévale." In *Mise en page et mise en texte du livre manuscrit,* edited by Henri-Jean Martin and Jean Vezin, 164–168. Paris: Éditions du Cercle de la Librairie-Promodis, 1990.

Boutemy, André. "Notes additionnelles à la notice de Ch. Fierville sur le manuscrit 115 de Saint Omer." *Revue belge de philologie et d'histoire*, 22 (1943): 5–33.

———. "Notice sur le recueil poétique du manuscrit Cotton Vitellius A xii, du British Museum." *Latomus* 1 (1937): 278–313.

———. "Le recueil poétique du manuscrit latin 5129 de la Bibliothèque nationale de Paris." *Scriptorium* 2 (1948): 47–55.

Brown, Michelle P. *A Guide to Western Historical Scripts from Antiquity to 1600*. Toronto: University of Toronto Press, 1990.

Bulst, Walther. "Studien zu Marbods *Carmina varia* und *Liber decem capitulorum*." *Nachrichten von der Akademie der Wissenschaften in Göttingen*. Philologisch-historische Klasse, Fachgruppe 4: Neuere Philologie und Literaturgeschichte 2 (1939): 173–241.

Chenu, M.-D. "*Auctor, actor, autor*." *Bulletin du Cange: Archivum Latinitatis medii aevi* 3 (1927): 81–86.

Chevalier, Ulysse. *Répertoire des sources historiques du Moyen Age: Topo-bibliographie*. 2 vols. Montbéliard: Société anonyme d'Imprimerie montbéliardaise, 1894–1903.

Colby, Alice M. *The Portrait in Twelfth-Century French Literature*. Geneva: Librairie Droz, 1965.

Curtius, Ernst Robert. *European Literature and the Latin Middle Ages*. Translated by Willard R. Trask. Bollingen Series 36. Princeton: Princeton University Press, 1990.

Dean, Ruth J., and Maureen B. M. Boulton. *Anglo-Norman Literature: A Guide to Texts and Manuscripts*. Occasional Publications 3. London: Anglo-Norman Text Society, 1999.

Delbouille, Maurice. "La chanson de Landri." *Revue belge de philologie et d'histoire* 5, nos. 2–3 (1926): 339–350.

Delisle, Léopold. "Notice sur les manuscrits disparus de la bibliothèque de Tours pendant la première moitié du XIXe siècle." In *Notices et extraits des manuscrits de la Bibliothèque nationale et autres bibliothèques*, vol. 31, no. 1, 157–356. Paris, 1884.

Derolez, Albert. *The Palaeography of Gothic Manuscript Books: From the Twelfth to the Early Sixteenth Century*. Cambridge Studies in Palaeography and Codicology 9. Cambridge: Cambridge University Press, 2003.

Dictionnaire des lettres françaises. Edited by Georges Grente. Vol. 1, *Le Moyen Age*, edited by Robert Bossuat, Louis Pichard, and Guy Raynaud de Lage. Paris: A. Fayard, 1964.

Drevin, Helmut. *Die französischen Sprachelemente in den lateinischen Urkunden des 11. und 12. Jahrhunderts*. Halle an der Saale: Hohmann, 1912.

Dronke, Peter. *Medieval Latin and the Rise of European Love-Lyric.* 2nd ed. 2 vols. Oxford: Clarendon Press, 1968.

———. "Thierry of Chartres." In *A History of Twelfth-Century Western Philosophy,* edited by Peter Dronke, 358–385, 455. Cambridge: Cambridge University Press, 1988.

Dunbabin, Jean. *France in the Making 843–1180.* Oxford: Oxford University Press, 1985.

———. "What's in a Name? Philip, King of France." *Speculum* 68 (1993): 949–968.

Dutton, Paul Edward. *Charlemagne's Mustache and Other Cultural Clusters of a Dark Age.* New York: Palgrave, 2004.

———. *The "Glosae super Platonem" of Bernard of Chartres.* Studies and Texts 107. Toronto: Pontifical Institute of Mediaeval Studies, 1991.

Edwards, Robert R. "Poetic Invention and the Medieval *Causae.*" *Mediaeval Studies* 55 (1993): 183–217.

Ehlers, Joachim, Heribert Müller, and Bernd Schneidmüller, eds. *Die französischen Könige des Mittelalters von Odo bis Karl VIII.* Munich: C. H. Beck, 1996.

Evans, M. W. *Medieval Drawings.* London: Paul Hamlyn, 1969.

Faral, Edmond. "Le manuscrit 511 du 'Hunterian Museum' de Glasgow." *Studi medievali,* n.s., 9 (1936): 18–119.

Fawtier, Robert. *The Capetian Kings of France.* Translated by L. Butler and R. J. Adam. London: McMillan, 1960.

Fierville, Charles. "Notices et extraits des manuscrits de la Bibliothèque de Saint-Omer, nos. 115 et 710." In *Notices et extraits des manuscrits de la Bibliothèque nationale et autres bibliothèques* vol. 31, part 1, 49–145. Paris: Imprimerie nationale, 1884.

Fliche, Augustin. *La réforme grégorienne.* 3 vols. Spicilegium sacrum Lovaniense: Etudes et documents 6, 9, 16. Louvain; Paris: E. Champion, 1924–1937.

———. *Le règne de Philippe 1er, roi de France.* Paris, 1912. Reprint, Geneva: Slatkine-Megariotis, 1975.

Franklin, C. F. "O sacrata dies: A New Typological Poem in Epanaleptic Elegiacs." *The Journal of Medieval Latin* 14 (2004): 69–72.

Gaeta, Franco. "L'avventura di Ercole." *Rinascimento* 5 (1954): 227–260.

Gallia christiana. Edited by Barthélemy Hauréau. 16 vols. Paris: V. Palme, 1856–1899.

Gasparri, Françoise. *L'écriture des actes de Louis VI, Louis VII et Philippe Auguste.* Centre de recherches d'histoire et de philologie de la IVe section de l'École Pratique des Hautes Études 5, Hautes Études Médiévales et Modernes 20. Geneva: Droz, 1973.

Georgi, Annette. *Das lateinische und deutsche Preisgedicht des Mittelalters.* Berlin: Erich Schmidt, 1969.

Ghisalberti, Fausto. "Arnolfo d'Orléans, un cultore di Ovidio nel secolo XII." *Memorie del R. Istituto Lombardo di Scienze e Lettere, Classe di Lettere, scienze morali e storiche* 24, fasc. 4 (1932): 157–234.

Gobry, Ivan. *Louis VI: père de Louis VII.* Histoire des rois de France. Paris: Pygmalion, 2003.

Graesse, Johann Georg Theodor. *Orbis Latinus: Lexikon lateinischer geographischer Namen; Lateinisch-deutsch, deutsch-lateinisch.* 4th ed. Handausgabe. Edited by Helmut Plechl, with Günter Spitzbart. Braunschweig: Klinckhardt & Biermann, 1971.

Guillot, Olivier. *Le comte d'Anjou et son entourage au XIe siècle.* 2 vols. Paris: A. & J. Picard, 1972.

Gumbert, J. Peter. "Codicological Units: Towards a Terminology for the Stratigraphy of the Non-Homogeneous Codex." *Segno e testo* 2 (2004): 17–42.

Günther, Otto. "Die Handschriften der Kirchenbibliothek von St. Marien in Danzig." In *Katalog der Danziger Stadtbibliothek verfertigt und herausgegeben im Auftrage der städtischen Behörden*, vol. 5, 375–381. Gdańsk: Kommissions-Verlag von A. W. Kafemann, 1921.

Halm, Karl, Friedrich Heinz, Wilhelm Meyer, and Georg Thomas, eds. "Codices latinos (Clm) 15121–21313 complectens." In *Catalogus codicum manu scriptorum Bibliothecae regiae monacensis*, vol. 4, part, 3, 87–89. Munich: Libraria Palmiana, 1878.

Halphen, Louis. *Le comté d'Anjou au XIe siècle.* Paris: A. Picard, 1906.

———. "France in the Eleventh Century." In *The Cambridge Medieval History,* edited by J. B. Bury, H. M. Gwatkin, and J. P. Whitney, 3:99-133. Cambridge: Cambridge University Press, 1922.

Hanna, Ralph. "Booklets in Medieval Manuscripts: Further Considerations." *Studies in Bibliography* 39 (1986): 100–111.

Hauréau, Barthélemy. *Les mélanges poétiques d'Hildebert de Lavardin.* Paris: G. Pedone-Lauriel, 1882.

Häussler, Reinhard, ed. *Nachträge zu A. Otto Sprichwörter und sprichwörtlichen Redensarten der Römer.* Hildesheim: Georg Olms, 1968.

Herman, József. *Vulgar Latin.* Translated by Roger Wright. University Park: Pennsylvania State University Press, 2000.

Hill, Thomas D. "The Crowning of Alfred and the Topos of *Sapientia et Fortitudo* in Asser's Life of King Alfred." *Neophilologus* 86 (2002): 471–476.

Histoire littéraire de la France. Vol. 10. Paris: Par les religieux Benedictins, 1756.

Hohl, Claude. "Le comte Landri de Nevers dans l'histoire et dans la geste de *Girart de Roussillon*." In *La Chanson de Geste et le Mythe carolingien: Mélanges René Louis publiés par ses collègues, ses amis et ses élèves à l'occasion de son 75e anniversaire*, 2 vols., edited by Emmanuèle Baumgartner, 2:779–806. Saint-Père-sous-Vézelay: [n.p.], 1982.

Holdenried, Anke. "The Bedan Recension of the *Sibylla Tiburtina*: New Manuscript Evidence and its Implications." In *Latin Culture in the Eleventh Century*, edited by Michael W. Herren, Christopher J. McDonough, and Ross G. Arthur, 410–443. Turnhout: Brepols, 2002.

———. *The Sibyl and her Scribes: Manuscripts and Interpretation of the Latin Sibylla Tiburtina c. 1050–1250*. Aldershot, Hants., England: Ashgate, 2006.

In principio: Incipit index of Latin texts. Turnhout: Brepols, 1993–.

Jaeger, C. Stephen. *The Origins of Courtliness: Civilizing Trends and the Formation of Courtly Ideals 939–1210*. Philadelphia: University of Pennsylvania Press, 1985.

Klopsch, Paul. *Einführung in die mittellateinische Verslehre*. Darmstadt: Wissenschaftliche Buchgesellschaft, 1972.

Krill, Richard M. "The *Vatican Mythographers*: Their Place in Ancient Mythography." *Manuscripta* 23 (1979): 173–177.

Lange, Klaus. "Geistliche Speise: Untersuchungen zur Metaphorik der Bibelhermeneutik." *Zeitschrift für deutsches Altertum und deutsche Literatur* 95 (1966): 81–122.

Latham, Ronald Edward, and David Howlett. *Dictionary of Medieval Latin from British Sources*. London: Oxford University Press, 1975–.

Lausberg, Heinrich. *Handbook of Literary Rhetoric*. Edited by D. E. Orton and R. D. Anderson. Translated by M. T. Bliss, A. Jansen, and D. E. Orton. Leiden: Brill, 1998.

Lehmann, Paul. "Eine Sammlung mittellateinischer Gedichte aus dem Ende des 12. Jahrhunderts." *Historische Vierteljahrsschrift* 30 (1935): 20–58.

Lemaire, Jacques. *Introduction à la codicologie*. Publications de l'Institut d'Études Médiévales: Textes, études, congrès 9. Louvain-la-Neuve: Institut d'Études Médiévales de l'Université Catholique de Louvain, 1989.

Lemaitre, Jean-Loup. "Amans-Alexis Monteil (1769–1850) et les manuscrits." *Bibliothèque de l'École des Chartes* (forthcoming).

Lewis, Andrew W. *Royal Succession in Capetian France: Studies on Familial Order and the State*. Cambridge, Mass.: Harvard University Press, 1981.

Lexikon für Theologie und Kirche. Edited by Josef Höfer and Karl Rahner. 11 vols. Freiburg i. B.: Herder, 1957–1965.

Lexicon musicum Latinum medii aevi = Wörterbuch der lateinischen Musikterminologie des Mittelalters bis zum Ausgang des 15. Jahrhunderts = Dictionary of Medieval Latin Music Terminology to the End of the 15th Century. Edited by Michael Bernhard. Munich: Verlag der Bayerischen Akademie der Wissenschaften in Kommission bei der C. H. Beck'schen Verlagsbuchhandlung, 1992–.

Lot, Ferdinand. "La chanson de Landri." *Romania* 32 (1903): 1–17.

Lugge, Margret. *"Gallia" und "Francia" im Mittelalter: Untersuchungen über den Zusammenhang zwischen geographisch-historischer Terminologie und politischem Denken vom 6.–15. Jahrhundert*. Bonner historische Forschungen 15. Bonn: L. Röhrscheid, 1960.

Manitius, Maximilian. *Geschichte der lateinischen Literatur des Mittelalters*. 3 vols. Handbuch der Altertumswissenschaft, neunte Abteilung, zweiter Teil, erster-zweiter-dritter Band. Munich: C. H. Beck, 1911–1931.

Mars, Noël. *Histoire du royal monastère de Sainct-Lomer de Blois de l'ordre de Sainct-Benoist*. Blois: J. Marchand, 1869.

McGinn, Bernard. "*Teste David cum Sibylla*: The Significance of the Sibylline Tradition in the Middle Ages." In *Women of the Medieval World: Essays in Honor of John H. Mundy*, edited by Julius Kirshner and Suzanne F. Wemple, 7–35. Oxford: Basil Blackwell, 1985.

Meyer, Wilhelm. "Radewins Gedichte über Theophilus und die Arten der gereimten Hexameter." In *Gesammelte Abhandlungen zur mittellateinischen Rythmik*, vol. 1, 59–135. Berlin: Weidmann, 1905. Reprint, Hildesheim and New York: Georg Olms, 1970.

Monteil, Amans-Alexis. *Catalogue des manuscrits et d'une partie des livres imprimés composant la bibliothèque de feu M. Amans Alexis Monteil*. Paris: P. Jannet, 1850.

———. *Histoire des Français des divers états aux cinq derniers siècles*. Paris: Janet et Cotelle, 1828–1844.

———. *Traité de matériaux manuscrits de divers genres d'histoire*. 2 vols. Paris: E. Duverger, 1836.

Moser, Thomas C., Jr. *A Cosmos of Desire: The Medieval Latin Erotic Lyric in English Manuscripts*. Ann Arbor: University of Michigan Press, 2004.

Munk Olsen, Birger. "La réception de Stace au moyen âge (du IXe au XIIe siècle)." In *Nova de veteribus: Mittel- und neulateinische Studien für Paul Gerhard Schmidt*, ed. Andreas Bihrer and Elisabeth Stein, 230–246. Munich: K. G. Saur, 2004.

Münxelhaus, Barbara. *Pythagoras musicus: Zur Rezeption der pythagoreischen Musiktheorie als quadrivialer Wissenschaft im lateinischen Mittelalter*. Orpheus: Schriftenreihe zu Grundfragen der Musik 19. Bonn: Verlag für systematische Musikwissenschaft, 1976.

Nees, Lawrence. *A Tainted Mantle: Hercules and the Classical Tradition at the Carolingian Court.* Philadelphia: University of Pennsylvania Press, 1991.

Norberg, Dag. *An Introduction to the Study of Medieval Latin Versification.* Translated by Grant C. Roti and Jacqueline Skubly. Edited by Jan Ziolkowski. Washington, D.C.: Catholic University of America Press, 2004.

Parkes, Malcolm B. "The Date of the Oxford Manuscript of *La Chanson de Roland* (Oxford, Bodleian Library, MS. Digby 23)." *Medioevo Romanzo* 10 (1985): 161–175.

Pepin, Ronald E. *Literature of Satire in the Twelfth Century: A Neglected Mediaeval Genre.* Studies in Mediaeval Literature 2. Lewiston, N.Y.: Edwin Mellen Press, 1988.

Rigg, A. G. "Anthologies and Florilegia." In *Medieval Latin: An Introduction and Bibliographical Guide*, edited by F. A.C. Mantello and A.G. Rigg, 709-712. Washington, D.C.: Catholic University of America Press, 1996.

———. *A History of Anglo-Latin Literature 1066–1422.* Cambridge: Cambridge University Press, 1992.

———. "Medieval Latin Poetic Anthologies (I)." *Mediaeval Studies* 39 (1977): 281–330.

———. "Medieval Latin Poetic Anthologies (II)." *Mediaeval Studies* 40 (1978): 387–407.

———. "Medieval Latin Poetic Anthologies (III)." *Mediaeval Studies* 41 (1979): 468–505.

———. "Medieval Latin Poetic Anthologies (IV)." *Mediaeval Studies* 43 (1981): 472–497.

Rigg, A. G., and David Townsend. "Medieval Latin Poetic Anthologies (V)." *Mediaeval Studies* 49 (1987): 352–390.

Robinson, P. R. "The 'Booklet': A Self-Contained Unit in Composite Manuscripts." *Codicologica* 3 (1980): 46–69.

———. "Self-Contained Units in Composite Manuscripts of the Anglo-Saxon Period." *Anglo-Saxon England* 7 (1978): 231–238.

Rodrigues, Vera. "Thierry de Chartres: Profil philosophique d'un maître Chartrain." In *Roma, Magistra Mundi: Itineraria Culturae Medievalis; Mélanges offerts à Père L. E. Boyle à l'occasion de son 75e anniversaire*, 3 vols., edited by Jacqueline Hamesse, 3:317–328. Fédération Internationale des Instituts d'Etudes Médiévales 10. Louvain-la-Neuve: Fédération Internationale des Instituts d'Etudes Médiévales, 1998.

Samaran, Charles. "Sur la date approximative du *Roland* d'Oxford." *Romania* 94 (1973): 523–527.

Sandler, Lucy Freeman. "The Study of Marginal Imagery: Past, Present, and Future." *Studies in Iconography* 18 (1997): 1–49.

Sannelli, Massimo. "Raccolta, canzoniere, *Liederbuch*: *Ratio* e *ordo* delle raccolte poetiche mediolatine." In *Poesía latina medieval (siglos V–XV): Actas del IV Congreso del "Internationales Mittellateinerkomitee" (Santiago de Compostela, 12–15 de septiembre de 2002)*, edited by Manuel C. Díaz y Díaz and José M. Díaz de Bustamante, 303–307. Millennio medievale 55. Atti di convegni 17. Florence: SISMEL, 2005.

Sauer, Hans. "Die 72 Völker und Sprachen der Welt: einige Ergänzungen." *Anglia: Zeitschrift für englische Philologie* 107 (1989): 61–64.

Savorelli, Mirella Brini. "Il 'Dictamen' di Bernardo Silvestre." *Rivista critica di storia della filosofia* 20 (1965): 182–230.

Scheller, Robert W. *Exemplum: Model-Book Drawings and the Practice of Artistic Transmission in the Middle Ages (ca. 900–ca. 1470)*. Translated by Michael Hoyle. Amsterdam: Amsterdam University Press, 1995.

Schieffer, Theodor. *Die päpstlichen Legaten in Frankreich vom Vertrage von Meersen (870) bis zum Schisma von 1130*. Historische Studien 263. Berlin: Emil Ebering, 1935.

Schmidt, Paul Gerhard. *Proverbia sententiaeque Latinitatis medii ac recentis aevi, nova series: Lateinische Sprichwörter und Sentenzen des Mittelalters und der frühen Neuzeit in alphabetischer Anordnung*. 3 vols. Carmina Medii Aevi Posterioris Latina, section 2/7–9. Göttingen: Vandenhoeck & Ruprecht, 1982–1986.

Schneidmüller, Bernd. "Constructing Identities of Medieval France." In *France in the Central Middle Ages 900–1200*, edited by Marcus Bull, 15–42. Oxford: Oxford University Press, 2002.

Schüppert, Helga. *Kirchenkritik in der lateinischen Lyrik des 12. und 13. Jahrhunderts*. Medium Aevum: Philologische Studien 23. Munich: Wilhelm Fink, 1972.

Scott, A. B. "The Biblical Allegories of Hildebert of Le Mans." *Sacris Erudiri* 16 (1965): 404–424.

Scott, A. B., Deirdre F. Baker, and A. G. Rigg. "The *Biblical Epigrams* of Hildebert of Le Mans: A Critical Edition." *Mediaeval Studies* 47 (1985): 272–316.

Short, Ian. "The Oxford Manuscript of the *Chanson de Roland*: A Palaeographic Note." *Romania* 94 (1973): 221–231.

Sørensen, Preben Meulengracht. *The Unmanly Man: Concepts of Sexual Defamation in Early Northern Society*. Viking Collection: Studies in Northern Civilization. Odense: Odense University Press, 1983.

Spiegel, Gabrielle M. *The Chronicle Tradition of Saint-Denis: A Survey.* Leiden: Brill, 1978.

Spitz, Hans-Jörg. *Die Metaphorik des geistigen Schriftsinns: Ein Beitrag zur allegorischen Bibelauslegung des ersten christlichen Jahrtausends.* Münstersche Mittelalter-Schriften 12. Munich: W. Fink, 1972.

Springer, Matthias. "Gab es ein Volk der Salier?" In *Nomen et gens: Zur historischen Aussagekraft frühmittelalterlicher Personennamen*, edited by Dieter Geuenich, Wolfgang Haubrichs, and Jörg Jarnut, 58–83. Berlin: Walter de Gruyter, 1997.

Stotz, Peter. *Handbuch zur lateinischen Sprache des Mittelalters.* 5 vols. Handbuch der Altertumswissenschaft, zweite Abteilung, fünfter Teil. Munich: C. H. Beck, 1996–2004.

Strayer, Joseph R. "France, the Holy Land, the Chosen People, and the Most Christian King." In *Medieval Statecraft and the Perspectives of History*, edited by Joseph R. Strayer, 300–314. Princeton, N.J.: Princeton University Press, 1971.

Thesaurus Linguae Latinae. Leipzig: B. G. Teubner, 1900–.

Thomson, S. Harrison. *Latin Bookhands of the Later Middle Ages, 1100–1500.* Cambridge: Cambridge University Press, 1969.

Tilliette, Jean-Yves. "Savants et poètes du moyen âge face à Ovide: les débuts de l'*aetas Ovidiana* (v. 1050–v. 1200)." In *Ovidius redivivus: Von Ovid zu Dante*, edited by Michelangelo Picone and Bernhard Zimmermann, 63–104. Stuttgart: M & P, Verlag für Wissenschaft und Forschung, 1994.

———. "Le sens et la composition du florilège de Zurich (Zentralbibliothek, ms. C 58): Hypothèses et propositions." In *Non recedet memoria eius: Beiträge zur lateinischen Philologie des Mittelalters im Gedenken an Jakob Werner (1861–1944); Akten der wissenschaftlichen Tagung vom 9./10. September 1994 am Mittellateinischen Seminar der Universität Zürich*, edited by Peter Stotz, 147–167. Bern and New York: Peter Lang, 1995.

Vernet, André. "Épitaphe de Thierry de Chartres." In *Recueil de travaux offert à M. Clovis Brunel, membre de l'Institut, Directeur honoraire de l'École des Chartes, par ses amis, collègues et élèves*, 2:660–670. Mémoires et documents 12. Paris: Société de l'École des Chartes, 1955.

———. "Séance du 16 avril." *Bulletin de la Société national des antiquaires de France* (1952–1953): 53–54.

Walther, Hans. *Initia carminum ac versuum medii aevi posterioris Latinorum: Alphabetisches Verzeichnis der Versanfänge mittellateinischer Dichtungen.* 2nd ed. Carmina Medii Aevi Posterioris Latina, section 1/1. Göttingen: Vandenhoeck & Ruprecht, 1969.

———. *Proverbia sententiaeque Latinitatis medii aevi: Lateinische Sprichwörter und Sentenzen des Mittelalters in alphabetischer Anordnung.* 5 vols. Carmina Medii Aevi Posterioris Latina, section 2/1–5. Göttingen: Vandenhoeck & Ruprecht, 1963–1967.

Warne, Chris. "Amateurs and Collectors: Amans-Alexis Monteil and the Emergence of a Professional Archive Culture in Nineteenth-Century France." *Australian Journal of French Studies* 33 (1996): 45–72.

Wattenbach, Wilhelm. "Beschreibung einer Handschrift der Stadtbibliothek zu Reims." *Neues Archiv der Gesellschaft für ältere deutsche Geschichtskunde* 18 (1893): 491–526.

Watson, Lindsay, and Patricia Watson, eds. *Martial: Select Epigrams.* Cambridge: Cambridge University Press, 2003.

Weitzmann, Kurt. "An Addendum to 'The Heracles Plaques of St. Peter's Cathedra.'" *The Art Bulletin* 56 (1974): 248–252.

———. "The Heracles Plaques of St. Peter's Cathedra." *The Art Bulletin* 55 (1973): 1–37.

Werner, Jakob. *Beiträge zur Kunde der lateinischen Literatur des Mittelalters aus Handschriften gesammelt.* 2nd ed. Aarau, 1905. Reprint, Hildesheim: Georg Olms, 1979.

Widmer, Berthe. "Thierry von Chartres, ein Gelehrtenschicksal des 12. Jahrhunderts." *Historische Zeitschrift* 200 (1965): 552–571.

Wilmart, André. "Le Florilège de Saint-Gatien: Contribution à l'étude des poèmes d'Hildebert et de Marbode." *Revue bénédictine* 48 (1936), 3–40; 147–181; 235–258.

Wood, Charles T. "*Regnum Francie*: A Problem in Capetian Administrative Usage." *Traditio* 23 (1976): 117–148.

Yunck, John A. *The Lineage of Lady Meed: The Development of Mediaeval Venality Satire.* Publications in Mediaeval Studies 17. Notre Dame, Ind.: University of Notre Dame Press, 1963.

Ziolkowski, Jan. "A Bouquet of Wisdom and Invective: Houghton MS. Lat 300." *Harvard Library Bulletin*, n.s., 1, no. 3 (1990): 20–48.

———. "Classical Influences on Medieval Latin Views of Poetic Inspiration." In *Latin Poetry and the Classical Tradition: Essays in Medieval and Renaissance Literature*, edited by Peter Godman and Oswyn Murray, 15–38. Oxford: Clarendon Press, 1990.

Manuscripts Cited

Contributors

BKB **Bridget K. Balint**, an assistant professor of classical studies at Indiana University–Bloomington, studies the Latin literature of the High Middle Ages.

JL **Justin Lake**, a PhD candidate in Medieval Latin at Harvard University, has interests in late antique and medieval historiography, rhetoric, and poetics.

LL **Laura Light** has catalogued medieval manuscripts at the Houghton Library, Harvard University; her publications focus on topics related to the medieval Vulgate, especially in the thirteenth century.

PP **Prydwyn O. Piper**, assistant editor of the *Dictionary of Medieval Latin from British Sources* in Oxford, is interested in the interaction between the Latin and vernacular languages and literatures in the Middle Ages, with a special focus on Middle Welsh.

JZ **Jan M. Ziolkowski,** Arthur Kingsley Porter Professor of Medieval Latin at Harvard University and Director of Dumbarton Oaks Research Library and Collection, has published extensively on medieval literature, especially Medieval Latin literature.

FACSIMILE

Introduction

HOUGHTON MS LAT 300, the manuscript presented in this facsimile, is also available on the web in a digitized form, freely accessible through the electronic catalog of Harvard College Library. Like the digitization, the facsimile in the present volume includes not only the eleven parchment leaves that are all we possess of the medieval manuscript, but also the nineteenth-century interleaves on which Amans-Alexis Monteil attempted to transcribe all or parts of some poems. The combination of the parchment and paper is what constitutes the body of the manuscript as it now exists. From one perspective it is lavish to reproduce the paper leaves, together with the cover and Monteil's title page. Then again, they could prove to be useful for understanding the nineteenth-century history of the manuscript, and they also shed light on Monteil's skills and interests in reading medieval manuscripts.

The eleven parchment leaves are foliated in pencil at the bottom on the inner corner of each recto. It is to this count that reference is made in this edition and translation. On the printed pages these numbers have been supplied at the bottom of the facsimile pages, to the left. The parchment and paper leaves have also been foliated continuously together. In the manuscript itself this foliation appears in pencil at the top on the outer corner of each recto. On the printed pages these numbers have been placed at the bottom of the facsimile pages, to the right. The reader should beware of becoming confused by the discrepancies between the two foliations, since the numberings diverge after the first folio and the numbers of the parchment leaves alone are progressively lower. One note of warning is in order: the manuscript has been reduced very slightly, to 95 percent of its original size. For precise information on the dimensions of MS Lat 300, remember to consult the codicological description on pp. 2–3 of the introduction.

The facsimile is intended to serve at least three functions. First, someday it may catch the eye of a reader who is familiar with one or more other codices related to this manuscript. Although MS Lat 300 may remain forever shrouded in mystery, there is always a possibility that by happy chance other gatherings from which it became separated have survived or that its scribes wrote in other extant manuscripts about which we have more information. A reader of our book may alight upon the missing link.

A second purpose of the reproductions is to provide materials for class study. For example, the poems in Groups Three and Four are not transcribed, edited, or translated here, although they are available in print elsewhere. With the help of the editions, English versions, and commentaries provided in this book, students could familiarize themselves with the peculiarities of the hands in MS Lat 300 by studying poems in Groups One, Two, or Five, or the prose in Group Six. Then they could set out to transcribe the other poems, in part or in toto. Although some may prefer the convenient anachronism of reading this book with the medieval manuscript glowing on a nearby computer screen, others may find it more congenial to experience the codex on printed pages. In either case, with the reproduction of the folios of the medieval manuscript, the nineteenth-century leaves and binding, and an early twenty-first century edition with philological trimmings, this book is meant to offer something to everyone.

The final aim of the facsimile is as a kind of *captatio benevolentiae*, to secure the goodwill of the Latinists who may be tempted to find fault with the editions that precede this section of the book. Those of us who have grappled with MS Lat 300 may not have always deciphered the manuscript in the best way possible, but we have given our all in an attempt to make sense of its many enigmas. Fair-minded readers who compare the text presented in the facsimile with our editions, translations, and commentaries may not always agree with our decisions, but we trust that they will credit us at least with having made an honest effort in coming to terms with scribes and scripts whose strong suit was not always clarity. May those who come after us carry forward the process of understanding, both the manuscript and the Latin, since we hope very much to furnish an honest and mostly reliable basis for further investigation rather than to pretend that our labors have precluded any additional discoveries. On the contrary, the time has now come for study of the *Carmina Houghtoniensia* to begin in earnest. [JZ]

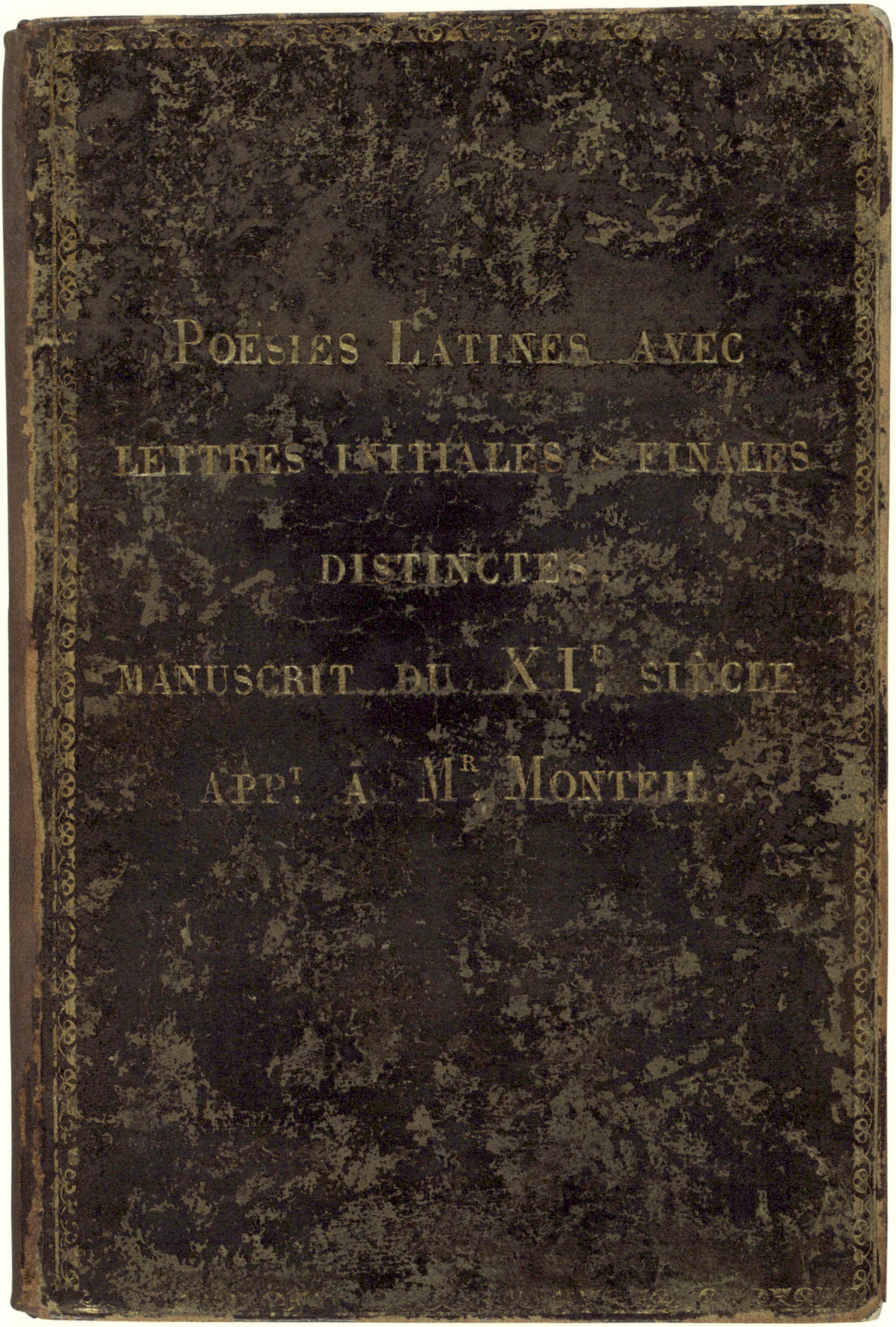
POESIES LATINES AVEC
LETTRES INITIALES & FINALES
DISTINCTES.
MANUSCRIT DU XI.E SIÈCLE
APP.T A M.R MONTEIL.

FRONT COVER

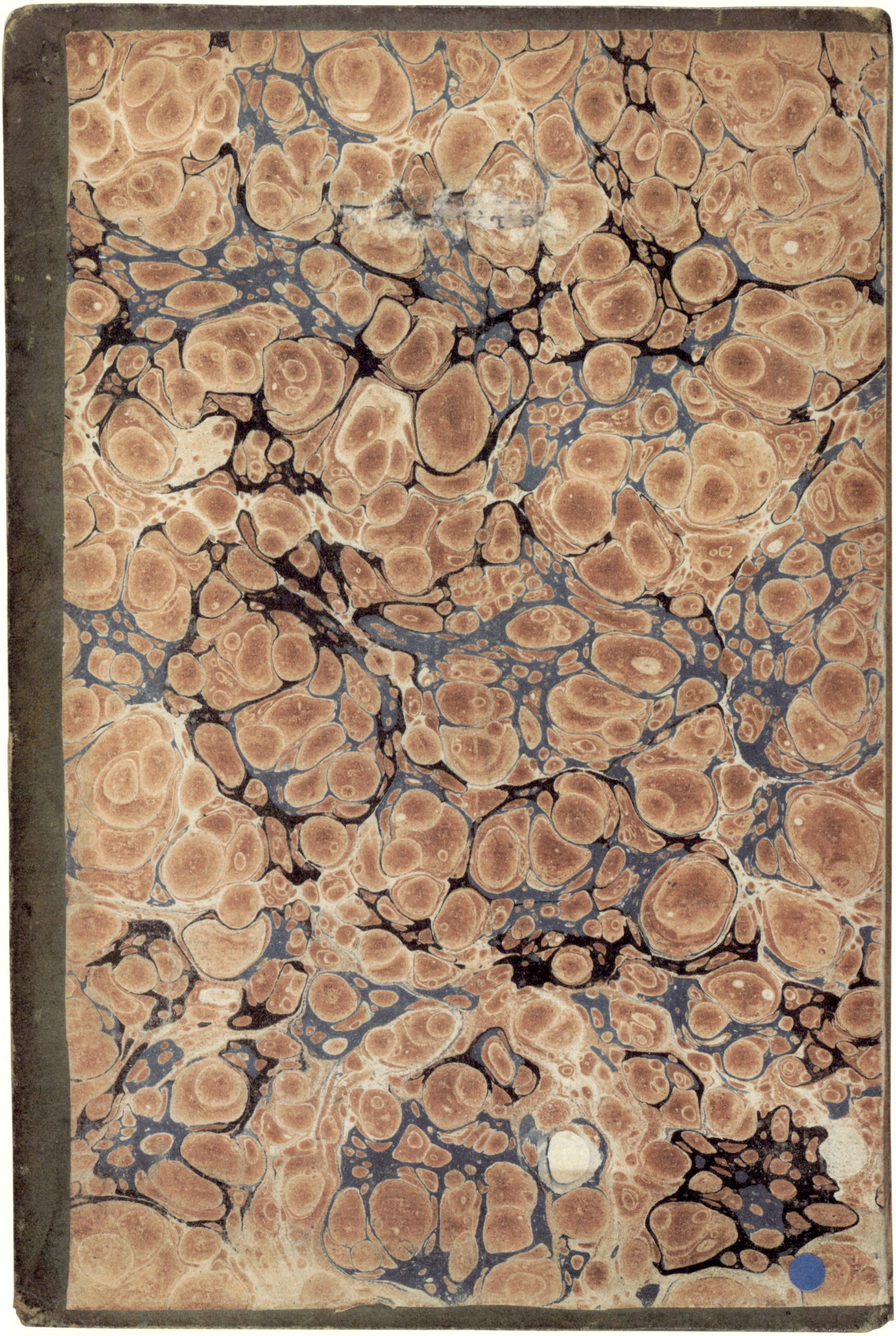

fol. i^{v} (PARCHMENT AND PAPER)

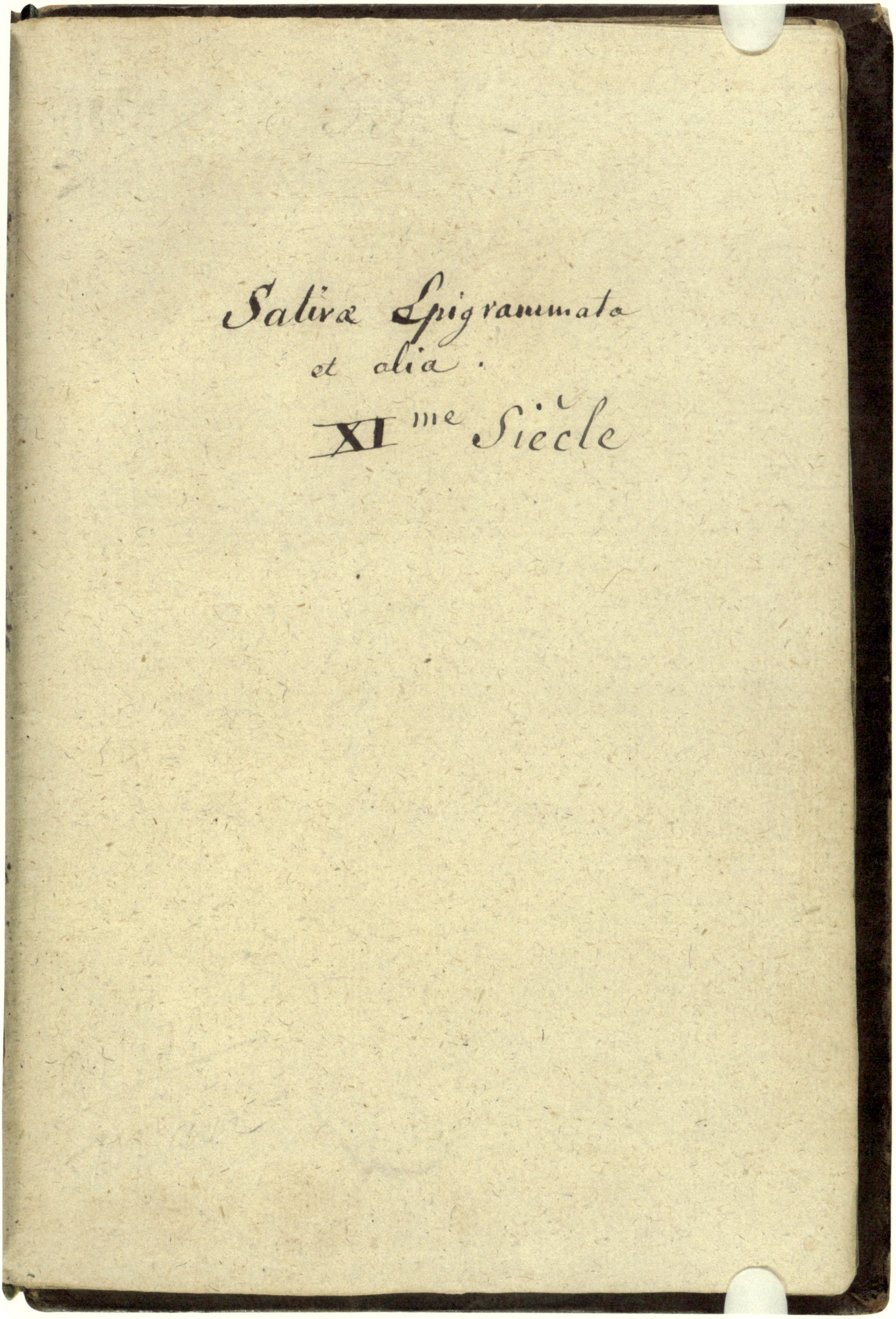
Satiræ Epigrammata
et alia.
XIme Siecle

fol. ii^{r} (PARCHMENT AND PAPER)

fol. ii^{v} (PARCHMENT AND PAPER)

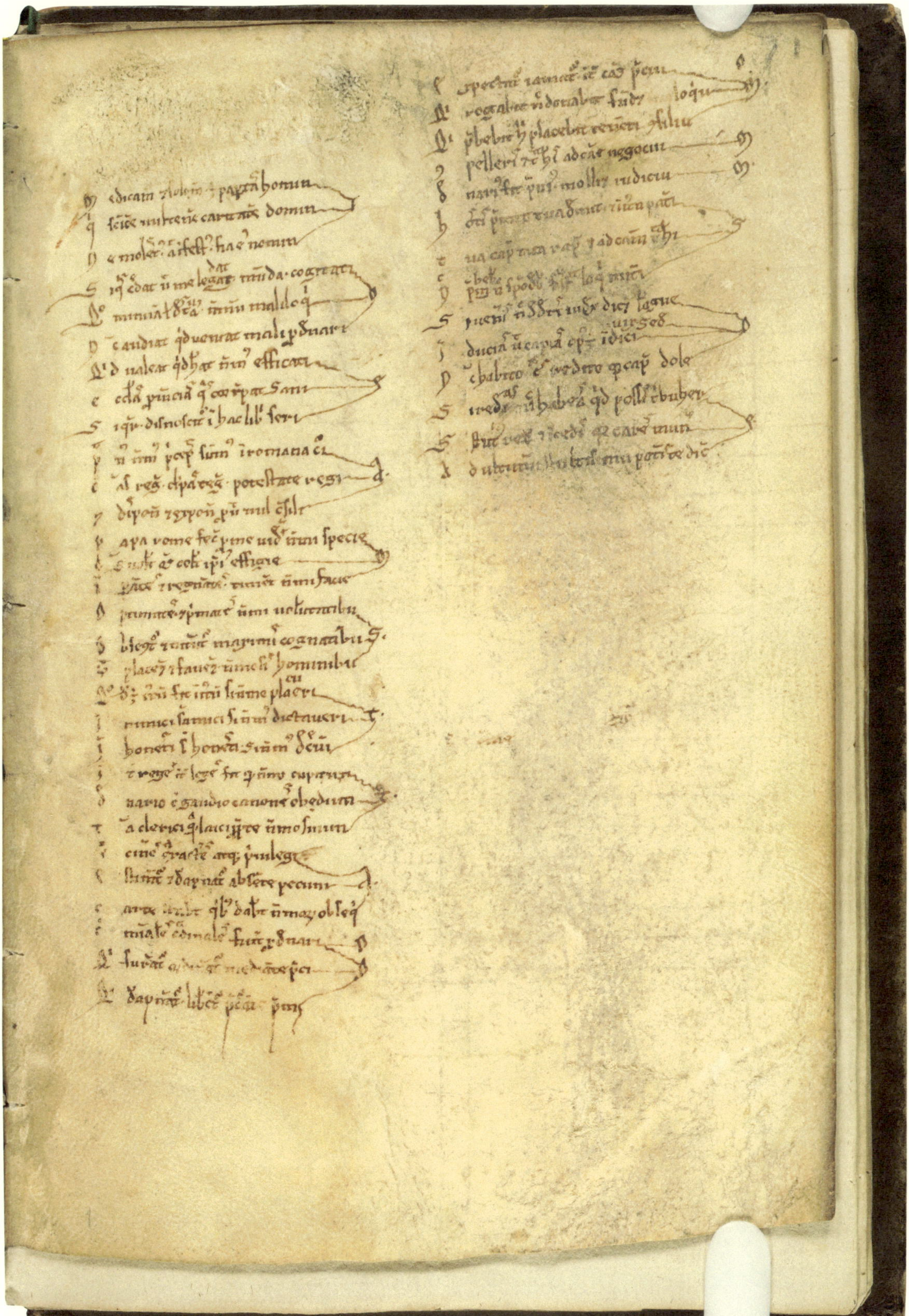

fol. 1r (PARCHMENT ONLY)

fol. 1r (PARCHMENT AND PAPER)

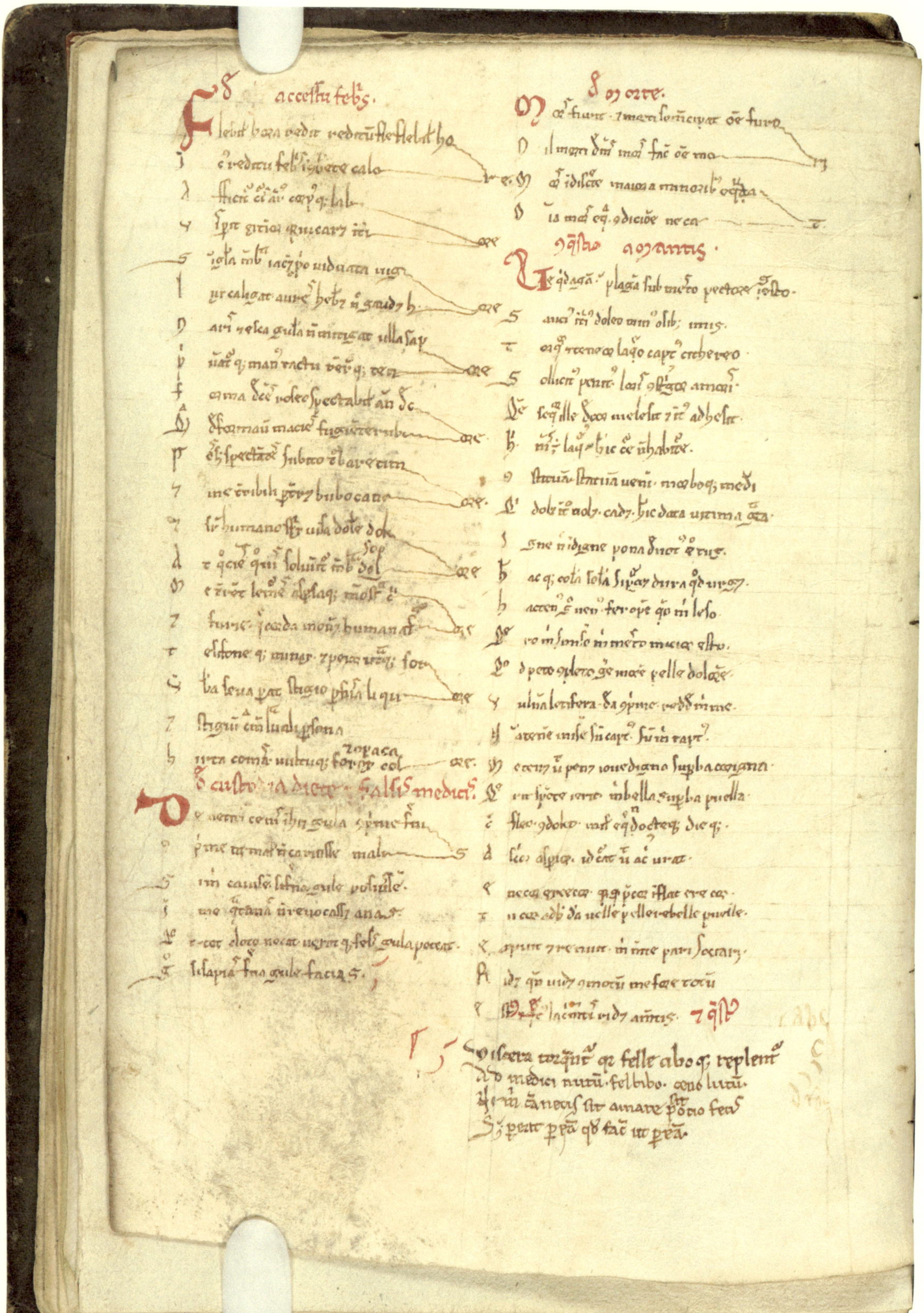

fol. 1v (PARCHMENT ONLY) fol. 1v (PARCHMENT AND PAPER)

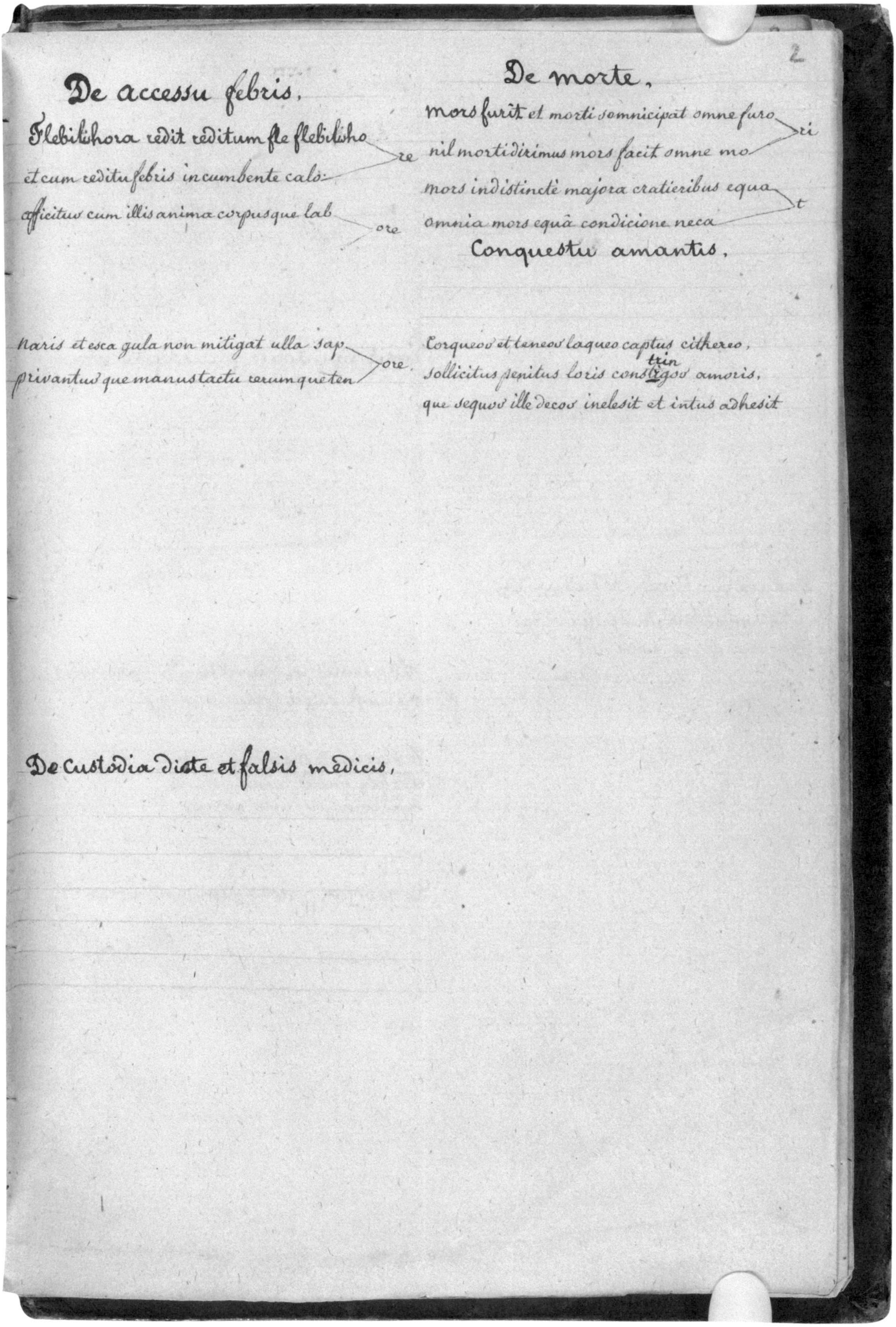
2

De accessu febris.

Flebilishora redit reditum fle flebilisho re
et cum reditu febris incumbente calo re
afficitur cum illis anima corpusque lab ore

naris et esca gula non mitigat ulla sap ore
privantur que manus tactu cerumque ten ore.

De morte.

mors furit et morti somnicipat omne furo ri
nil morti dirimus mors facit omne mo ri
mors indistincte majora cratieribus equa t
omnia mors equâ condicione neca t

Conquestu amantis.

Torqueor et teneor laqueo captus cithereo,
sollicitus penitus loris constr[trin]gor amoris,
que sequor ille decor inelesit et intus adhesit

De custodia diete et falsis medicis.

fol. 2r (PARCHMENT AND PAPER)

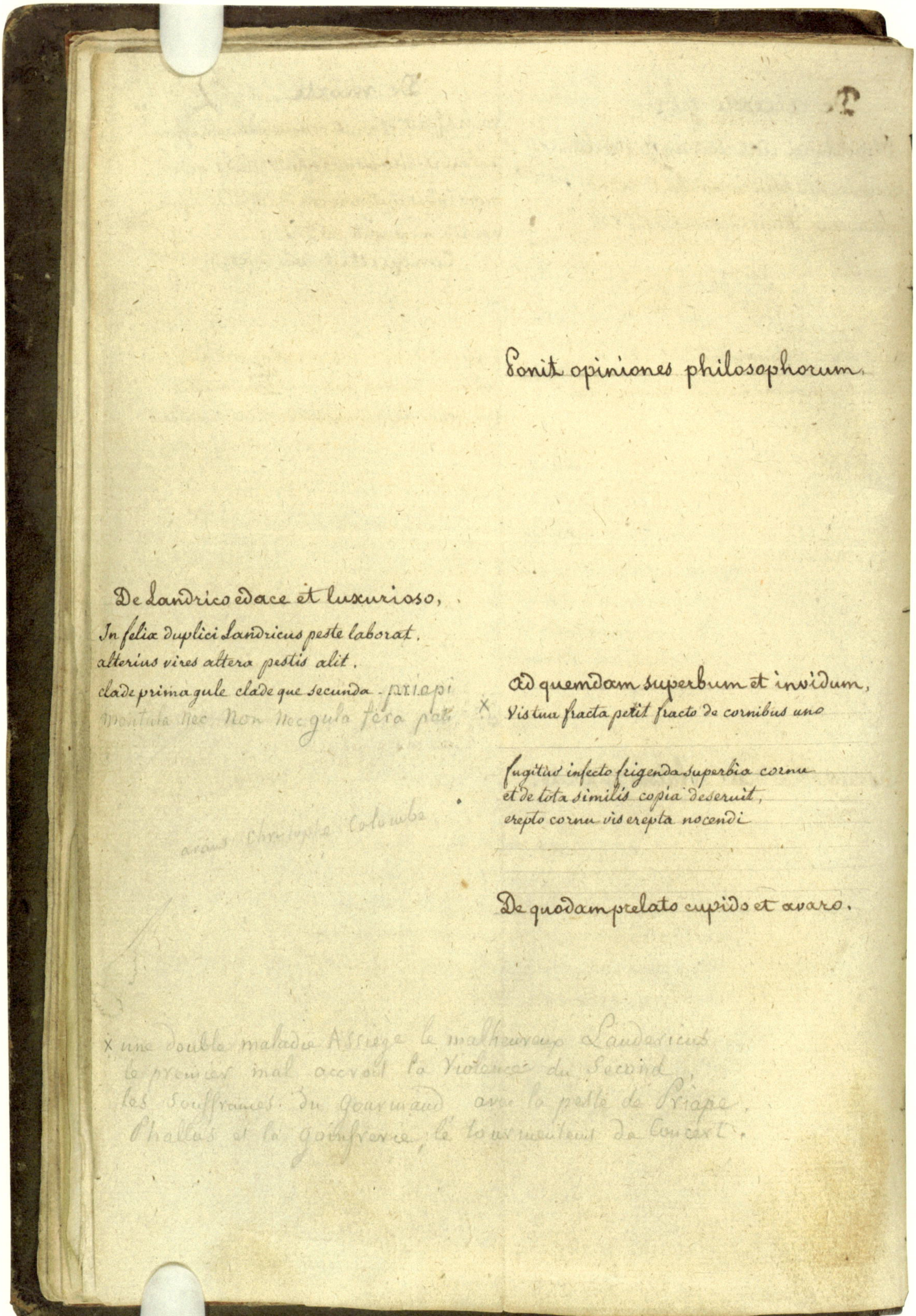

Ponit opiniones philosophorum.

De Landrico edace et luxurioso,
In felix duplici Landricus peste laborat,
alterius vires altera pestis alit.
clade prima gule clade que secunda priapi
mentula nec. Non nec gula fera pati

avant Christophe Colombe

Ad quemdam superbum et invidum,
Vis tua fracta petit fracto de cornibus uno
fugitiv infecto frigenda superbia cornu
et de tota similis copia deseruit,
erepto cornu vis erepta nocendi

De quodam prelato cupido et avaro.

x une double maladie Assiege le malheureux Landaricus
le premier mal accroit la Violence du Second
les Souffrances du Gourmand avec la peste de Priape
Phallas et la goinfrerie, le tourmenteur du Concert.

fol. 2v (PARCHMENT AND PAPER)

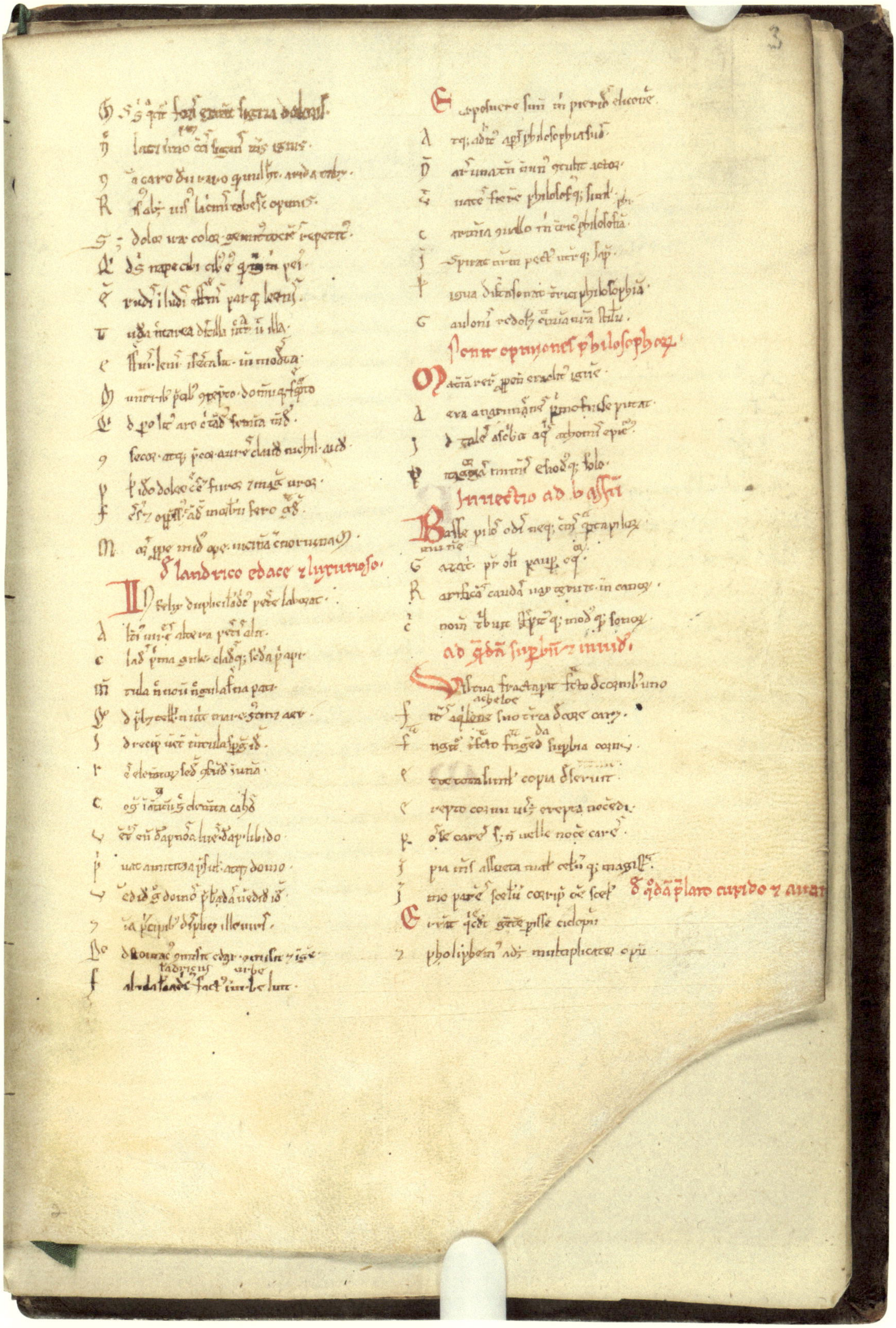

fol. 2r (PARCHMENT ONLY)

fol. 3r (PARCHMENT AND PAPER)

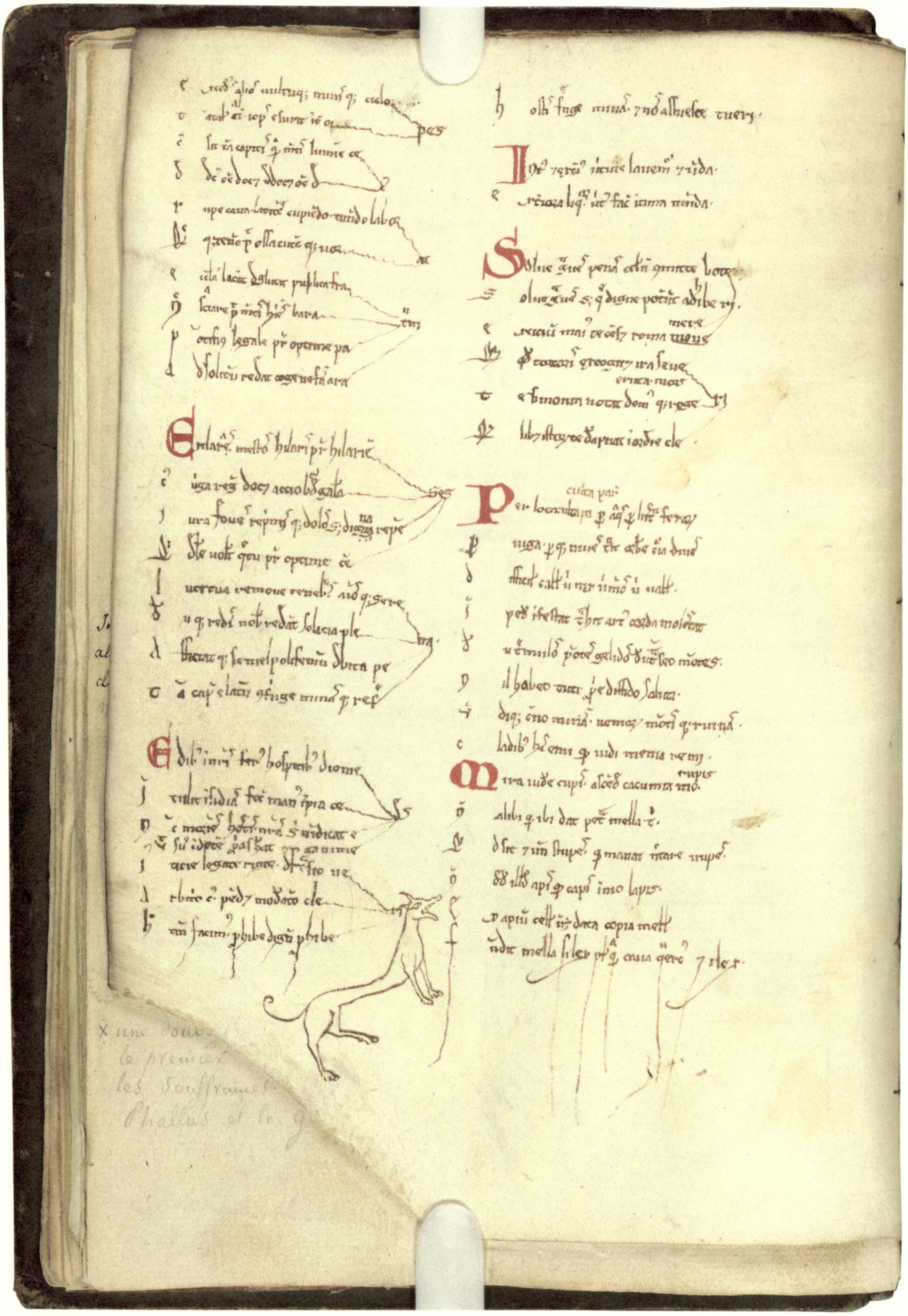

fol. 2v (PARCHMENT ONLY)

fol. 3v (PARCHMENT AND PAPER)

fol. 4r (PARCHMENT AND PAPER)

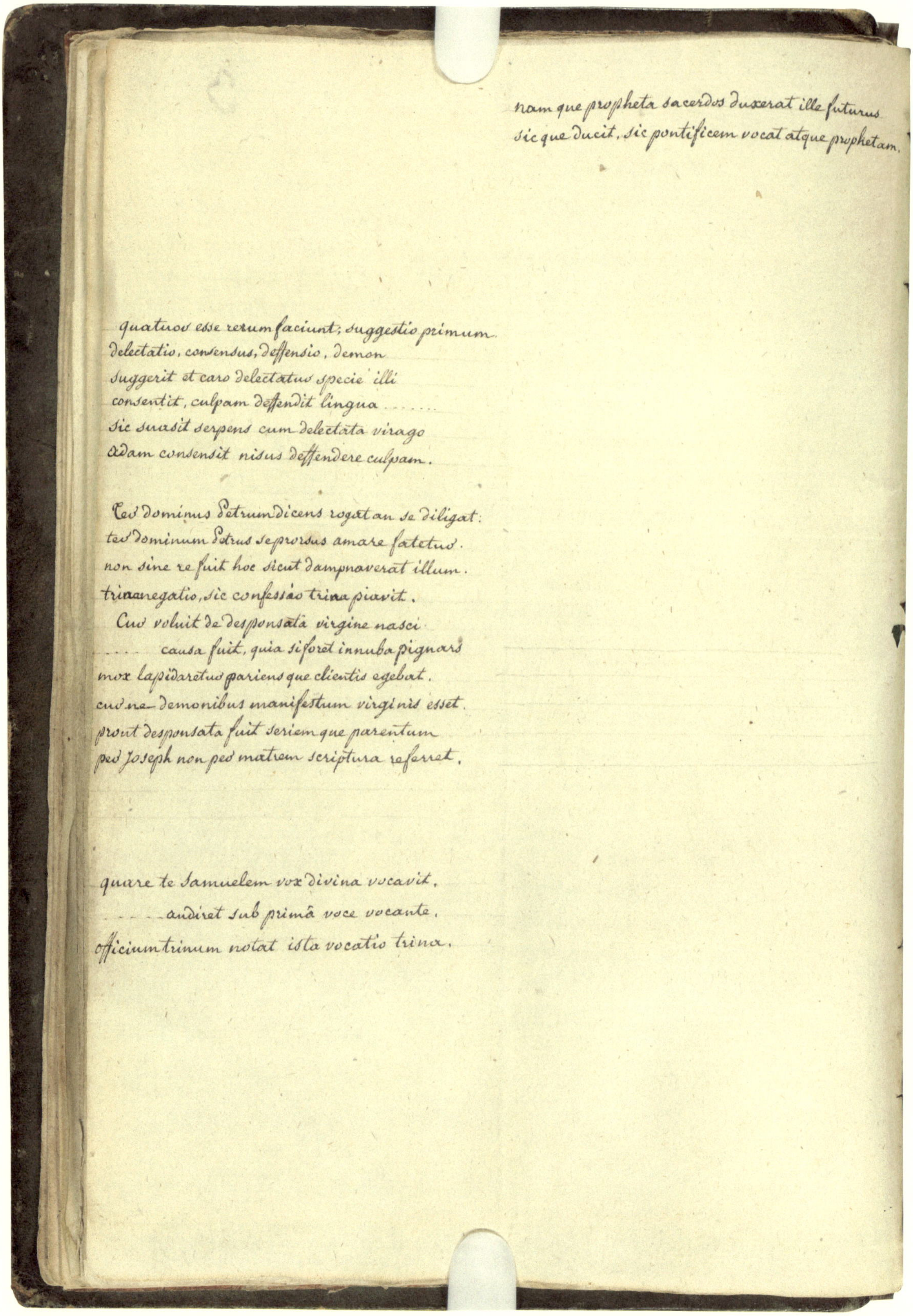

nam que propheta sacerdos duxerat ille futurus
sic que ducit, sic pontificem vocat atque prophetam.

quatuor esse rerum faciunt; suggestio primum
delectatio, consensus, deffensio, demon
suggerit et caro delectatus specie illi
consentit, culpam deffendit lingua ......
sic suasit serpens cum delectata virago
adam consensit nisus deffendere culpam.

Ter dominus Petrum dicens rogat an se diligat:
ter dominum Petrus se prorsus amare fatetur.
non sine re fuit hoc sicut dampnaverat illum.
trina negatio, sic confessio trina piavit.
Cur voluit de desponsata virgine nasci
.... causa fuit, quia si foret innuba pignaris
mox lapidaretur pariens que clientis egebat.
cur ne demonibus manifestum virginis esset.
prout desponsata fuit seriem que parentum
per Joseph non per matrem scriptura referret.

quare te Samuelem vox divina vocavit.
.... audiret sub prima voce vocante.
officium trinum notat ista vocatio trina.

fol. 4v (PARCHMENT AND PAPER)

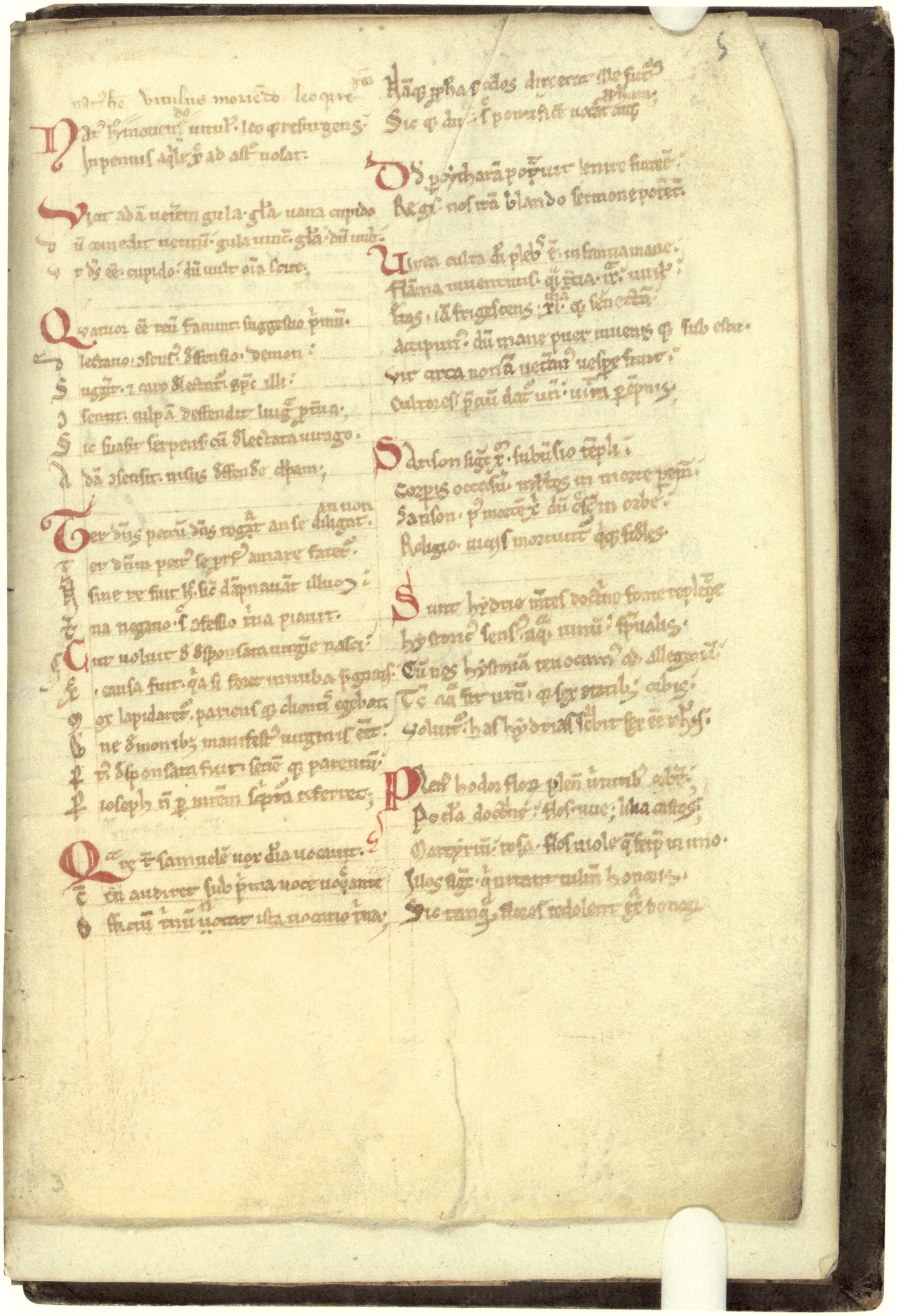

fol. 3r (PARCHMENT ONLY) fol. 5r (PARCHMENT AND PAPER)

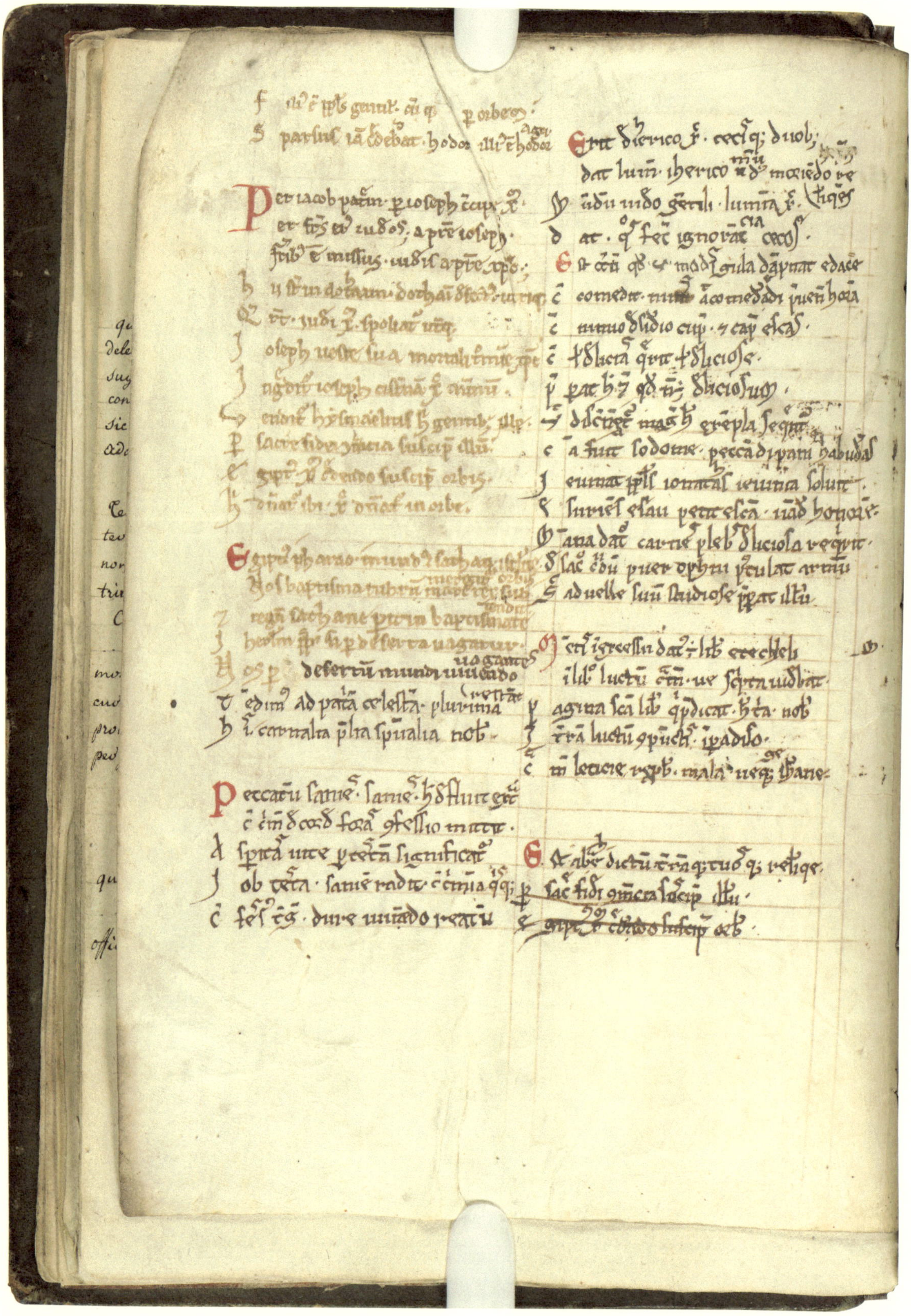

fol. 3v (PARCHMENT ONLY)

fol. 5v (PARCHMENT AND PAPER)

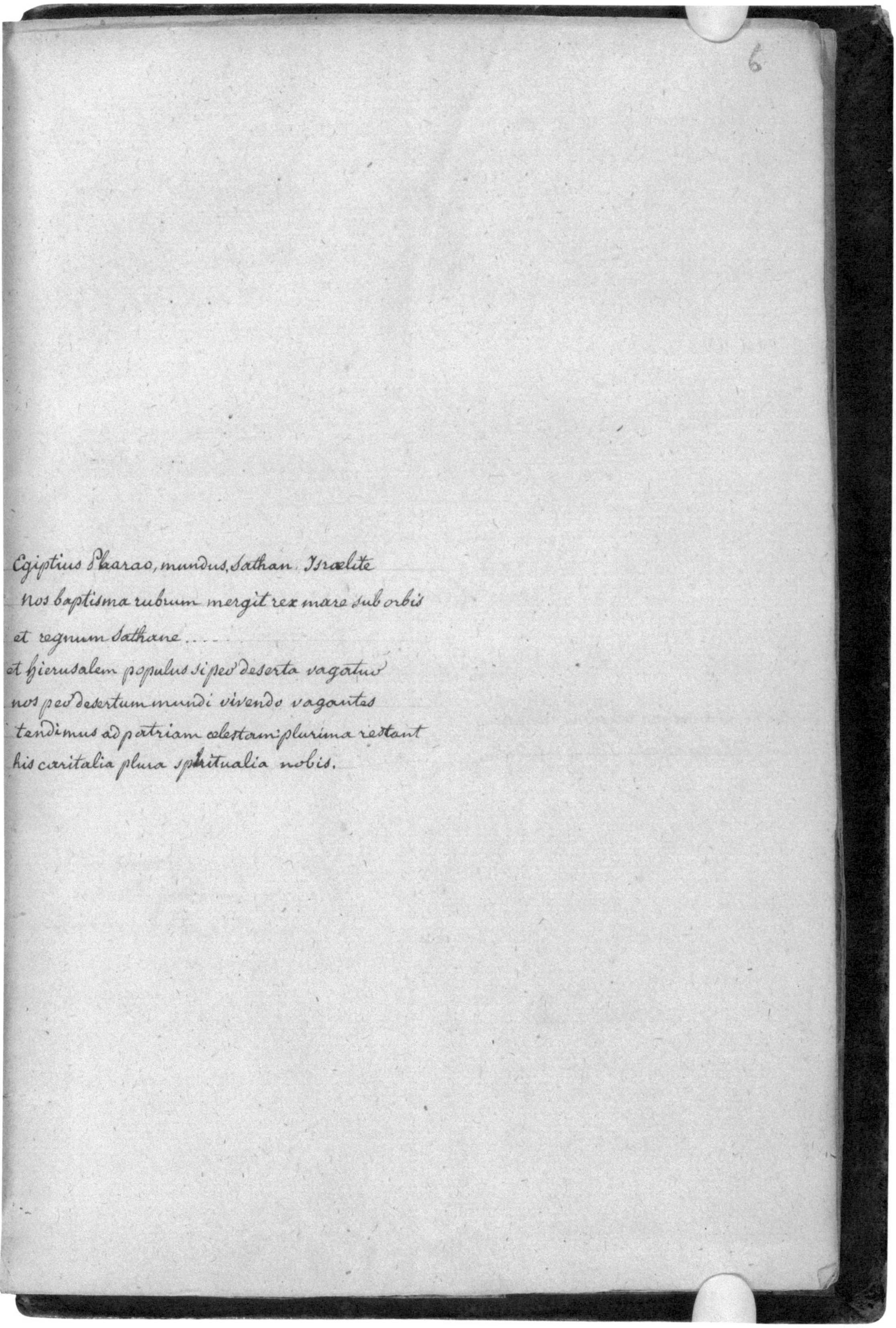

6

Egiptius Pharao, mundus, Sathan. Israelite
nos baptisma rubrum mergit rex mare sub orbis
et regnum Sathane....
et hierusalem populus si per deserta vagatur
nos per desertum mundi vivendo vagantes
tendimus ad patriam celestam: plurima restant
his caritalia plura spiritualia nobis.

fol. 6r (PARCHMENT AND PAPER)

qui res mundanas pro religione relinquit.
effugiunt hi hostes abjectâ Sidone crudeli.

fol. 6v (PARCHMENT AND PAPER)

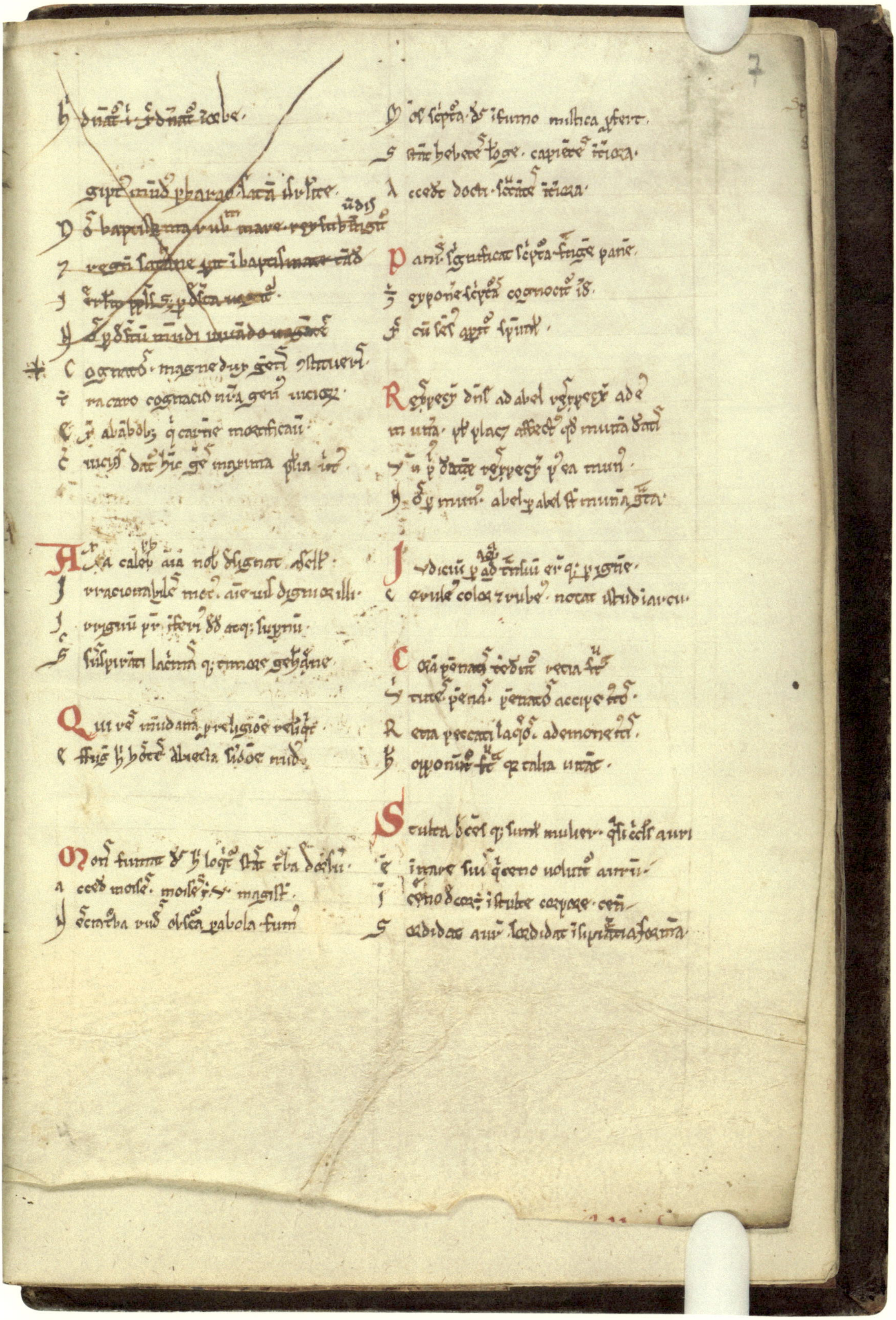

fol. 4r (PARCHMENT ONLY)

fol. 7r (PARCHMENT AND PAPER)

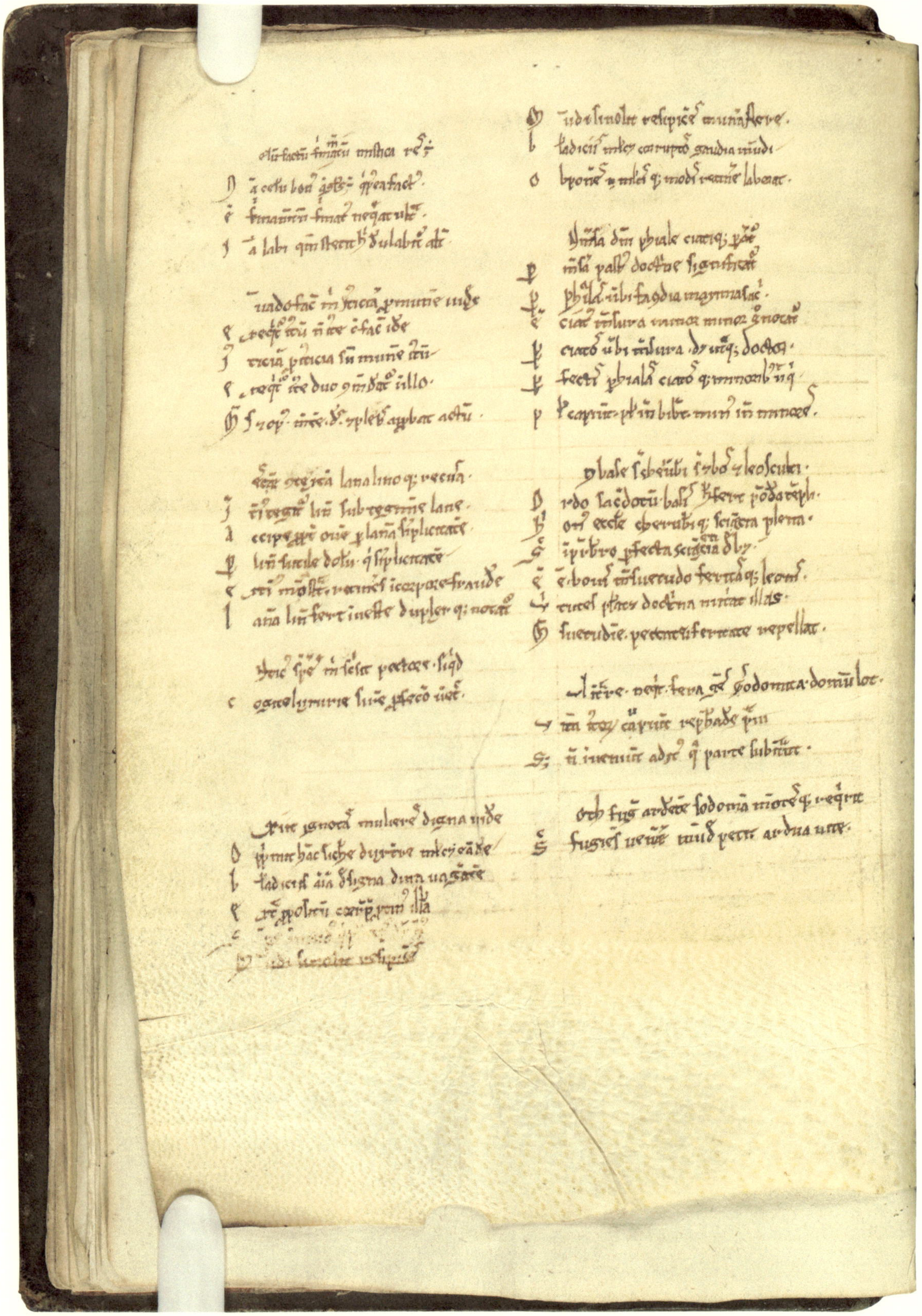

fol. 4v (PARCHMENT ONLY) fol. 7v (PARCHMENT AND PAPER)

8

mundi si nolit resipicens. . . . . . flere
blandiciis mulctet corruptos, gaudia mundi
obponens multis que modis retinere laborat.

Exiit ignotas mulieres digna videre
opprimit hanc Sichem dux terre mulctet easdem
blandiciis anima designa dura vagantes
exit propositum corruptum protinus illas

Loth fugit ardentem Sodomam, montes que requirit,
se fugiens vertere mundum petit ardua vite

fol. 8r (PARCHMENT AND PAPER)

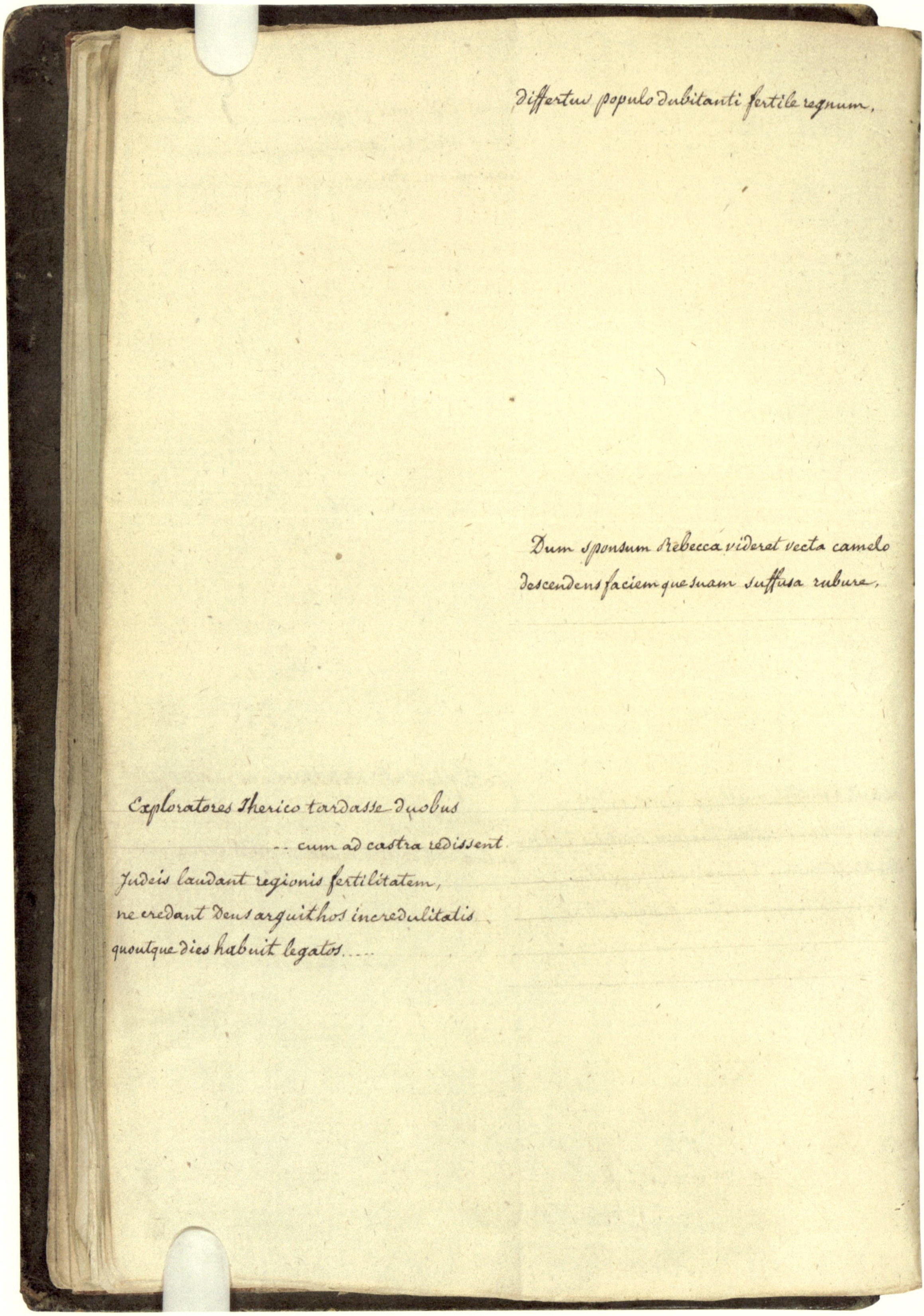

differtur populo dubitanti fertile regnum,

Dum sponsum Rebecca videret vecta camelo
descendens faciemque suam suffusa rubore,

Exploratores Iherico tardasse duobus
.. cum ad castra redissent.
Judeis laudant regionis fertilitatem,
ne credant Deus arguit hos incredulitatis.
quoutque dies habuit legatos.....

fol. 8v (PARCHMENT AND PAPER)

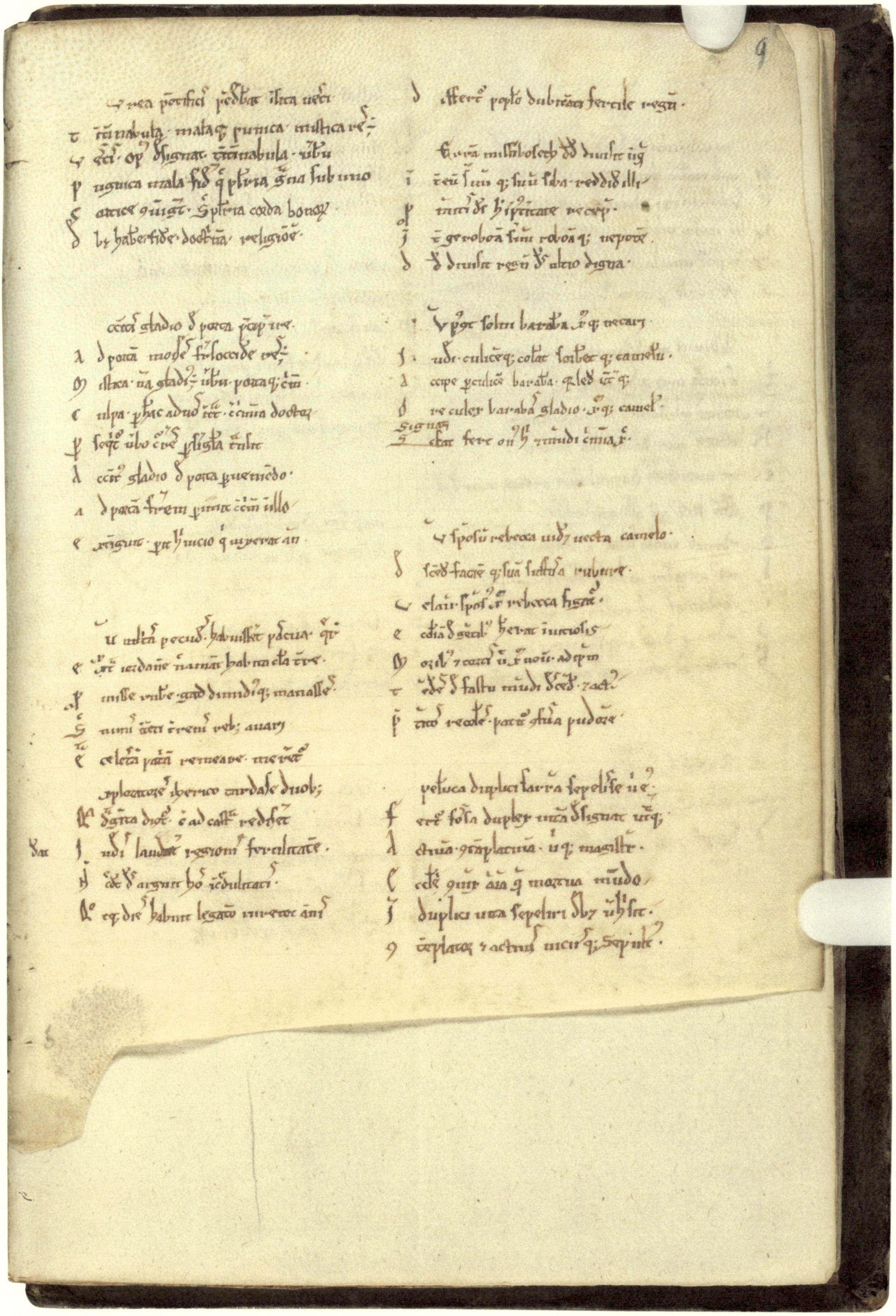

fol. 5r (PARCHMENT ONLY) fol. 9r (PARCHMENT AND PAPER)

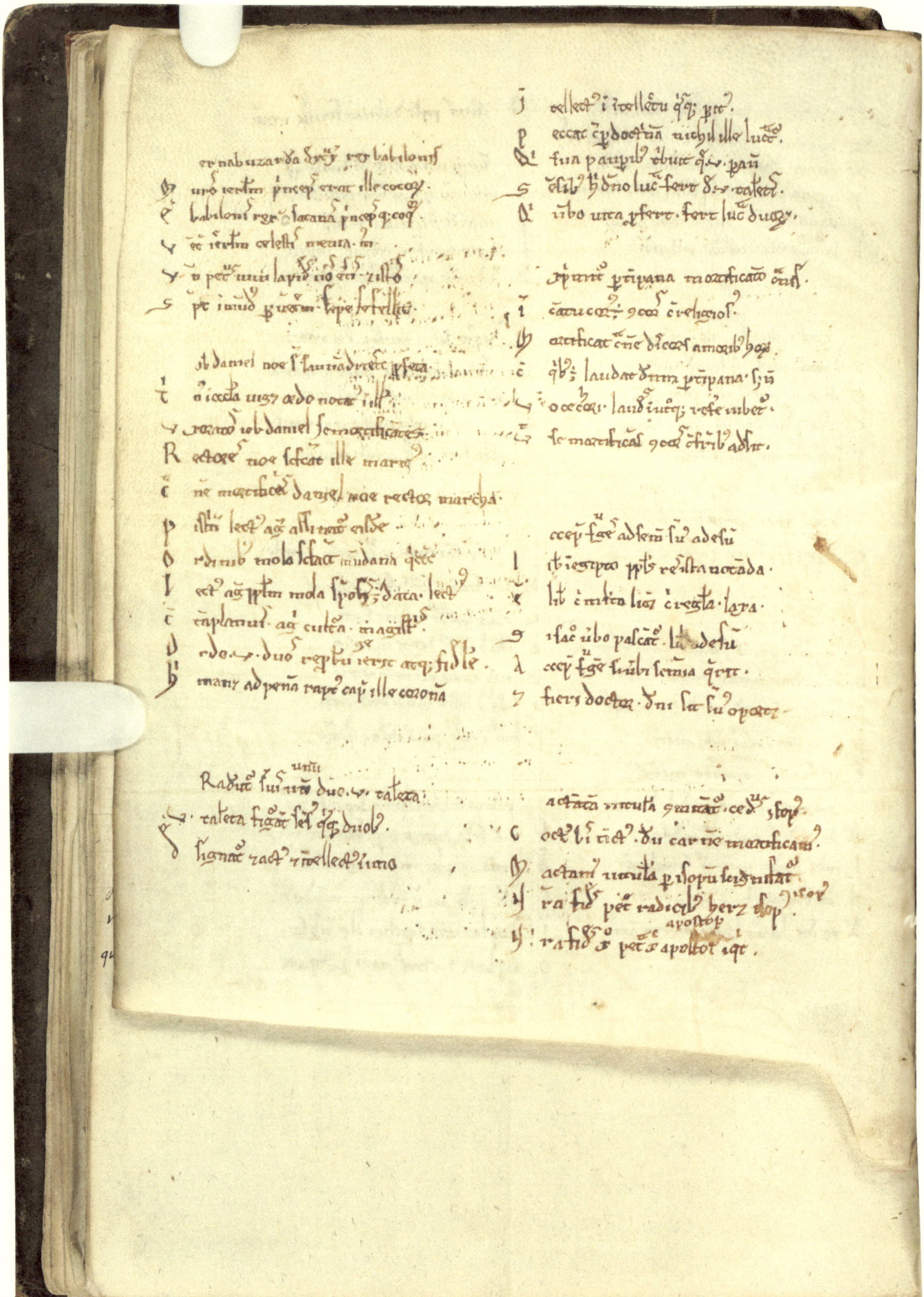

fol. 5v (PARCHMENT ONLY) fol. 9v (PARCHMENT AND PAPER)

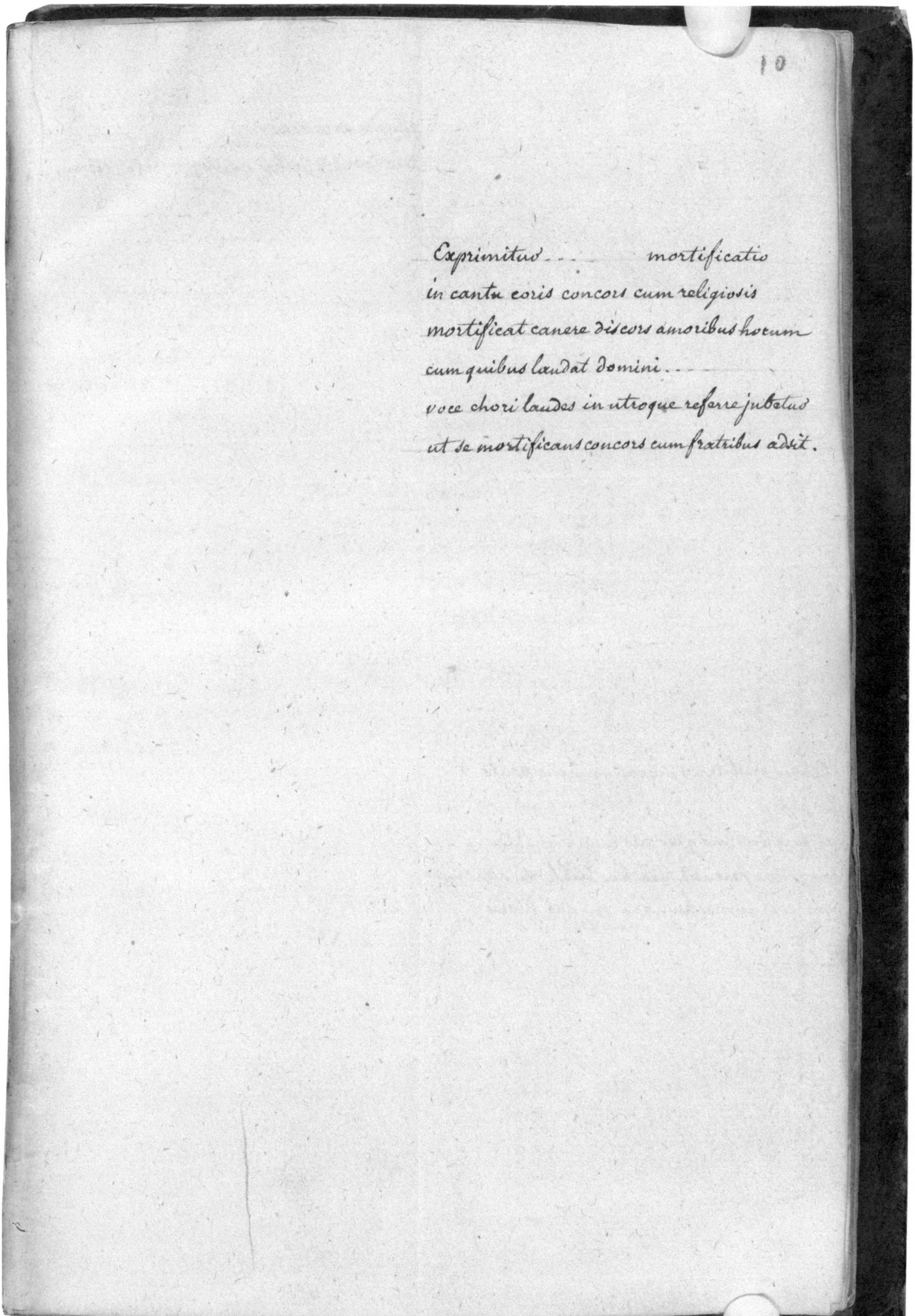

10

Exprimitur . . . mortificatio
in cantu coris concors cum religiosis
mortificat canere discors amoribus horum
cum quibus laudat domini . . .
voce chori laudes in utroque referre jubetur
ut se mortificans concors cum fratribus adsit.

fol. 10r (PARCHMENT AND PAPER)

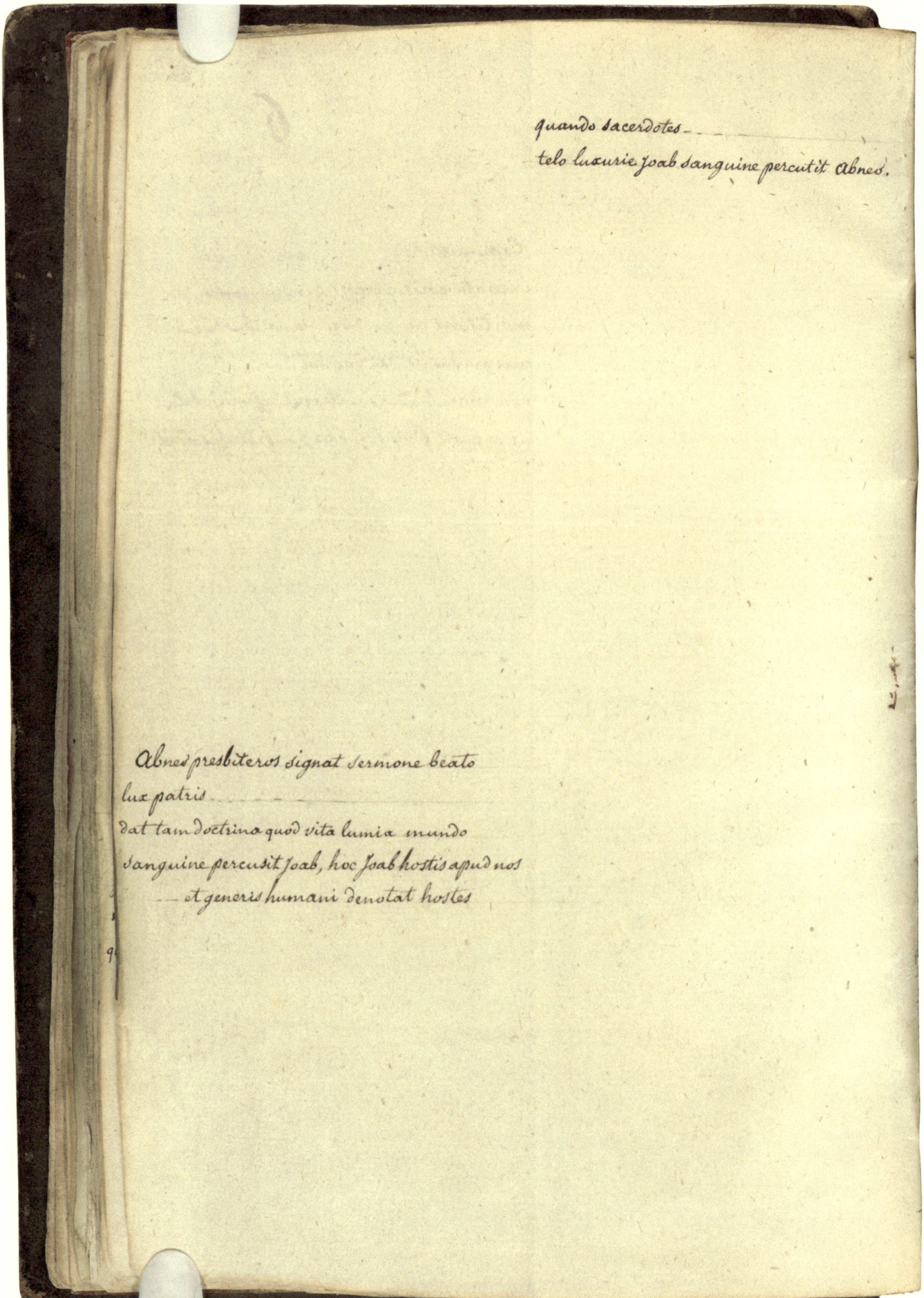
quando sacerdotes ——
telo luxurie Joab sanguine percutit Abnes.

Abnes presbiteros signat sermone beato
lux patris ——
dat tam doctrina quod vita lumia mundo
sanguine percusit Joab, hoc Joab hostis apud nos
—— et generis humani denotat hostes

fol. 10v (PARCHMENT AND PAPER)

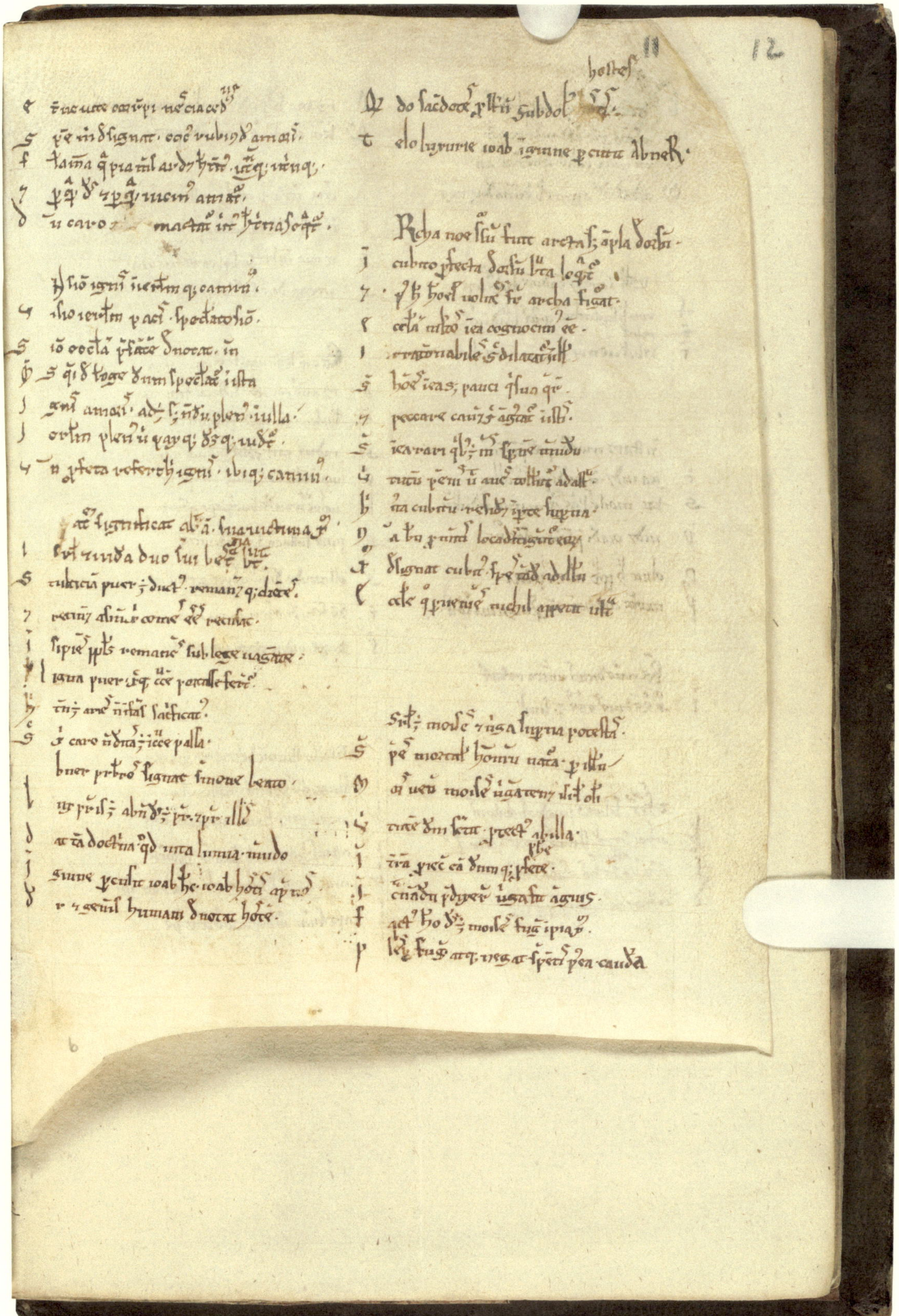

fol. 6r (PARCHMENT ONLY) fol. 11r (PARCHMENT AND PAPER)

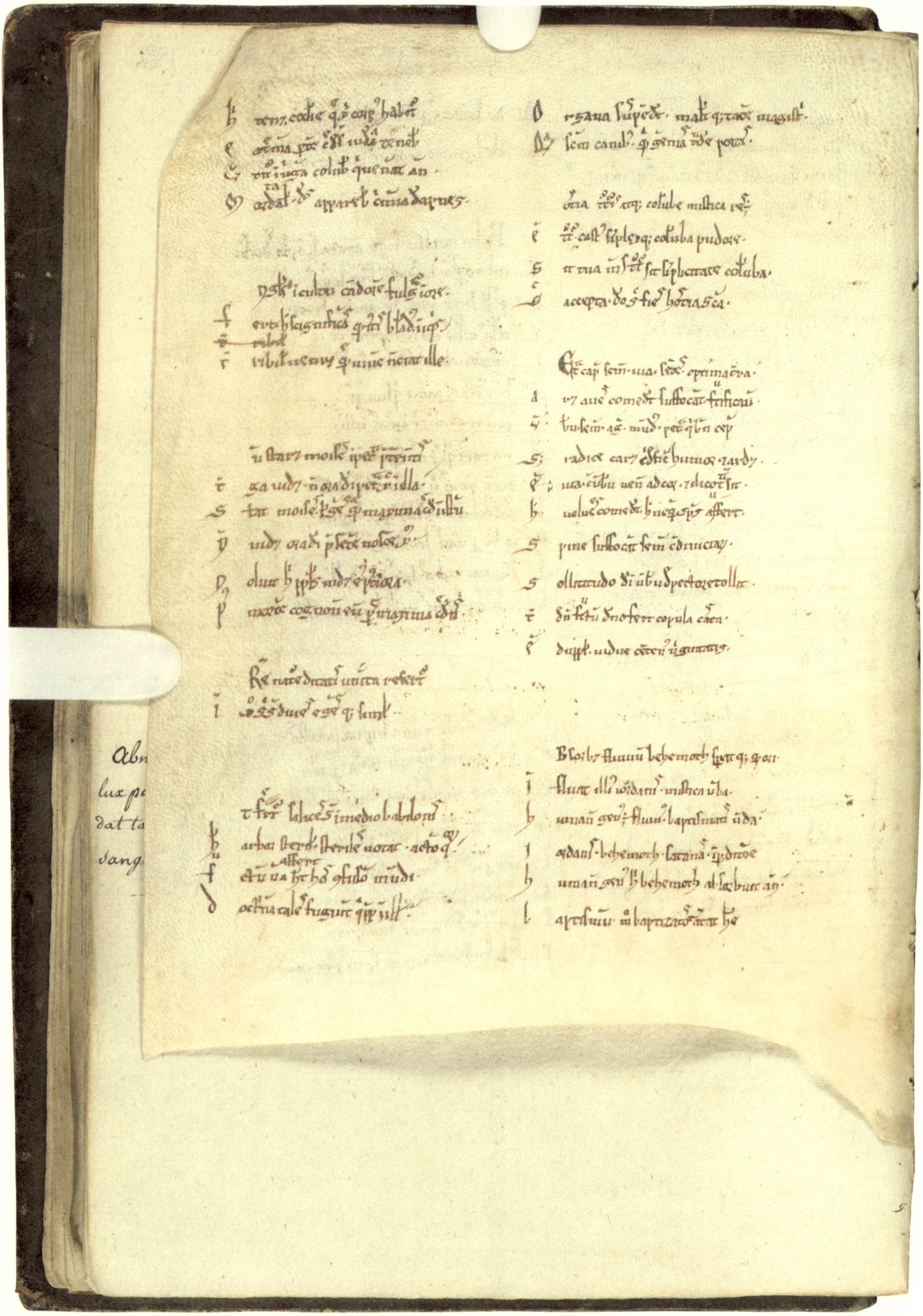

fol. 6v (PARCHMENT ONLY) fol. 11v (PARCHMENT AND PAPER)

fol. 12r (PARCHMENT AND PAPER)

fol. 12v (PARCHMENT AND PAPER)

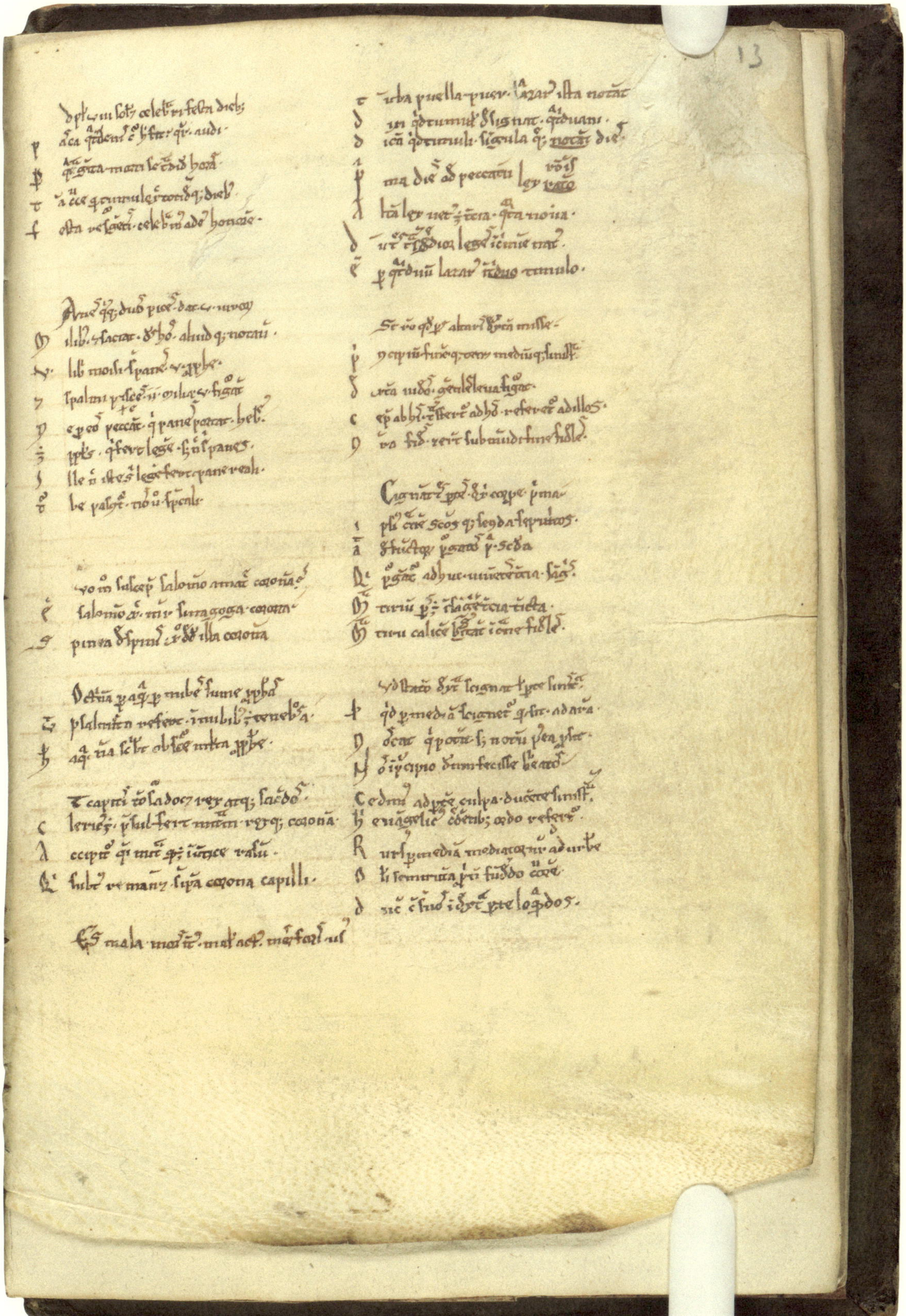

fol. 7r (PARCHMENT ONLY)

fol. 13r (PARCHMENT AND PAPER)

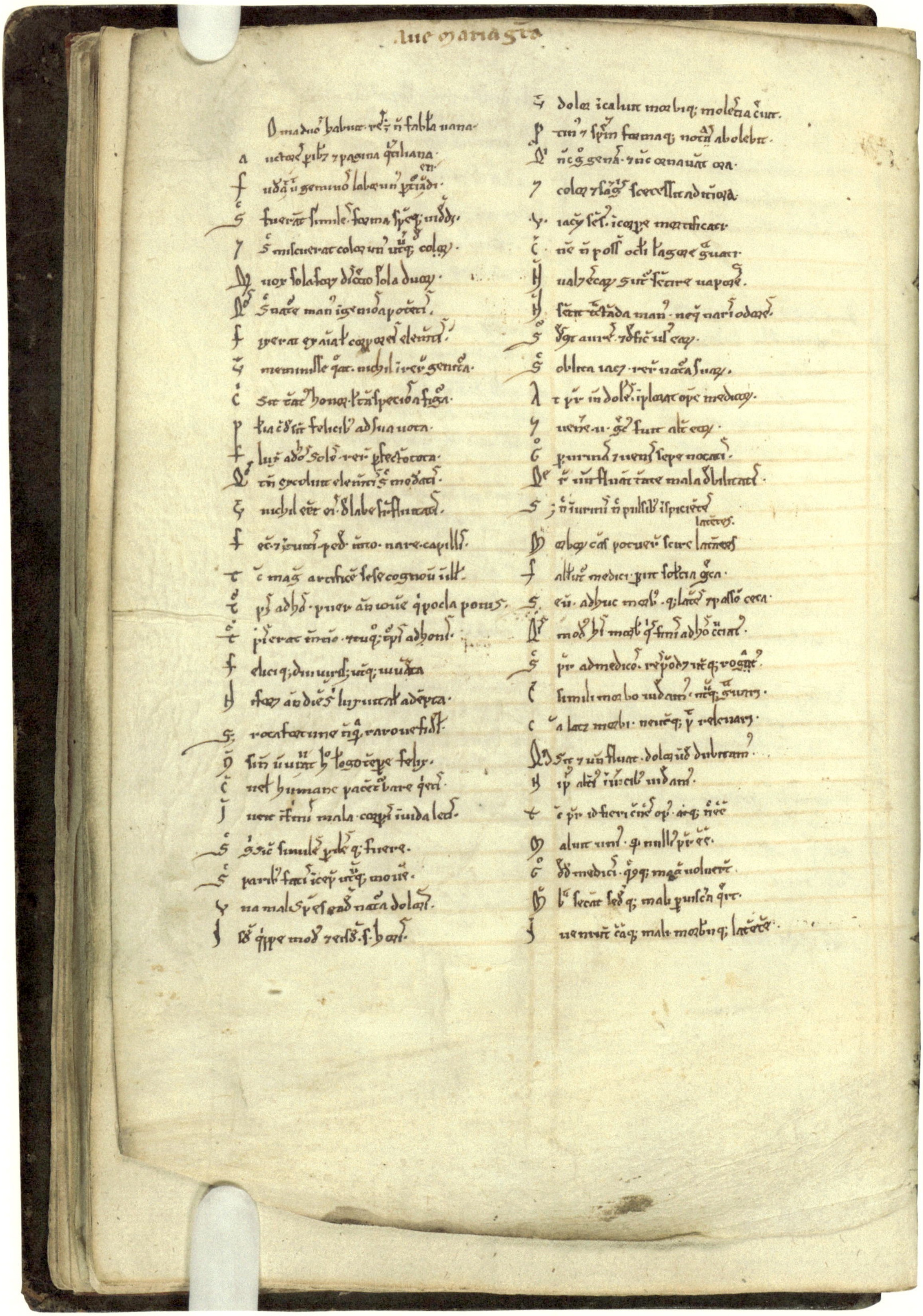

fol. 7v (PARCHMENT ONLY)

fol. 13v (PARCHMENT AND PAPER)

fol. 14r (PARCHMENT AND PAPER)

fol. 14v (PARCHMENT AND PAPER)

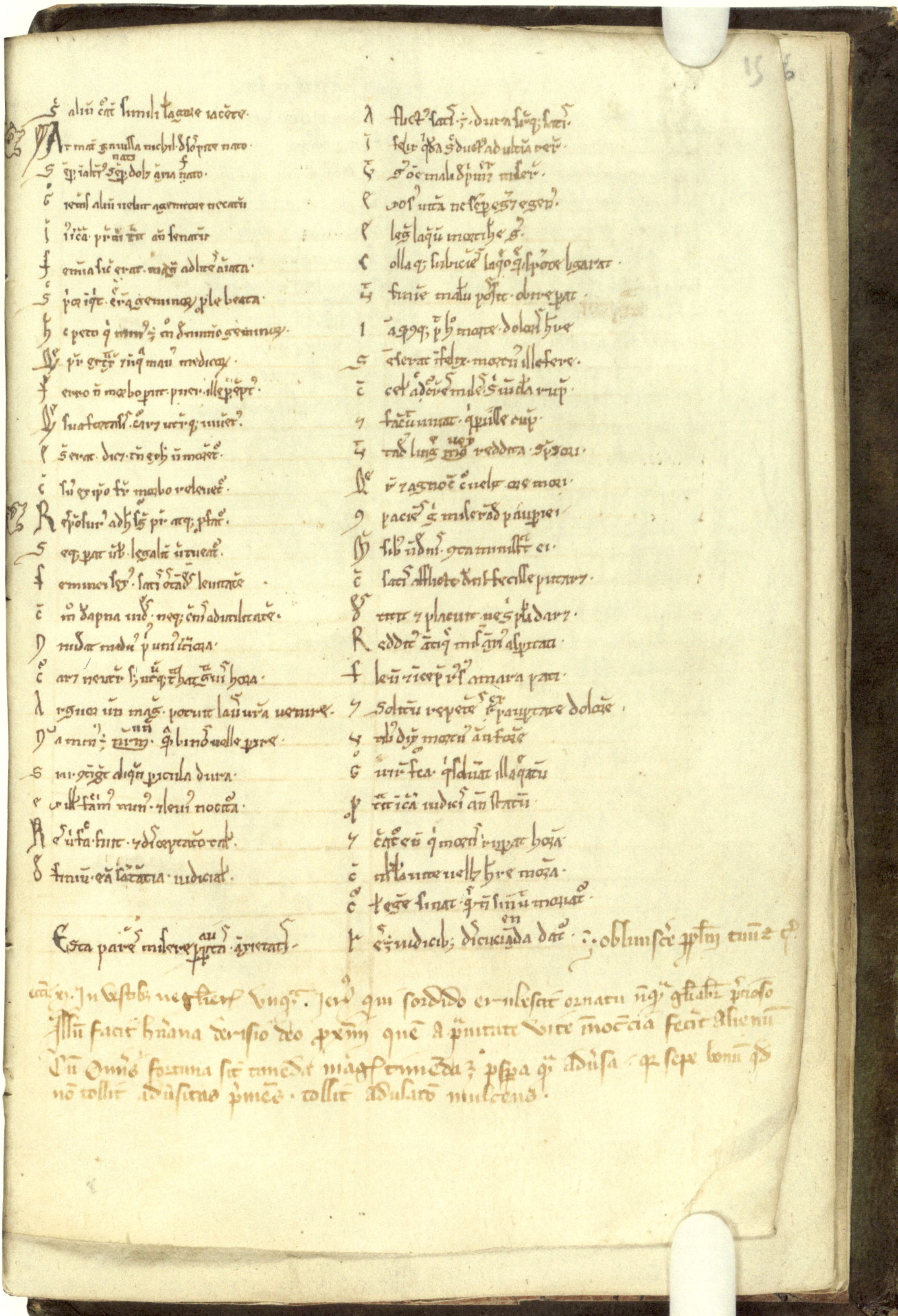

fol. 8r (PARCHMENT ONLY)

fol. 15r (PARCHMENT AND PAPER)

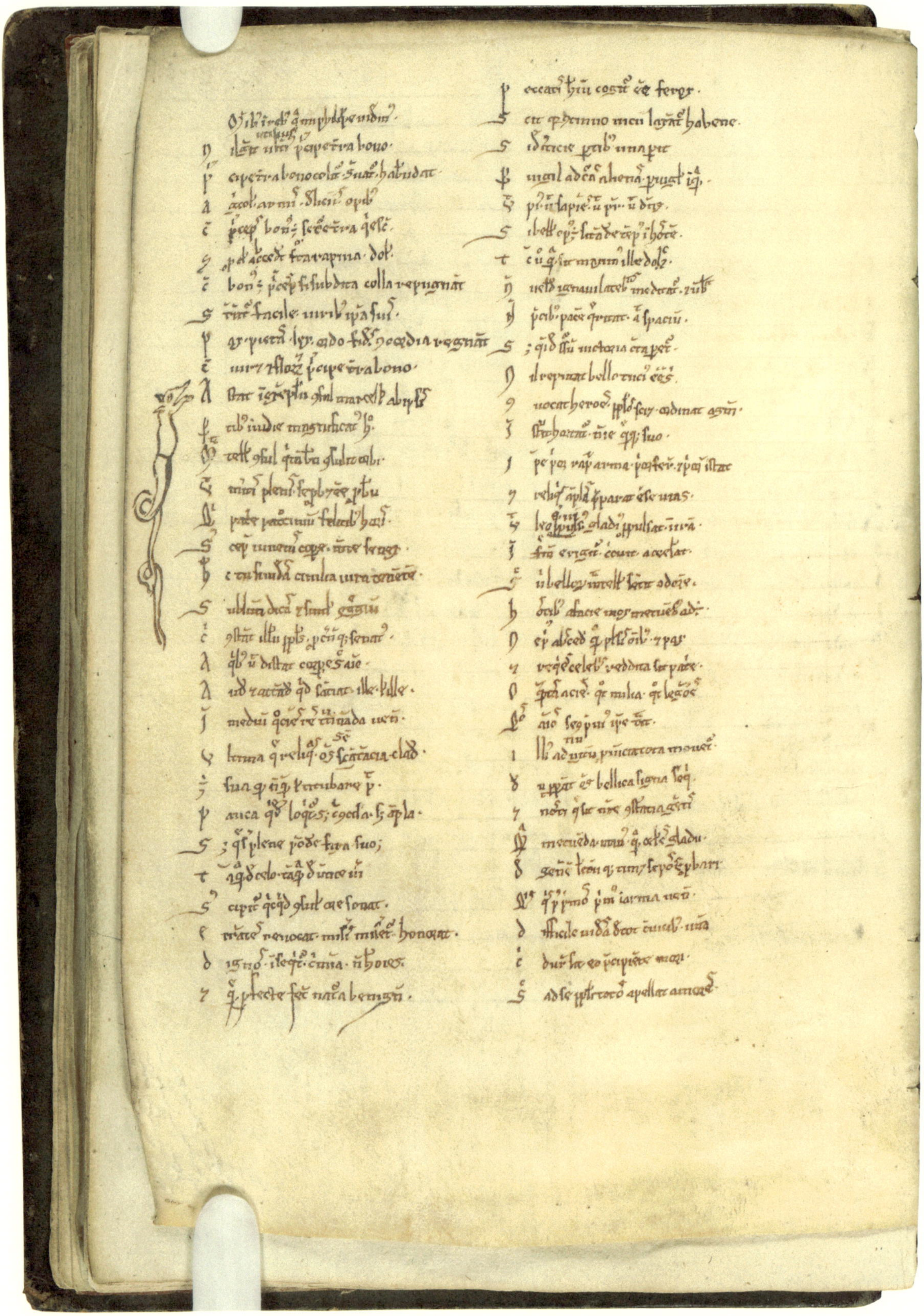

fol. 8v (PARCHMENT ONLY)

fol. 15v (PARCHMENT AND PAPER)

fol. 16r (PARCHMENT AND PAPER)

fol. 16v (PARCHMENT AND PAPER)

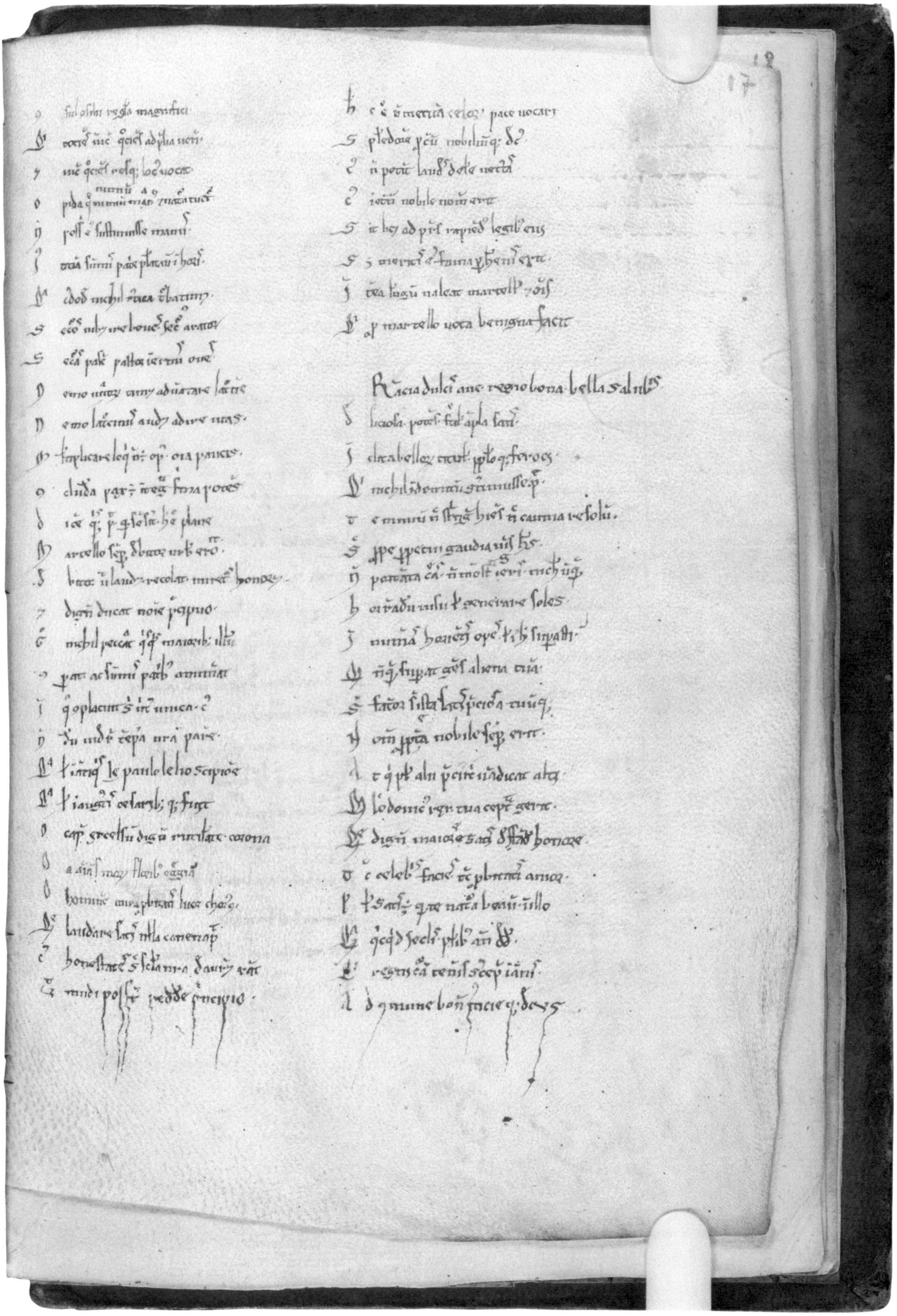

fol. 9r (PARCHMENT ONLY)

fol. 17r (PARCHMENT AND PAPER)

fol. 9v (PARCHMENT ONLY)

fol. 17v (PARCHMENT AND PAPER)

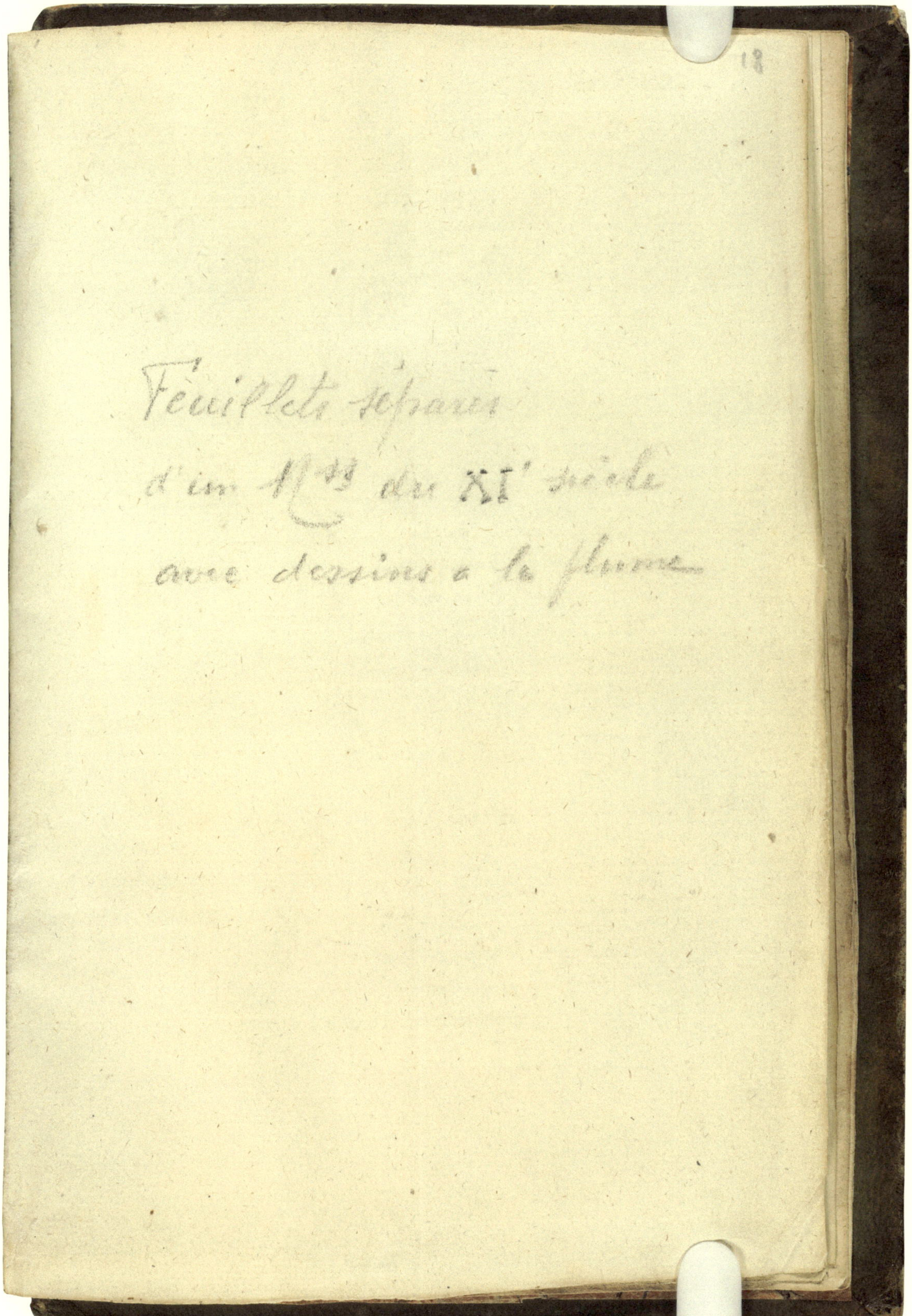

fol. 18r (PARCHMENT AND PAPER)

fol. 18v (PARCHMENT AND PAPER)

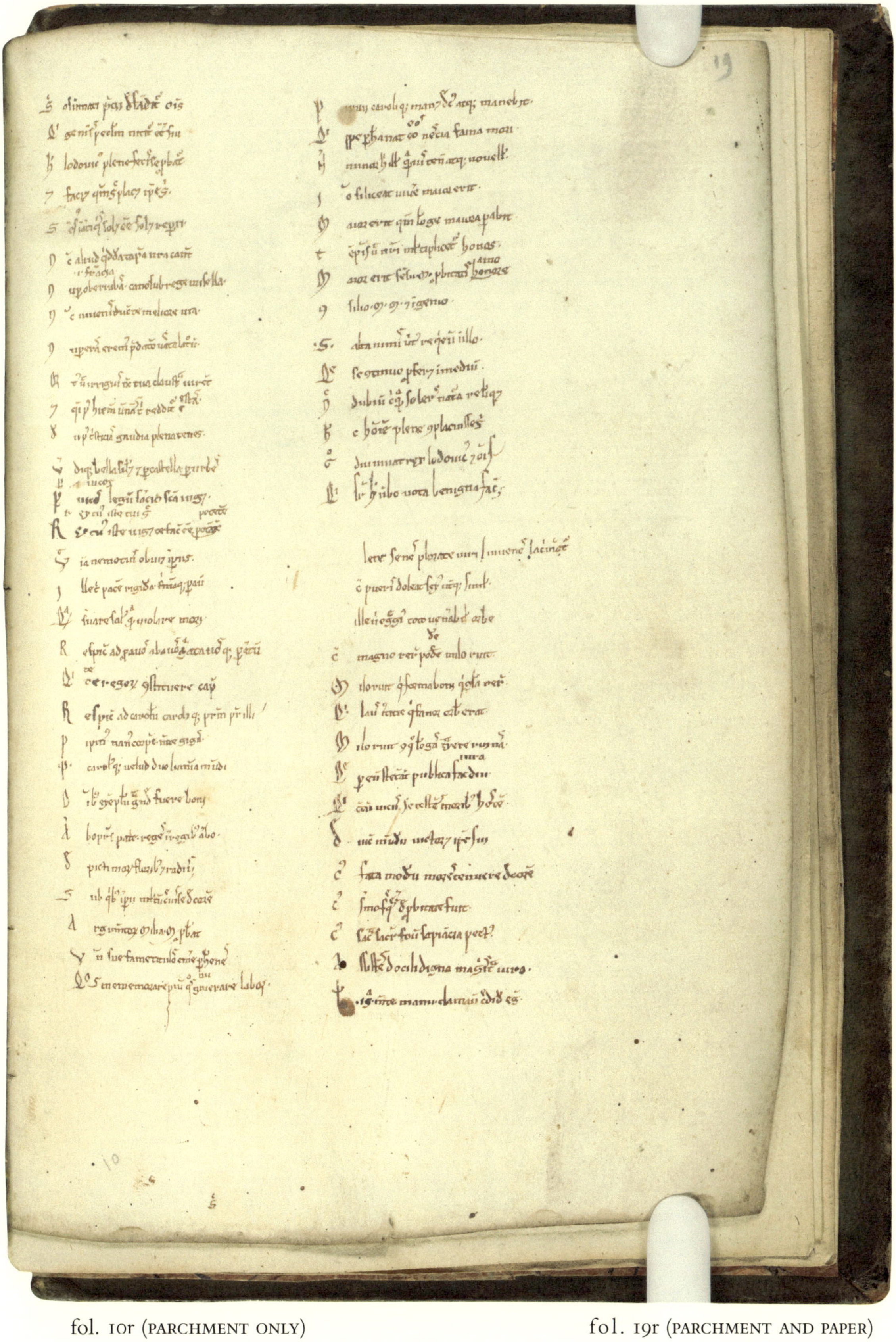

fol. 10r (PARCHMENT ONLY) fol. 19r (PARCHMENT AND PAPER)

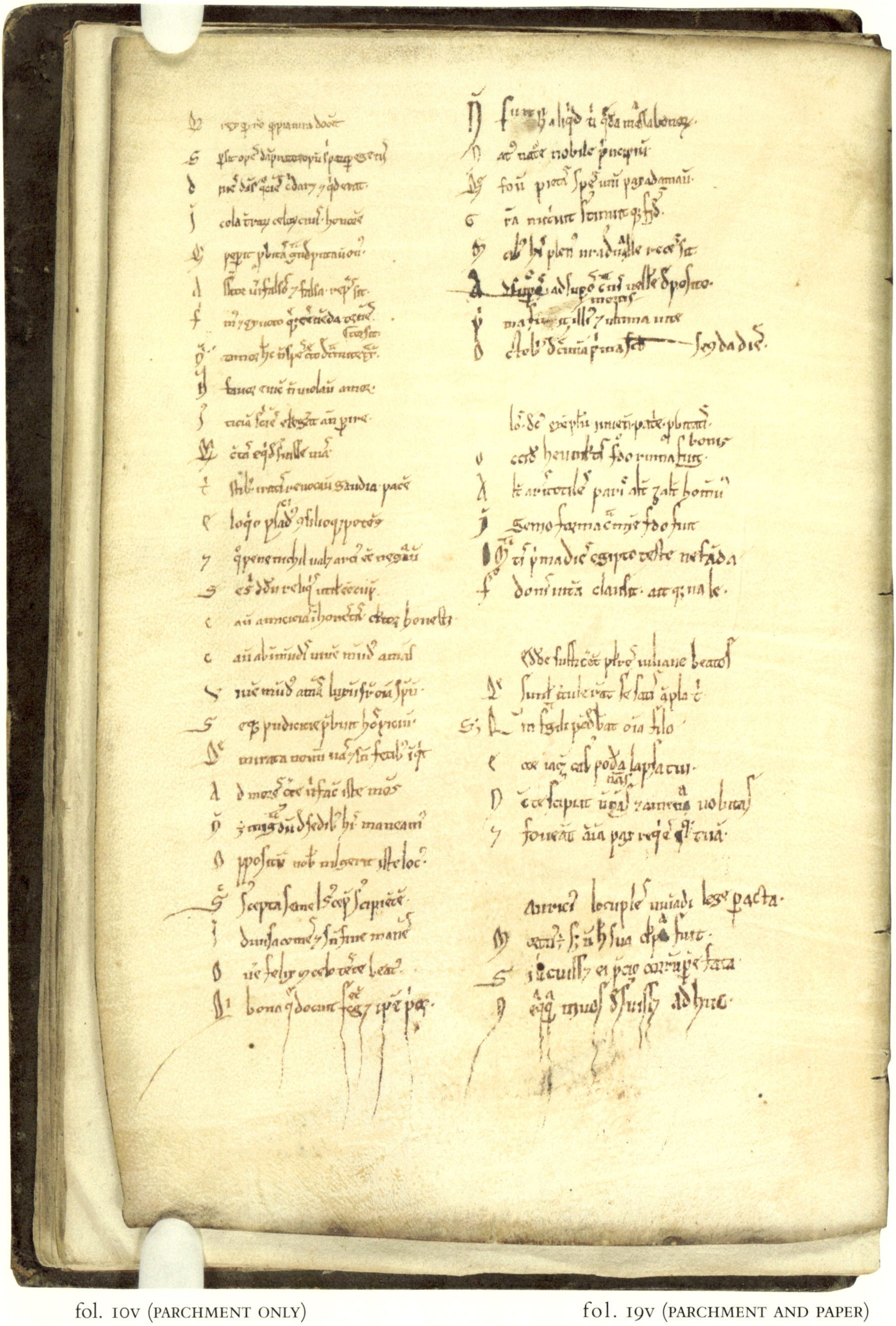

fol. 10v (PARCHMENT ONLY) fol. 19v (PARCHMENT AND PAPER)

fol. 20r (PARCHMENT AND PAPER)

fol. 20v (PARCHMENT AND PAPER)

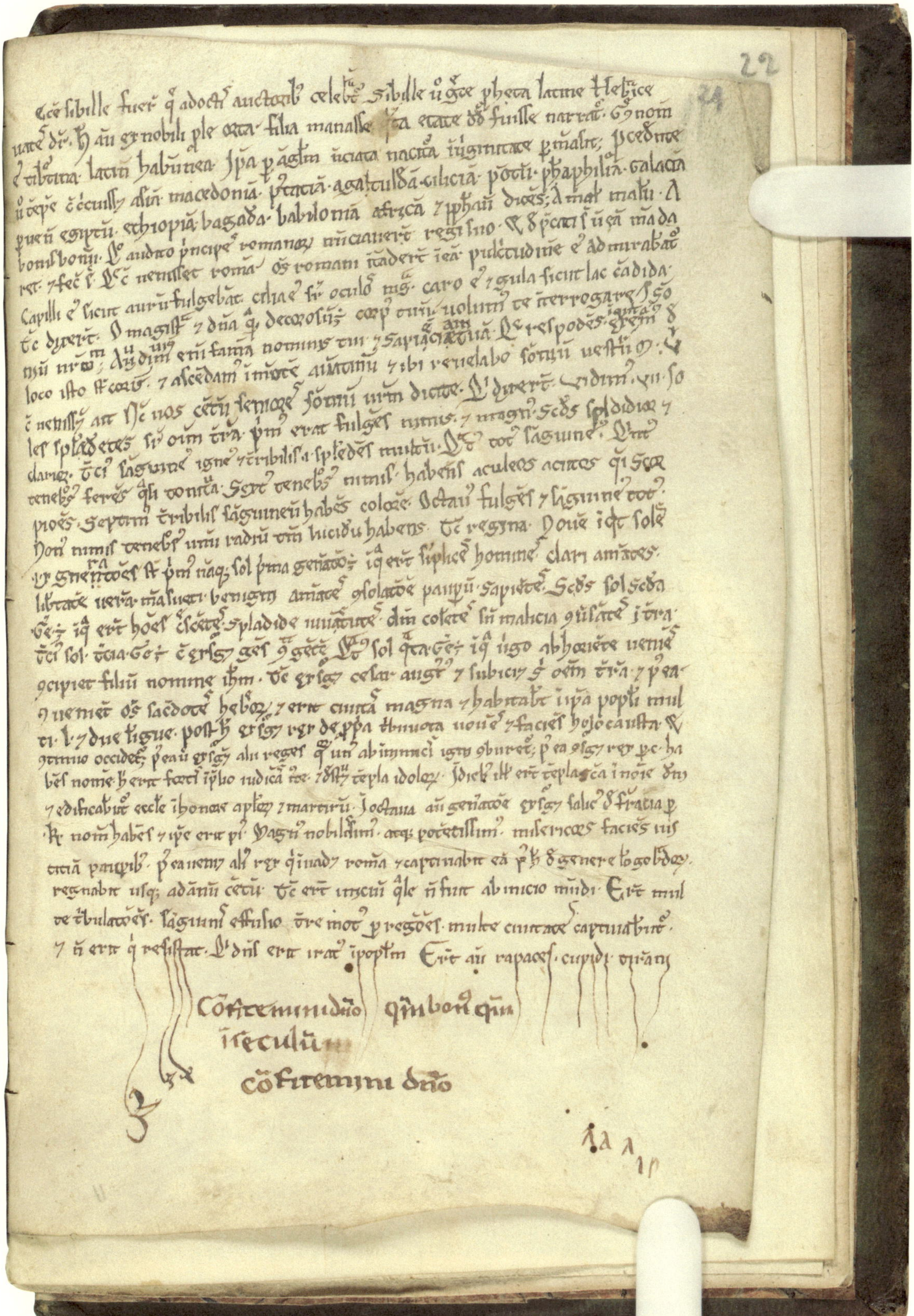

fol. 11r (PARCHMENT ONLY) fol. 21r (PARCHMENT AND PAPER)

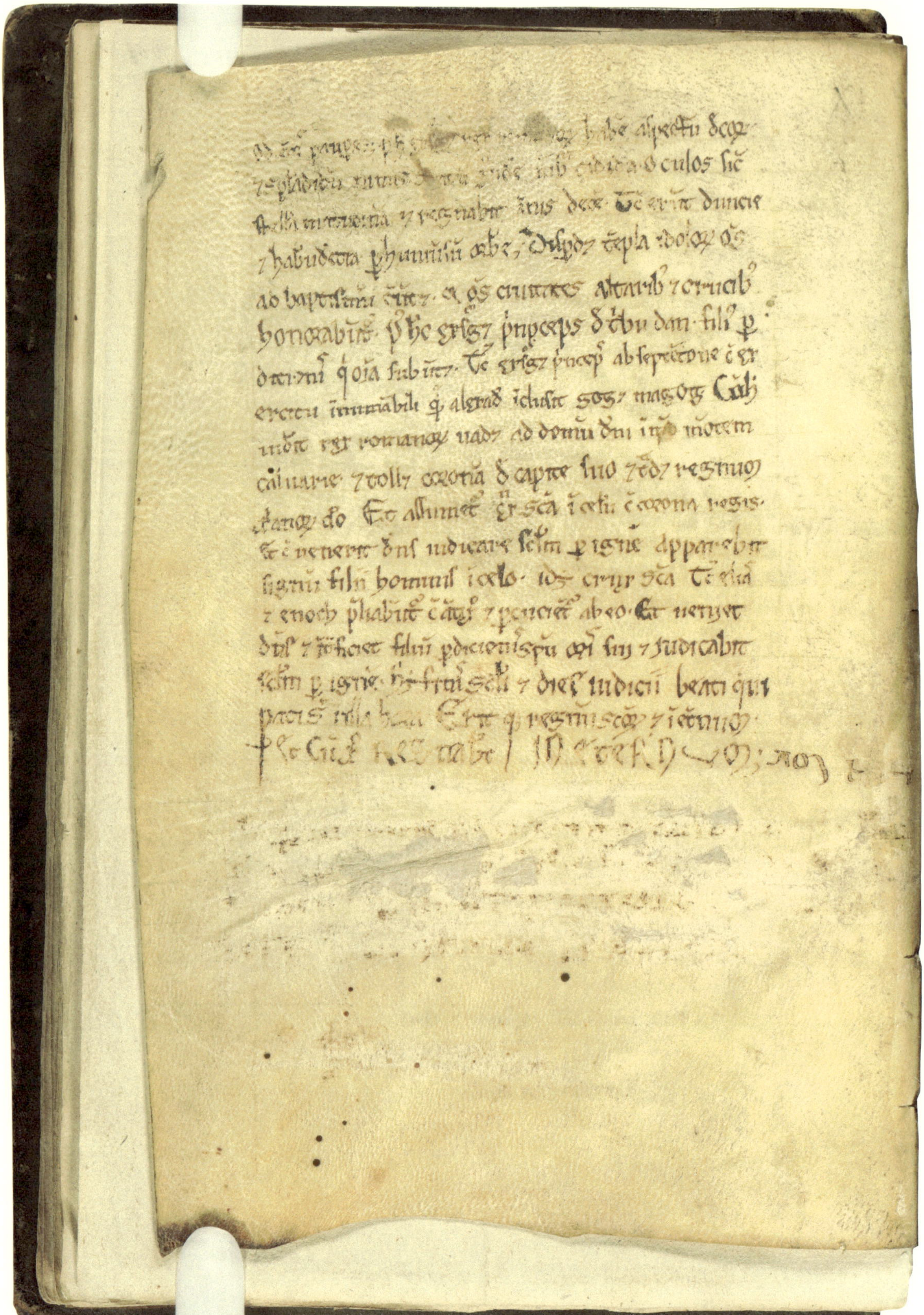

fol. 11v (parchment only) fol. 21v (parchment and paper)

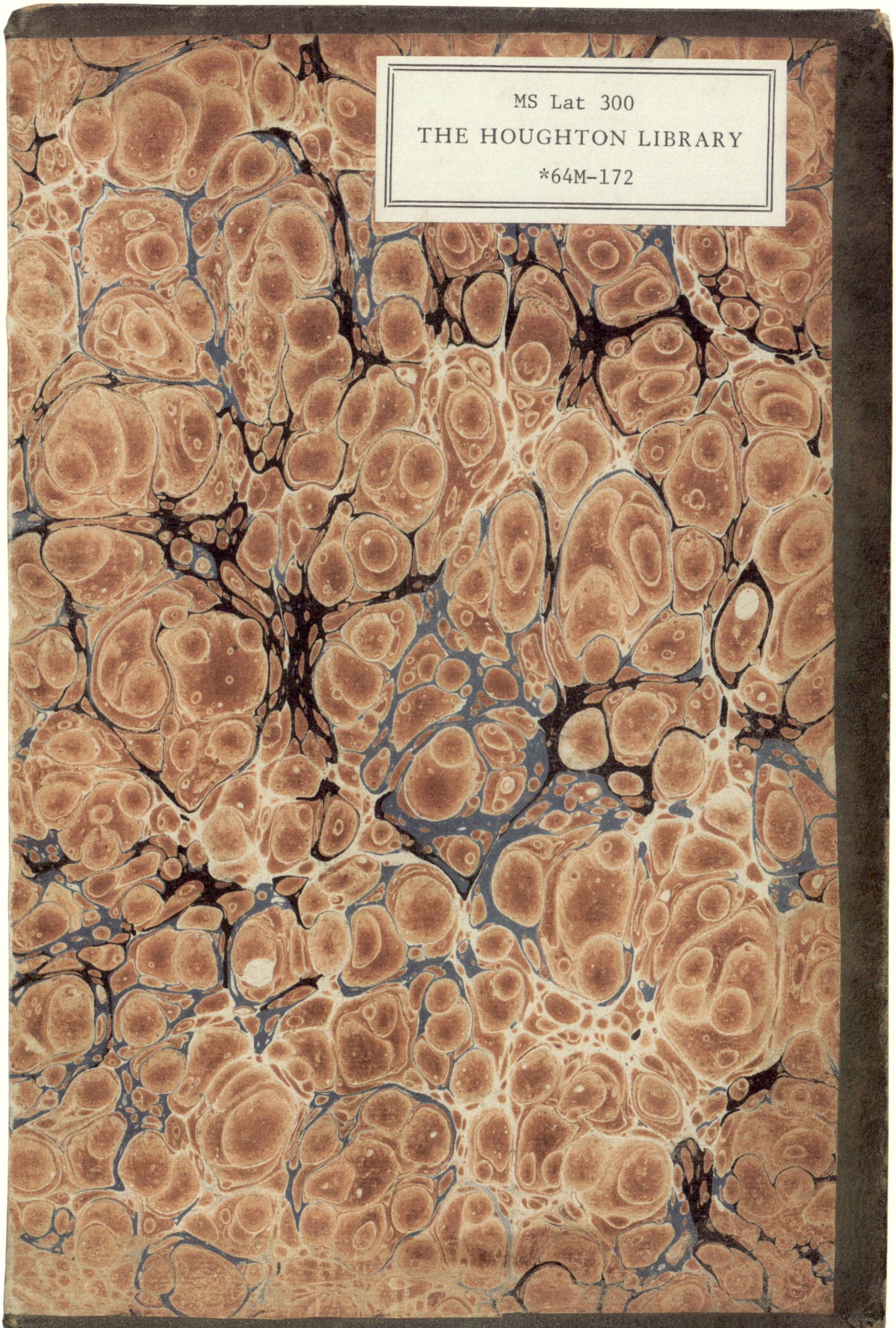

INSIDE BACK COVER

OUTSIDE BACK COVER

Index of Latin Words and Phrases

Index of Latin Incipits and Titles

Page numbers in italics indicate editions of texts, with translations and commentaries.

F

G

H

I

K

L

General Index

N

O

P

A Garland of Satire, Wisdom, and History:
Latin Verse from Twelfth-Century France
(Carmina Houghtoniensia)
is the first volume of the
HOUGHTON LIBRARY SERIES
and was
designed and typeset
in Bembo by Duncan G. Todd
and printed by Universal Millennium, Inc.